MY PAST AND THOUGHTS

MY PAST AND THOUGHTS
The Memoirs of Alexander Herzen

VOLUME IV

*Translated from the Russian
by Constance Garnett*

faber and faber

This edition first published in 2008
by Faber and Faber Ltd
3 Queen Square, London WC1N 3AU

Printed by Books on Demand GmbH, Norderstedt

All rights reserved
Translation © Constance Garnett, 1925

The right of Constance Garnett to be identified as translator of this work
has been asserted in accordance with Section 77 of the
Copyright, Designs and Patents Act 1988

This book is sold subject to the condition that it shall not, by way of
trade or otherwise, be lent, resold, hired out or otherwise circulated
without the publisher's prior consent in any form of binding or cover other than
that in which it is published and without a similar condition including this
condition being imposed on the subsequent purchaser

A CIP record for this book is available from the British Library

ISBN 978–0–571–24544–4

CONTENTS

SECTION THREE
A FAMILY DRAMA

I. THE YEAR 1848 — *page* 1

II. THE YEAR 1849 — *page* 39

III. THE YEAR 1851 — *page* 47

IV. THE YEAR 1852 — *page* 75

ADDENDA TO SECTION THREE—EXTRACTS FROM A DIARY *page* 110

SELECTIONS FROM CORRESPONDENCE RELATING TO SECTION THREE *page* 114

SECTION FOUR
ENGLAND
(1852-1855)

CHAPTER I :—The Fogs of London *page* 138

CHAPTER II :—The Mountain Heights—The Central European Committee—Mazzini—Ledru-Rollin—Kossuth

page 144

APPENDIX (TO CHAPTER II) *page* 163

CHAPTER III:—I. The Exiles in London—The Germans and the French—Parties—Victor Hugo—Felix Pyat—Louis Blanc and Armand Barbès—II. Felix Pyat—Victor Hugo and Others—Louis Blanc and the French Refugees *page* 167

CHAPTER IV :—1. POLISH REFUGEES: Aloysius Bernacki—Stanislaw Worcell—The Polish Agitators between 1854 and 1856—The Death of Worcell.—11. Pater V. Petcherin *page* 206

Three Trials—1. The Duel—11. Barthélemy—111. Not Guilty *page* 250

CHAPTER V :—Golovin *page* 301

SECTION THREE[1]
A FAMILY DRAMA

I

THE YEAR 1848

I

'TO understand so much' (Natalie wrote to Ogaryov at the end of 1846) 'and not to have the strength to deal with it—not to have the fortitude to accept bitter and sweet alike, but to stop short at the first—it is pitiful! And I understand all that as well as possible, and yet I cannot arrive at enjoying myself or even being indulgent. I understand what is good outside myself, I do it justice —but only what is gloomy is reflected in my soul and torments me. Give me your hand and say with me that nothing satisfies you, that there is nothing you are content with, and then teach me to rejoice, to be gay, to enjoy myself—I have everything to make me happy, if only I could develop the faculty.' These lines and the fragment of her diary relating to the same period, and quoted elsewhere, were written under the influence of our Moscow misunderstandings. Her gloomy side had come uppermost again; the estrangement of the Granovskys terrified Natalie; it seemed to her that our whole circle was falling to pieces and that we were being left alone with Ogaryov. . . . A girl hardly more than a child, whom she loved like a younger sister, was drifting further from us than any. At all costs to break out of this circle became at that time a passionate *idée fixe* with Natalie,

We went away.

---

[1] This is the section of which Turgenev wrote: 'It is written in tears and blood.'—(*Translator's Note*.)

At first the novelty of Paris, then awakening Italy and revolutionary France, occupied our whole souls. Personal doubts and hesitations were eclipsed by history.

So we lived up to the days of June. Even before those terrible days of bloodshed, the 15th of May had cut down our hopes that had risen once again. . . .

'Three full months had not passed since the 24th of February, men were still wearing the same shoes as when they built the barricades, but France, already worn out, was asking to be subjugated.'[1] No blood was spilt on that day; it was a thunderclap from a cloudless sky foretelling a fearful storm. On that day I seemed to look with a sort of clairvoyance into the soul of the bourgeois, into the soul of the workman—and felt horror-stricken. I saw the savage lust of blood on both sides—concentrated hatred on the side of the workman, and fierce, rapacious self-preservation on the side of the bourgeois. Two such camps could not stand side by side, jostling each other every day in the closest proximity—in the home, in the street, in the workshop, in the market-place. A terrible bloody conflict, foreboding nothing good, was close upon us. This was seen by none except the Conservatives who were working to bring it about; my nearest friends spoke with a smile of my nervous pessimism. It was easier for them to snatch up a gun and to go to die on a barricade than to look facts boldly in the face; they did not want as a rule to understand things, but to triumph over their opponents; they wanted to establish their own point of view.

I drifted further and further away from every one. There was the menace of emptiness in that—but all at once the beating of drums, the clatter of crowds in the streets in the early morning, announced the beginning of the catastrophe.

Those June days—and the days that followed after

[1] *Letters from France and Italy*, ix.

them—were awful; they made the turning-point in my life. I will repeat a few lines I wrote a month later.

'Women weep to relieve their hearts, we do not know how to weep. Instead of tears I want to write—not in order to describe and explain the bloody events, but simply to talk about them, to give vent to speech, to tears, to thoughts, to bitterness. How is one to describe, to collect evidence, to judge!—One's ears are still ringing with the sound of shots, the tramp of racing cavalry, the heavy rumblings of cannon-wheels through the dead streets; individual details flash upon the memory—a wounded man holding on to the stretcher, with his hand to his side, and a few drops of blood trickling down it; the omnibuses filled with corpses, the prisoners with bound hands, the cannon on the Place de la Bastille, the camp at the Porte St. Denis in the Champs-Élysées, and the gloomy night: "*Sentinelle, prenez garde à vous!*" How can one describe things when the brain is inflamed and the blood is on fire?

'To sit at home with one's hands folded, unable to go out beyond the gate, and to hear far and near all around one firing, cannonades, screams, drums beating, and to know that blood is flowing, men are being hacked and stabbed and dying at your side—that is enough to kill a man, to drive him mad. I did not die, but it made me old, and I am recovering after the days of June as after a terrible illness.

'And yet the beginning was impressive. On the 23rd, at four o'clock, before dinner, I was walking along the bank of the Seine towards the Hotel de Ville; the shops were shutting, columns of the National Guard with sinister faces were marching in different directions, the sky was covered with storm-clouds, a fine rain was falling. I stopped at the Pont Neuf, a vivid flash of lightning gleamed out of a storm-cloud, claps of thunder followed one after another, and, in the midst of all that, the drawn-out measured sound of the alarm-bell rang out from the belfry of St. Sulpice, and with it the deceived proletariat once more summoned their brothers to arms. The cathedral and all the buildings on the river bank were wonderfully lighted up by a few rays of sunshine, gleaming brightly from under a storm-cloud, the drums sounded from all sides, the artillery filed along from the Place du Carrousel. I heard the thunder and the bell ringing, and could not gaze enough at the panorama of Paris, as though I were taking leave of it; I passionately loved Paris at that moment; it was the last homage I paid to the great city—after the days of June it grew hateful to me.

'On the other side of the river barricades were being thrown up in all the streets and alleys. I can see now those gloomy figures dragging the stones, women and children helping them. A young Polytechnic student climbed one barricade that apparently was finished, unfurled the flag and began singing the Marseillaise in a mournfully solemn voice, all who were working joined in, and the chorus of the grand song resounding over the stones of the barricades made the heart throb. . . . The alarm bell still rang out. Meanwhile, there was the thud of artillery over the bridge, and General Beguot on the bridge scanned through a field-glass the *enemy's* position. . . .'

At that moment it was still possible to prevent it all, then it was still possible to save the republic and the freedom of all Europe, then it was still possible to have made peace. The dull-witted and tactless government could not do this, the Assembly would not, the reactionaries sought revenge, blood, atonement for the 24th of February, and the enactments of the Nationale gave them the instruments to carry out their will.

On the evening of the 26th of June, after the victory

AFTER THE FIGHTING

of the Nationale over Paris, we heard shots being fired at short intervals. . . . We glanced at one another, all our faces were livid. . . .

'They are shooting prisoners,' we said with one voice, and turned away from one another. I pressed my forehead against the window-pane. Such moments provoke ten years of hatred, a lifetime of revenge: *woe to him who forgives at such moments!*

After the fighting, which lasted four days and four nights, there followed the calm and stillness of a state of siege; the streets were still surrounded by cordons, only very rarely here and there one came upon a carriage; the haughty National Guards, with brutal and stupid ferocity in their faces, guarded their shops, threatening with bayonets and butt-ends of rifles. Triumphant crowds of drunken *gardes mobiles* paraded the streets singing *Mourir pour la Patrie*; lads of sixteen or seventeen boasted of their brothers' blood, with which their hands were stained; shopgirls ran out from behind the counter and threw flowers to them, to greet the conquerors. Cavaignac took round with him in a carriage a monster who had killed dozens of Frenchmen. The bourgeoisie was triumphant. Yet the houses of the Faubourg St. Antoine were still smoking, the walls battered by bullets were in ruins, the interior of rooms thrown open displayed wounds in the stones, broken furniture was still smouldering, bits of shattered looking-glass glittered . . . and where were the owners? The inhabitants? No one even thought of them. . . . In places they were scattering sand, but still there was blood to be seen. People were not allowed to approach the Panthéon, which had been damaged by cannon-balls; there were tents pitched in the boulevards, horses were nibbling the carefully tended trees of the Champs-Élysées; hay, cuirassiers, breastplates, and saddles were lying about everywhere in the Place de la Concorde; soldiers were making soup in the Jardin des Tuileries, by the fence. Paris had not seen this even in 1814.

A few more days passed—and Paris began to assume its customary aspect. Crowds of idlers appeared again on the boulevards, smartly-dressed ladies drove about in carriages and cabriolets *to look* at the ruins of houses and the traces of desperate fighting. . . . It was only the frequent patrols and gangs of prisoners that reminded one of the terrible days, only then the past began to grow clear. Byron has a description of a battlefield at night; its blood-stained details are hidden in the darkness; at dawn, when the battle has long been over, its traces—a sword-blade and bloodstained clothes—are seen. It was just such a dawn that rose now in the soul, it lighted up a scene of fearful desolation. Half of our hopes, half of our beliefs were slain, ideas of scepticism and despair haunted the brain and took root in it. One could never have supposed that, after passing through so many trials, after being schooled by contemporary scepticism, we had so much left in our souls to be destroyed.

Natalie wrote about this time to Moscow: 'I look at the children and weep, I am terrified. I no longer dare to wish them to live, perhaps there is a fate as awful in store for them too.'

In these words is the echo of all she had been through, in them one seems to see the omnibuses piled up with dead, and prisoners with bound hands, followed by oaths, and the poor deaf-and-dumb boy shot a few steps from our gate because he did not hear: '*Passez, au large!*' And how could it fail to make this impression on the heart of a woman who had unhappily so profound an understanding of everything sorrowful? . . . Even joyous natures grew gloomy and full of bitterness, the heart ached with a sort of angry pain, and an overwhelming shame made daily life seem out of place.

It was not a fantastic grief for ideals, not a revival of the tears and romantic religion of her girlhood, which once more flooded Natalie's soul, but a real sorrow, too heavy a burden for a woman's shoulders. Natalie's living interest in public affairs did not grow colder; on the contrary, it turned into a living agony. It was the distress of a sister, the tears of a mother, on the sorrowful field of the battle that had just been lost. She was in reality what Rachel falsely played at being with her Marseillaise.

Weary of fruitless discussions, I snatched up my pen and, with a sort of inner fury, slew my own old dreams and hopes. The energy that was breaking and fretting me spent itself in these pages of cursing and resentment, in which even now, when I read them over, I am conscious of the fevered blood and indignation that passed beyond all bounds . . . it was an outlet.

She had no such outlet. In the morning there were the children, in the evening our irritable, vindictive discussions, the post-mortem arguments of dissectors with doctors who had failed.

She was suffering—and I, in place of healing, offered her the bitter cup of scepticism and irony. If I had tended her sick soul with half the care I lavished afterwards on her sick body, I should never have let this rankling sorrow send out roots in all directions. I helped to feed and strengthen them without making sure whether she could bear it, could cope with it.

Our life itself was strangely ordered. We rarely had quiet evenings of intimate talk and peaceful rest. We had not yet learnt to close our doors on outsiders. Towards the end of the year, fugitives from all countries, homeless refugees, began to arrive from all parts. In their dullness and isolation they sought a friendly roof and a warm welcome.

Here is what she wrote of that:

November 21, 1848.—'I am sick of Chinese shadows. I do not know whom I see and why I see them, I only know that I see too many people — all good people; I fancy I might take pleasure in their company *sometimes*, but that it is too often, life is so like the dripping water in springtime, drip, drip, drip.

'All the morning I am looking after Sasha, after Tata, and that goes on all day. I cannot concentrate for one minute. I am so distracted that it sometimes makes me ill and frightened; the evening comes, the children are put to bed—well, one might think I should rest. . . . No, good people begin strolling in, and that they are good people makes it even harder to bear; otherwise, I should be quite alone, and, as it is, I am not alone—and I do not feel their presence, it 's as though the room were full of smoke, one's eyes smart, and it is hard to breathe—and they go away and nothing is left. . . . To-morrow comes, always the same thing, the day after comes, always the same thing. To no one else could I say this, others would think I am complaining, would imagine I am dissatisfied with my life; you understand me, you know that I would not change with any one on earth. This is a moment's indignation, weariness—a breath of fresh air, and I rise up again as strong as ever. If I am to say all that passes in my mind, I am sometimes terrified looking at the children . . . what boldness, what audacity, to bring a new creature into life, and to have nothing, nothing to make its life happy—it is fearful, sometimes I seem to myself a criminal; it would be easier to take life than to give it, if it were done with full consciousness. I have never yet met any one of whom I could say, "If my child were such as he, that is, if his life were such as his . . ." My views grow more and more humble. Soon after Sasna's birth, I wanted him to be a great man, later on, to be this or that, now all I want is . . .'

At this point the letter was cut short by our little girl Tata's having typhoid fever; on the 15th of December the words were added: 'Well, what I meant to say was that now I don't care about making anything of the children; so long as their lives are bright and happy, the rest is of no consequence....'

January 24, 1849.—'How I should sometimes like to run about like a mouse as others do, and to find that trotting to and fro interesting, instead of being so idle, so idle in the midst of this bustle, in the midst of these necessary things, while the work that I should like is out of the question; how agonising it is always to feel oneself in such disharmony with those surrounding one—I am not speaking of our most intimate circle, but if only one could confine oneself to it; one cannot.

'One longs to get away, far away! . . . It was all right to feel like that when we were in Italy.

'But now! there 's no sense in it! At thirty to have the same yearnings, the same thirst, and the same dissatisfaction—yes, I said that aloud—and Tata came up at that word and kissed me so warmly. Dissatisfaction? —I am too happy, *la vie déborde* . . . But

> '"Why is it on the world
> One longs to gaze,
> Why to fly over it
> Does the soul crave?"

'It is only to you that I talk like this—you will understand me, because you are just as weak as I am—but with others, whether stronger or weaker, I should not care to speak like this, I should not care for them to hear what I am saying. I find something else for them. Then I am frightened by my indifference, so few things, so few people interest me. . . . Nature—only not in the kitchen; history—only not in the law-courts; and then my own family, then two or three others—that's all.

And yet how kind they all are—they take so much trouble over my health and Kolya's deafness.'

January 27.— 'No, I really have not the strength to go on watching the death-agonies—they last too long, and life is so short; I am possessed by egoism, because one does no good by self-sacrifice, at the most it shows the truth of the proverb, "Even death is agreeable in good company!" But enough of dying. I should like to. live . . . I should like to escape to America. . . . What we believed in, what we took for reality, was only a prophecy of the future, and a very premature one. How bitter, how comfortless it is! I want to cry like a child. What is personal happiness? . . . public life is all around one like the atmosphere, and that atmosphere is full now of the breath of death and pestilence.'

February 1.—'Natasha,[1] if you knew, my dear, how dark, how comfortless it is outside our personal private circle! Oh, if one could shut oneself inside it, and forget, forget everything except that narrow circle. . . . How insufferable is the ferment, the result of which won't come for some centuries! I am too weak to rise above that ferment and look so far into the future—I shrink into myself and am crushed.'

This letter ends with the words: 'I should like to have so little strength as not to feel my own existence; when I do feel it, I feel all the disharmony of everything that exists. . . .'

The reaction was triumphant; through the pale blue republic could be seen the features of pretenders to the throne, the National Guards went hunting after workmen in blouses, the Prefect of Police sent search-parties through the woods and catacombs, hunting for those who were in hiding. Men of a less martial type preferred eavesdropping and sending secret reports.

[1] All this was written to Natalya Alexeyevna Tutchkov, who married Ogaryov in 1850.—(*Translator's Note.*)

PARTING

Until the autumn we were surrounded by our own friends, and gave vent to our grief and our anger in our own language; the Tutchkovs[1] were living in the same house, Mariya Fyodorovna Korsh[2] was with us, Annenkov[3] and Turgenev used to come every day; but all were looking away into the distance, our little circle was breaking up. After its bath of blood, Paris had no hold on them; all prepared to go away, from no special necessity, probably thinking to escape from the spiritual oppression, from the days of June which had become part of them, and which they took with them.

Why did not I go too? Much would have been saved, and I should not have had to offer up such human sacrifices and so much of myself, as an offering to a cruel and merciless god.

The day of our parting with the Tutchkovs and Mariya Fyodorovna struck a particularly ominous note in my life, but I let that note of warning pass unheeded like hundreds of others.

Every man who has gone through a great deal remembers days, hours, a succession of scarcely noticed points with which a crisis begins, with which the wind shifts to a different quarter; these signs or warnings do not come by chance at all, they are sequences, rudimentary germs of what is ready to burst into life, revelations of what is secretly fermenting and already existing. We do not notice these psychological signs, but laugh at them as we do over spilled salt, or a candle being blown out, because we consider ourselves immeasurably more independent than we really are, and proudly desire to guide our lives ourselves.

---

[1] Natalie (afterwards wife of Ogaryov) and Yelena (afterwards wife of Satin, one of the Herzens' circle), with their parents.

[2] A great friend of the Herzens, sister of Yevgeny Korsh.

[3]a A literary critic, intimate friend of Turgenev, editor of Pushkin.—(*Translator's Notes.*)

On the eve of our friends' departure, they gathered at our house together with three or four other intimate friends. The travellers were to be at the railway-station at seven o'clock in the morning; it was not worth while going to bed, we all preferred to spend the last hours together. At first all were lively with that nervous excitement which is always seen at moments of separation, but by degrees a cloud of depression seemed to come over all of us. . . . Conversation flagged, every one began to feel dispirited, the wine was left untouched in our glasses, the efforts at jesting no longer cheered us. Some one, seeing the daybreak, pulled back the curtain and threw a pale bluish light on all our faces that suggested the Roman orgies of Couture.[1] All were melancholy. I was so sad I could hardly breathe. My wife was sitting on a little sofa, while Tutchkov's younger daughter, '*Consuelo di sua alma*,'[2] as Natalie used to call her, was kneeling with her face on Natalie's bosom. She was passionately fond of my wife, and was unwillingly leaving her to go into the wilds of the country; her sister stood mournfully beside her. Consuelo was whispering something through her tears, while two paces away Mariya Fyodorovna was sitting in gloomy silence; she had learnt through years to submit to destiny, she knew life, and in her eyes one could simply read 'good-bye,' while through the young girl's tears there still gleamed 'till we meet again.' Then we went to see them off. It was piercingly cold in the high, empty, stone station, the doors slammed incessantly, and the draught blew in all directions. We sat down on a seat in the corner. Tutchkov went to look after the luggage. Suddenly the door opened, and two drunken old men burst noisily into the

[1] Couture, Thomas (1815-79), historical painter, and author of the *Romains de la Décadence*.—(*Translator's Note*.)
[2] Natalya Alexeyevna Tutchkov, to whom the preceding letters were addressed.—(*Note to Russian edition*.)

station. Their clothes were muddy, their faces distorted, everything about them was suggestive of brutal debauchery. They came in, swearing. One tried to strike the other, the latter dodged and, swinging his fist with all his might, hit him in the face. The old drunkard was sent flying. His head struck the stone floor with the sharp sound of something cracking; he shrieked and raised his head, while the blood poured in streams over his grey hair and the stone floor. The police and passengers fell with fury upon the other old man. Though we had been overwrought and excited ever since the previous evening, and our nerves were over-strained, we maintained our self-control, but the fearful echo that resounded through the hall when the skull struck the floor had almost an hysterical effect upon all of us. Our household and all our circle were at all times sane and free from neurotic and hysterical exhibitions, but this was more than we could bear. I felt myself shuddering all over, and my wife was almost fainting. And then the bell—time was up! And we were left suddenly at the barrier—alone.

Nothing could be coarser and more mortifying for parting friends than the police arrangements at railway-stations in France; they rob those left behind of the last two or three minutes; the friends are still there, the engine has not yet whistled, the train has not moved off, but between you is a fence, a barrier, and the arm of a policeman—while you long to see them settled, to see the train move off, then to watch it in the distance turn to a cloud of dust, of smoke, a point, to watch until you can see nothing. . . .

In silence we reached home. My wife was weeping quietly all the way—she was sorry to lose her Consuelo; at times, wrapping herself in her shawl, she asked me, 'Do you remember that sound?—it is ringing in my ears still.'

At home I persuaded her to lie down, while I sat down to read the newspapers; I read, read the *premier Paris* and the *feuilletons* and the short paragraphs, and glanced at my watch—it was not yet twelve; what a day! I went to see Annenkov; he, too, was going in a few days. We went for a walk together, the streets were even more dreary than reading; I was weighed down by misery that was like the gnawing of conscience. 'Come to dinner with me,' I said, and we went home. My wife was really ill, the evening was disjointed and stupid. 'And so it is settled,' I asked as we parted, 'that you go at the end of the week?'

'Yes.'

'You'll be wretched in Russia.'

'I can't help that, I must go. I shall not stay in Petersburg, I shall go into the country. Why, it's not so wonderfully nice here now. You may yet regret staying.'

At that time I could still have returned, I had not yet burnt my ships. Rebillaud and Carlier had not yet written their secret police reports, but in my mind the matter was settled. Yet Annenkov's words jarred unpleasantly on my overwrought nerves; I thought a moment and answered: 'No, there is no choice for me, I must stay; and if I regret anything, it is rather that I did not take the gun when a workman offered it to me at a barricade on the Place Maubert.'

Many times in moments of weakness and despair, when the cup of bitterness was too full, when my whole life seemed to me nothing but one prolonged blunder, when I doubted of myself, of 'the last thing, all that is left,' those words came back to my mind, 'Why did I not take the gun from the workman and stay at the barricade?' Struck by a chance bullet, I should have borne two or three convictions with me to the grave.

. . . . . .

And again the time lagged on . . . day after day . . . grey and wearisome. . . . People flitted in, made friends for a day, passed by, vanished, were lost. Towards the winter, exiles from other lands, survivors from other shipwrecks, began to arrive; full of hope and self-confidence, they took the reaction that had sprung up all over Europe for a passing squall, a minor reverse; they expected their turn would come, next day, next week.

I felt that they were wrong, but I was glad of their mistake. I tried to be inconsistent, struggled with myself, and lived in a state of nervous irritability. That time has remained in my memory like a day of stupefaction and delirium. . . . In my misery I turned hither and thither, restlessly seeking distraction—in books, in noise, in solitude, at home, in company, but always there was something lacking, laughter did not make me merry, wine only made me heavy, music cut me to the heart, and lively talk almost always ended in gloomy silence. Everything within was outraged, everything was turned upside down, all was chaos, full of glaring contradictions; again I was pulling everything to pieces, again there was nothing. The principles of one's moral existence, worked out long ago, were turned again into questions, facts had risen up sullenly on all sides and refuted them. Doubt trampled under foot the little we had gained, it was now tearing to shreds, not the vestments of the Church nor the robes of learned doctors, but the flags of the revolution. . . . From abstract ideas doubt was turned upon life. There is a deep gulf between theoretical scepticism and doubt that passes over into conduct; thought is bold, the tongue is reckless, it readily utters words which the heart dreads; hopes and convictions still smoulder in the breast while the mind, racing on ahead, refuses assent. The heart lags behind because it loves; and while the mind delivers sentence and verdict, it is still taking leave.

Perhaps in youth, when all is ferment and commotion, when there is so much in the future, when the loss of some convictions only makes room for others, perhaps in old age, when all grows indistinct from weariness, these crises are easier—but *nel mezzo del cammin di nostra vita*,[1] we paid dearly for them.

What does it all mean—is it a jest? Everything sacred that we loved, for which we struggled, for which we made sacrifices, has been betrayed by life, betrayed by history, betrayed for her own ends—she needs madmen as a ferment, and cares not what becomes of them when they recover; they have served her turn—let them live out their crippled lives in hospital! The shame, the mortification! And here at one's side simple-hearted friends shrug their shoulders, wonder at one's poor-spiritedness, at one's impatience, look forward to the morrow, and for ever fussing, for ever busy with the same thing, see nothing, stop before nothing, go on for ever and are never a step forwarder. . . . They judge you, comfort you, scold you—oh wearisome, insufferable infliction! 'Men of faith, men of love,' as they call themselves in contradistinction to us men 'of doubt and negation,' do not know what it is to tear out by the roots the cherished convictions of a lifetime, they know nothing of the sickness of truth, they have surrendered no treasure with that loud lamentation of which the poet speaks:

> 'Ich riss sie blutend aus dem wunden Herzen
> Und weinte laut und gab sie hin.'

Happy are the lunatics who have no lucid intervals; they know nothing of the inner conflict, they suffer from external causes, from evil men and evil chances, but within, all is whole, conscience is at rest, they are content. And so the gnawing despair of others seems to them

---

[1] The first line of the *Divine Comedy*.—(*Author's Note*.)

caprice, the self-indulgence of a too well-fed mind, idle irony. They see that the wounded man laughs at his crutch, and conclude that the operation meant nothing to him; it does not enter their heads to wonder why he is prematurely old and whether the stump aches at the change of the weather and the blowing of the wind.

My logical confession, the history of the disease through which my wounded thoughts struggled, remains in the series of articles that make up *From the Other Side*. In them I attacked the last idols I had left. With irony I revenged myself on them for the pain and the betrayal. I did not jeer at my neighbours, but at myself, and, carried away again, was already dreaming of being free, but there, too, I came to grief. Losing faith in words and banners, in canonised humanity and the one church of salvation, that is, Western civilisation, I still believed in a few persons, I believed in myself. Seeing that all was tumbling into ruins, I tried to save myself, to begin a new life, to get away with two or three others, to run, to hide from . . . superfluous people. And haughtily I headed my last article: *Omnia mea mecum porto!*

Life, burnt up, losing shape and colour in the abyss of events, in the vortex of public interests, became self-centred, shrank back into youthful lyricism, without youth, without faith. With this *faro da me*, my boat was bound to be wrecked on submerged rocks, and it was wrecked. I survived, it is true, but lost everything. . . .

2

Typhoid

In the winter of 1848 my little girl, Tata, was ill. She had been ailing for a long time, then had a slight attack of fever, and it seemed to have passed off. Rayer, the well-known doctor, advised that she should be taken a drive in spite of the wintry weather. It was a fine day, but not warm. When she was brought home, she was unusually pale; she asked for something to eat and fell asleep beside us on the sofa before the broth was brought; several hours passed, she went on sleeping. Adolf Vogt, a medical student, a brother of the naturalist, happened to be with us.

'Look at the child,' he said; 'why, that's not natural sleep.' The deathly, almost bluish, pallor of the face alarmed me; I put my hand on the child's forehead, it was stone-cold. I rushed myself to Ray er, luckily found him at home and brought him back with me. The little creature was still asleep. Rayer lifted her up, shook her violently and made me call her loudly by her name. . . . She opened her eyes, said a couple of words and dropped back again into the same heavy deathlike sleep; her breathing was hardly perceptible. She remained in that condition, with slight changes, for several days, without food and almost without drink. Her lips turned black, her nails were dark blue and spots came out over the body—it was typhoid. Rayer did scarcely anything, waited, watched the illness and gave us little hope.

The appearance of the child was terrible; I expected the end from hour to hour. Pale and silent, my wife sat day and night by the little bed, her eyes covered with that pearly lustre which betrays fatigue, suffering, exhausted strength and unnaturally strained nerves. Once, between one and two o'clock at night, I fancied that Tata was not breathing. I looked at her, concealing my horror. Natalie guessed it. 'My head is going round,' she said, 'give me some water.' When I handed her the glass, she was unconscious. Ivan Turgenev, who had come to share our gloomy hours, ran to the chemist's for spirits of ammonia. I stood motionless

TYPHOID

between two unconscious bodies, gazed at them, but did nothing. Our maid rubbed Natalie's hands and moistened her temples; in a few minutes she came to herself. 'Well?' she asked. 'I thought Tata opened her eyes,' said good, kind Luise. I looked, she seemed to be waking; I spoke her name in a whisper; she opened her eyes and smiled with her black, dry and cracked lips. From that minute she began to recover.

There are poisons which destroy a man more cruelly, more agonisingly than children's illnesses. I know them, but there is nothing worse than the slow poison that works by exhaustion, that saps the strength in the stillness and humiliates one with the impotence of an idle spectator.

The man who has once carried a little creature in his arms and felt it growing cold and heavy, turning to stone, who has heard the last moan with which the frail creature begs for mercy, for help, imploring for its life, who has seen the pretty little coffin covered with pink satin, and the little white frock, with lace on it, which contrasts so with the little yellow face, will think at every childish illness, may there not be another little coffin on that table!

Misfortune is a bad school! Of course, a man who has gone through a great deal is better able to bear misfortunes, but that is only because his soul has been bruised and weakened. A man slowly wears out and grows more cowardly from the troubles he has endured. He loses that confidence in the morrow without which nothing can be done: he grows more indifferent because he is used to terrible thoughts, and in the end he is selfishly afraid of suffering, that is, he is afraid of feeling again the succession of acute miseries, the succession of pangs to the heart, of which the memories never pass away as storm-clouds do from the sky.

The moan of a sick child causes such inward terror in

me, sends such a cold shiver through me, that I have to make great efforts to overcome this purely nervous effect of memory.

It was on the morning after that same night that I went out for the first time for a walk; it was cold, the pavements were lightly powdered with hoar frost, but in spite of the cold and the early hour the boulevards were crowded with people; shouting streets-boys were selling *bulletins*—over five million voices laid France bound at the feet of Louis Napoleon. The bereaved servants' hall had found a master again at last! It was just at this time of bitter trial and strain that a person came into our circle who brought with him another train of misfortunes, who brought more ruin into our private life than the black days of June into our public. This person approached us rapidly, forced himself upon us without giving us time for consideration. . . . At ordinary times I am quick to become acquainted and slow to become intimate, but that, I repeat again, was not an ordinary time. All our nerves were laid bare and smarting; trivial meetings, insignificant reminders of the past, made one quiver in every fibre. I remember, for instance, that three days after the cannonade, I was strolling along the Faubourg St. Antoine; everything still bore fresh traces of fierce fighting, there were broken walls, barricades still standing, pale, frightened women looking for something, and children rummaging in the *débris*. . . .

I sat down before a little café and looked, with an aching heart, at the terrible scene. A quarter of an hour passed—some one softly laid a hand on my shoulder— it was Doviat, a young enthusiast who had preached some sort of Neo-catholicism *à la* Ruge in Germany, and had, in 1847, emigrated to America.

He was pale, his face was working, his long hair was in disorder, he was dressed as though for a journey.

'My God!' he said, 'how we meet again!'

'When did you come?'

'To-day. Having heard in New York of the revolution of February and of all that was being done in Europe, I hurriedly sold everything I could, took all my money, and rushed for a steamer with a light heart full of hope. Yesterday, at Havre, I heard of what has just happened, but I could never have imagined anything as bad as this.'

We looked at each other once more, and our eyes were full of tears.

'Not a day, not one single day in this accursed city!' said the excited Doviat, and he was really like some prophesying Levite.

'Hence! Away! Farewell, I go to Germany!'

He did go, and fell into a Prussian prison, where he spent six years.

I remember, too, the performance of *Catiline* which the strong-nerved Dumas put on the stage at that time in his historic theatre. The forts were packed to overflowing with prisoners, some were sent by herds to the Château d'If and deported, their relations wandered like uneasy spirits from one police office to another, imploring to be told who was killed, and who had survived, and who had been shot; but Alexandre Dumas was already producing the days of June in a Roman setting on the stage. I went to have a look at it. At first it was nothing much; Ledru-Rollin as Catiline and Cicero as Lamartine, classical sentences with rhetorical padding. The rising is put down. Lamartine marches across the stage with his 'Vixerunt'; the scene changes. The market-place is covered with corpses, in the distance is a red glow—the dying, in death agonies, are lying among the dead; the dead are covered with bloody rags—I could hardly breathe. So lately behind the walls of that playhouse, in the streets leading up to it, we had seen the thing itself, and the corpses were not of cardboard, and the streaming blood was not coloured water, but trickled from live young bodies.

I rushed away almost hysterical, cursing the wildly applauding bourgeois. . . .

In such agonising days, when a man cannot stay in restaurant or theatre, at home or in his study, but goes out in a fever, with brain distraught, inwardly crushed, deeply wounded, and ready to wound any one he meets, then every word of sympathy, every tear over the same grief, every curse that springs from the same hatred, has wonderful power. Sore places quickly grow together when the wounds are alike.

In the early days of my youth I was struck by a French novel, which I have not met since—it was called *Arminius*. Possibly it has no great merits, but at the time it had a great influence on me, and it haunted my mind for years afterwards. I remember its chief incidents to this day.

From the history of the early ages of Christendom we all know something of the meeting and conflict between two different worlds—one, the ancient and classical world of culture, corrupt and effete, the other savage as a wild beast of the forest, but full of slumbering forces and a disorderly chaos of tendencies—that is, we all know the official public side of this contact, but not that side which was concerned with details and the stillness of home life. We know the events as a whole, but have no record of the lives of the persons who were directly dependent on them, though it was through those events that lives unchronicled were broken and ruined, blood was replaced by tears, devastated towns by desolate families, the field of battle by forgotten tombs.

The author of *Arminius*—I have forgotten his name—tried to reproduce these two worlds—one coming from the forest into history, the other going from history to the tomb—as they met at the domestic hearth. Universal history, when reduced to personal gossip, comes nearer to us, more within our grasp, more living. I was so interested by *Arminius* that I began writing a series of historical scenes in the same style, and the Chief Police-master, Tsinsky, made a critical analysis of them in 1834. But I need hardly say that when I wrote those it never entered my head that I should come into a similar conflict, and that my own hearth would be devastated, crushed at the meeting of two historic worlds. Whatever may be said, there are points of resemblance in our relation to Europeans. Our civilisation is skin-deep, our corruption is crude, our coarse hair bristles under the powder on our heads, and the sunburn shows through the powder on our cheeks; we have the cunning of savages, the vice of animals, the evasiveness of slaves, everywhere we are beginning to have money and money-grubbers, but we are very far behind the hereditary, intangible subtleties of West European corruption. Among us intellectual development[1] serves as a purification and a guarantee. Exceptions are rare. Culture among us, until lately, was a barrier which much that was infamous and vicious never crossed.

In Western Europe this is not so. And that is how it is that we readily surrender to a man who touches upon our holy things, who understands our cherished thoughts, who boldly utters what we are wont to pass over in silence or to speak of in whispers to a friend. We do not take into account that half the sayings which set our hearts beating and our bosoms heaving have become for Europe truisms or phrases; we forget how many corrupt passions, the artificial passions of old age, are entangled in the soul of a modern man belonging to that effete civilisation. From his earliest years he is trying to get in first, rotten through and through with self-seeking, sick with envy and *amour-propre*, with insatiable self-indulgence and petty egoism to which every relation, every feeling is

[1] Written in 1857.—(*Author's Note.*)

subordinated. . . . He wants to play a part, to pose on the stage, he wants at all costs to keep his place, to satisfy his passions. We sons of the Steppes, receiving one blow and a second, often not seeing whence they come, stupefied by them, are long before we come to our senses, and then fling ourselves like wounded bears, tearing up trees and howling and flinging up the earth—but too late, and our opponent points a finger of scorn at us. Much hatred yet will be engendered and much blood yet will flow through this difference in the two stages of growth and education.

There was a time when I sternly and passionately judged the man who shattered my life. There was a time when I earnestly desired to kill him. Seven years have passed since then; a true son of the age, I have worn out all desire of vengeance, and have cooled my passionate view by prolonged persistent analysis. In those seven years I have learnt both my own limit and the limits of many, and instead of a knife I have a scalpel in my hand, and instead of curses and abuse I set to work to tell my story of psychological pathology.

On coming home one evening, a few days before the 23rd of June 1848, I found in my room an unknown person who came to meet me with a mournful and embarrassed air. 'Why, is it you?' I said at last, laughing and holding out my hands to him. 'Is it possible? I should never have known you. . . .' It was Herwegh, shaven, shorn, with no moustache or beard. His luck had very quickly turned. Two months before, surrounded by admirers, he and his wife had driven in a comfortable *dormeuse* from Paris to the Baden campaign, at the invitation of the German republic. Now he had come back, fleeing from the field of battle, pursued by showers of caricatures, ridiculed by his enemies, blamed by his friends.

In a trice everything had changed, everything had fallen to pieces, and to complete it all, behind the wrecked scenery there was a prospect of ruin.

When I left Russia, Ogaryov gave me a letter of introduction to Herwegh, whom he had known in the days of his greatest glory. Ogaryov, always penetrating in questions of thought and of art, had no judgment of men. To him all who were not boring or vulgar were excellent people, and particularly all artists. I found Herwegh an intimate friend of Bakunin's and Sazonov's, and was soon on terms rather of familiarity than of intimacy with him. In the autumn of 1847 I went away to Italy. On my return to Paris I did not find him there. I read of his misfortunes in the newspapers. Almost on the eve of the days of June, he arrived in Paris, and as it was from me that he first met with a friendly reception after his Baden blunders, he took to coming more and more often to see us. There was a good deal at first to prevent my becoming intimate with the man. He had not that simple open nature, that complete *abandon* which is so in keeping with everything strong and gifted, and which in Russians almost invariably accompanies talent. He was reserved and furtive, afraid of other people, and liked to enjoy himself on the sly; he had a sort of unmanly effeminacy, a pitiful dependence on trifles, on comforts, and an unbounded *rücksichtslos* egoism to the degree of *naïveté* and cynicism. For all that I threw only half the blame on him. Fate had put beside him a woman who by her sophisticated love and her exaggerated solicitude fanned his egoistic propensities and encouraged his weaknesses by making them seem something fine in his eyes. Before his marriage he had been poor—she had brought him wealth, surrounded him with luxury, had become his nurse, his housekeeper, his attendant, a permanent necessity of the lowest order. Humbled to the dust in a sort of perpetual worship,

Huldigung, before the poet 'come to fill the place of Goethe and Heine,' she at the same time destroyed, stifled his talent—in the feather-bed of bourgeois luxury. It used to annoy me to see him accept so readily the position of a *kept* husband, and I must own it was not without satisfaction that I saw the financial ruin for which they were inevitably making, and I looked rather unsympathetically at Emma's tears when she had to give up her 'gilt-edged 'lodging, as we used to call it, and to sell, one by one, at half price, her 'amors and cupids'—happily not serfs, but bronze figures. I will pause here to say a few words about their previous life and about their marriage itself, which is wonderfully typical of modern German sentiment. . . .

.   .   .   .   .   .

Germans, and especially German women, have a mass of false passions—that is, invented, fantastic and affected literary passions. It is a sort of *Ueberspanntheit* . . . a bookish proneness to enthusiasm, an artificial, cold exaltation, always ready to be immensely impressed or touched without sufficient reason.

It is not hypocrisy, but a false truth, a psychological incontinence, ethical hysterics costing them nothing but inducing many tears, much joy and grief, many distractions and sensations, *Wonne*. Even an intelligent woman like Bettina von Arnim was unable to get rid of this German malady all her life. The forms it takes may change, the subjects with which it deals may be different, but the psychological treatment of the material, so to speak, is always the same. Everything is reduced to different variations, to different *nuances* of voluptuous pantheism, that is, of a religiously erotic and theoretically enamoured attitude to nature and to men, which by no means excludes romantic chastity or theoretical sensuality, either in the secular devotees of the cosmos or the monastic brides of Christ, abandoning themselves to the erotic ecstasies of prayer. They are both struggling to be the spiritual sisters . . . of the real Magdalens. They do this from curiosity and sympathy for transgressions to which they never bring themselves, and they are always ready to absolve the sins of others, even when these latter do not ask for it. The most enthusiastic of them pass through the whole programme of passions without descending to practice, and they experience all the sins, as it were by proxy—*per contumaciam*—in the books of others and their own manuscripts.

One almost universal feature of all ecstatic German ladies is their idolatrous worship of genius and of all great men; this religion dates from Weimar, from the days of Wieland, Schiller, and Goethe. But as men of genius are rare, and Heine lived in Paris, whilst Humboldt was too old and too realistic, they flung themselves, with a sort of hungry despair, on any good musician or decent painter. The image of Franz Liszt passed like an electric shock through the hearts of all the women of Germany, branding on them the high forehead and long hair combed back from it.

For lack in the end of great men common to all Germany, they accepted any, so to speak, local genius, who had distinguished himself in any way; all the women were in love with him, all the girls *schwärmten für ihn*. They all embroidered braces and slippers for him, and sent him all sorts of souvenirs in secret, anonymously. In the 'forties there was great mental excitement in Germany.

It might have been expected that that people, grown grey over books, might wish, like Faust, to come out into the market-place and look upon the light of day. We know now that these were fruitless efforts, that the new Faust from Auerbach's cellar went back to the *Studienzimmer*. It seemed otherwise at the time, particularly to the Germans, and so every manifestation of the revolutionary spirit met with ardent recognition.

It was in the very heyday of this period that Herwegh's political poems appeared. I never saw much talent in them; no one but his wife could compare Herwegh with Heine, but Heine's malicious scepticism was out of harmony with the mood of the day. The Germans, between 1840 and 1850, did not want Goethes or Voltaires, but Béranger's songs and the Marseillaise, adapted to the German fashion. Herwegh's verses ended sometimes *in crudo* with a French shout, with the refrain, *Vive la République!*, and that put people into ecstasies in 1842. In 1852 they were forgotten. They cannot be read over again. Herwegh—the poet-laureate of democracy—went from one banquet to another all over Germany, and at last appeared in Berlin. Every one rushed to invite him, dinners and parties were given in his honour, every one wanted to see him, even the King had such a desire to speak to him that the Court doctor, Schenlein, thought it necessary to present him to the King.

A few yards away from the palace in Berlin lived a banker. His daughter had for a long time been in love with Herwegh. She had never seen him and had no definite idea of him, but as she read his verses she felt that it was her vocation to make him happy and to twine the roses of domestic bliss in his laurel wreath. When she did actually see him for the first time at an evening party given by her father, she became finally convinced that this was *he*, and he did in fact become her *he*.

The enterprising, resolute girl made her attack vigorously. At first the poet, aged twenty-four, shied at the thought of marriage, and especially of marriage with a very plain young person, with a loud voice and rather *Junker* manners; the portals of a brilliant future stood wide open before him—what need had he of family peace, or a wife? But the banker's daughter, on her side, offered in the *present* a sack of gold, a tour in Italy, Paris, Strasbourg pies, and Clos de Vougeot: the poet was poor as a church mouse; he could not go on living at the Vollens' for ever—he hesitated and hesitated—and . . . accepted the offer, forgetting to say thank you to old Vollen, Vogt's grandfather.

Emma herself used to tell me how minutely and carefully the poet conducted negotiations about the dowry. He even sent sketches of the furniture, the curtains, and so on, from Zurich, and would have it all despatched before the wedding—he insisted upon that.

There was no thought of love; there had to be something to take its place. Emma understood that and made up her mind to secure her power by other measures. They spent some time in Zurich, she took her husband to Italy and then settled with him in Paris. There she assigned her Schatz a study with soft sofas, heavy velvet hangings, expensive rugs and bronze statuettes, and arranged for him a whole life of empty idleness. This was new to him and he liked it, but meanwhile his talent died down, and he produced nothing; she was vexed at this, scolded him for it and at the same time drew him more and more into bourgeois luxury. Here is an example of the extremes to which her solicitude would go. On one occasion in Italy, Herwegh was dissatisfied with the eau de Cologne. At once his wife wrote to Jean Marie Farina to send the very purest eau de Cologne to her husband in Rome. Meanwhile, he went away from Rome, leaving instructions that letters and parcels should be sent on to Naples; in the same way he left Naples shortly afterwards. . . . Some months later a box containing the eau de Cologne reached them in Paris, with an immense bill to pay for its travelling expenses.

She was in her own way not at all stupid and had far more strength and energy than he. Her culture was typically German—she had read an immense amount, but not what is necessary, and had studied all manner of subjects without reaching a clear grasp of anything.

Her complete lack of feminine grace made an unpleasant impression. From her abrupt voice to her angular gestures and angular features, from her cold eyes to her eagerness to drag the conversation down to ambiguous topics, everything about her was masculine. Openly, before every one, she dangled about her husband as elderly men dangle about young girls; she looked into his eyes, glanced at him to draw our attention to him, straightened his necktie, smoothed his hair and praised him with revolting indiscretion. Before strangers he was embarrassed by this, but in his own circle paid no attention to it, as a man absorbed in his work does not notice the devotion with which his dog licks his boots and fawns upon him. They sometimes had scenes over this after visitors had gone away; but next day the adoring Emma would begin the same fond pestering again, and he would put up with it again for the sake of his comforts and for the sake of her zealous supervision of everything. The following anecdote will show better than anything the extremes to which she went in spoiling her darling. Ivan Turgenev went in to see them one evening after dinner. He found Herwegh lying on the sofa. Emma was rubbing his foot; she left off when their visitor entered. 'Why have you stopped? Go on!' said the poet wearily. 'Are you ill?' asked Turgenev. 'No, not at all, but it's very pleasant. Well, what's the news?' They went on talking while Emma went on rubbing his feet.

Fully persuaded that every one admired her husband, she chattered about him incessantly, without observing either that it was very boring to others, or that she did him no good by her anecdotes of his delicate nerves and capricious exactingness; to her all that seemed very charming and quite worth being imprinted for ever and ever in the memory of men; other people were revolted by it.

EMMA'S INFATUATION

'My Georg is a fearful egoist and quite spoilt (*zu verwöhnt*),' she used to say; 'but who has more right to be spoilt than he? All great poets have been capricious children all their lives, and they have always been spoilt. The other day he bought me a superb camellia; when he got it home he was so loth to part with it that he did not even show it me, but hid it in his cupboard and kept it there till it was quite withered—*so kindisch!*'

That is word for word what she told us. By this idolatrous worship Emma brought her Georg to the edge of an abyss; he fell into it, indeed, and if he did not perish, covered himself with shame and disgrace.

The news of the February revolution roused Germany. Hearts were set throbbing, talk and murmuring were heard from one end to another of the one United German Fatherland divided into thirty parts. The German workmen in Paris formed themselves into a club, and considered what they were to do. The Provisional Government encouraged them, not to rise, but to leave France; their sleep was somewhat troubled as it was by the French workmen. Of course, it might well happen that after Flocon's[1] parting blessing, and Caussidière's[2] strong language about tyrants and despots, these poor fellows would be shot or hanged, or thrown for twenty years into prison; but they did not care about that.

A campaign in Baden was resolved upon; but who was to be their deliverer? Who was to lead this new *armée du Rhin*, consisting of a few hundred peaceful workmen and craftsmen? Who, thought Emma, if not the great poet, with his lyre on his back and his sword in his hand, on the 'battle steed' of which he dreamed in his poems? He would sing after battle and conquer

[1] Flocon, Ferdinand (1800-1866), was secretary of the Provisional Government of February 1848.
[2] Caussidière, Marc (1808-1861), a French politician and revolutionist.—(*Translator's Notes*.)

after singing; he would be chosen dictator, he would be in the assembly of kings and dictate to them the will of his Germany; in Berlin, *Unter den Linden*, his statue would be set up, and would be visible from the old banker's house, his name would be sung through the ages, and... in those songs the good, devoted Emma, who had accompanied him as sword-bearer, page, orderly, and watched over him *in der Schwertfahrt*, would perhaps not be forgotten. And she ordered herself, in the Rue Neuve-des-Petits-Champs, a martial riding-habit of the three national colours—black, red, and gold, and bought herself a black velvet béret with a cockade of the same three colours.

Through friends, Emma suggested the poet to the workmen; having no one in view and remembering Herwegh's poems calling them to rebellion, they chose him their leader. Emma persuaded him to accept the position.

What led this woman to thrust the man she so loved into this dangerous position? Where, how, when had he shown that presence of mind, that faculty of being stimulated by a crisis which gives a man control over it, that rapidity of reflection, that clearness of vision, and that spirit of defiance, in fact, without which no surgeon can perform an operation, no guerilla chief lead his followers? Where was this weakling to find strength to rouse one side of his nerves to redoubled activity and to suppress the other into insensibility? She herself had both determination and self-control, and that makes it the more unpardonable in her to have forgotten how he started at the slightest sound, turned pale at the least misadventure, how depressed he was at the slightest physical pain and how he lost his head at the sight of danger.

What made her lead him into the terrible ordeal, where pretence is useless, where there is no saving yourself by prose or verse, where the choice lies between the laurel wreath upon the tomb on one hand, and flight and the pillory of disgrace on the other? Her expectations were utterly different—she unconsciously described them in conversations and letters afterwards.

The republic in Paris had been proclaimed almost without fighting, the revolution was getting the upper hand in Italy, the news from Berlin and even from Vienna showed clearly that those thrones were tottering; it was difficult to imagine that the Duke of Baden or the King of Würtemberg could stand firm against the onrush of revolutionary ideas. It might have been expected that at the first shout of freedom the soldiers would fling away their weapons, and the people would open their arms to the insurgents, the poet would proclaim the republic, the republic would proclaim the poet dictator—had not Lamartine been dictator! All that would be left then would be for the dictator-poet to pass in triumphal procession through the whole of Germany, with his black, red, and gold Emma in her béret, to be covered with military and civic glory. . . .

In reality things turned out otherwise. The dull-witted soldier of Baden or Swabia knows nothing of poets or republics, but he knows his discipline and his corporal very well indeed and, from his innate servility, loves them, and blindly obeys his officers. The peasants were taken unawares, the revolutionaries moved without a serious plan and with nothing prepared. Even brave men like Hecker[1] and Willich[2] could do nothing—

[1] Hecker, F. K. F. (1811-1881), one of the leaders of the democratic and Socialist party of Germany, attempted on the outbreak of the German revolution to convert the preliminary convention (*Das Vorparlament*) into a permanent assembly. At the head of a band of revolutionists he invaded Baden, was defeated and fled to Switzerland and from there to America, where he took to farming. In the Civil War he raised a regiment of Germans and commanded a brigade.

[2] See page 256.—(*Translator's Notes.*)

they too were defeated, but they did not flee from the field of battle and, luckily for them, had no adoring German woman beside them.

When firing began, Emma saw her pale and terrified Georg with tears of terror in his eyes, ready to fling away his sword and hide anywhere—and she completed his ruin. She stood in front of him under fire and called on his comrades to save the poet. The soldiers were victorious. Emma, covering her husband's flight, ran the risk of being wounded, killed, or taken prisoner, that is, sent for twenty years to Spandau or Rastadt, besides a preliminary flogging.

He hid in a neighbouring village at the very beginning of the battle. There he rushed to a peasant, beseeching and imploring the latter to hide him. The peasant hesitated at first, fearing the soldiers, but at last called him into his yard and, looking round, hid the future dictator in an empty barrel and covered him with straw, exposing his house to the risk of pillage and himself to the risk of *Fuchtel* and imprisonment. The soldiers appeared—the peasant did not betray him, but sent word to Emma, who came to fetch him, hid her husband in a cart, changed her clothes, seated herself on the box and drove him over the frontier. 'What was the name of the man who saved you?' we asked him. 'I forgot to ask him,' Herwegh answered calmly.

His irritated comrades fell upon the luckless poet with fury, paying him out at the same time for having grown rich and for his lodgings being covered with 'gilt carving' and for his aristocratic effeminacy, and so on. His wife so utterly failed to see the *portée* of what she had done that four months later she published, in her husband's defence, a brochure, in which she described her own heroic deeds, oblivious of the light this threw on him.

Soon charges were made against him, not only of running away, but of wasting and concealing the party funds.

I think that the money was not appropriated by him, but at the same time I feel sure that it was aimlessly squandered and on utterly unnecessary fancies of the martial pair. P. Annenkov was an eye-witness of the purchase of pasties and turkeys stuffed with truffles, at Chevet's, and wines and so on being packed in the leader's travelling carriage. Money was given by Flocon in accordance with the instructions of the Provisional Government: there are very strange variations in the estimate of this sum; the French talked of thirty thousand francs, Herwegh declared that he had not received even half that, but that the government had paid his railway fare. To this charge the returning insurgents added, that when they reached Strasbourg, hungry, ragged, and without a farthing, after the defeat, they applied to Herwegh for assistance, and were refused—Emma did not even allow them to see him—while he was living in an expensive hotel and wearing 'yellow morocco slippers.' Why they regarded that as a sign of luxury, I do not know, but I heard of those yellow slippers a dozen times.

All this happened as in a dream. At the beginning of March the deliverers of their country, *in spe*, had been still feasting in Paris; by the middle of May, defeated, they crossed the French frontier back again. Herwegh, coming to his senses in Paris, saw his old garden path to glory choked up—real life had sternly reminded him of his limits. He realised that his position—the poet of his wife, and the dictator who had fled the field of battle— was awkward. . . . He had to begin his life afresh, or go to the bottom. I fancied—and that was where I made my worst mistake—that he would outgrow the petty side of his character. I fancied that I could help him in this more than any one.

And how could I help thinking it when the man said to me every day (and later on wrote it): 'I know the pitiful weakness of my character—your character is clearer and stronger than mine—support me, be an elder brother, a father to me. . . . I have no one near or dear to me—I concentrate on you all my affections—you can make anything of me by love and friendship—do not be severe, but kind and indulgent. Let me keep your hand . . . and, indeed, I shall not let it go, I cling to you. . . . In one thing I am not inferior to you, perhaps, indeed, go beyond you—in my unbounded love for any one dear to my heart.'

He was not lying, but all this laid no obligation upon him. He was not lying, but the truth cost him nothing. Why, he did not go to the Baden rising either, meaning to desert his comrades in the hour of conflict, but at the sight of danger he fled. So long as there is no hindrance, no conflict, so long as neither effort nor sacrifice is needed, all may go swimmingly—for whole years, for a whole lifetime . . . but if there is any stumbling-block in the path, then there will be trouble, crime, or shame. Why did I not understand that then!

Towards the end of 1848, Herwegh took to spending almost every evening with us. It was dull for him at home. Emma did, indeed, bother him dreadfully. She had come back from the Baden expedition exactly the same as she went. She had no inner misgivings over what had happened. As before, she was in love, satisfied, talkative, as though they had come back from a victory, or at any rate with no wounds in the back. Only one thing worried her—shortage of money and the certain expectation of soon having none at all. The revolution at which he had so unsuccessfully assisted had not freed Germany, nor covered the poet's brow with laurels, but it had completely ruined the old banker, her father. She was for ever trying to dissipate her husband's gloomy thoughts; it never entered her head that only these mournful reflections might perhaps be his salvation.

The superficial, volatile Emma had no yearnings for deep spiritual thought, productive apparently of nothing but pain. Hers was one of those natures (like simple tunes in two time) which cut every Gordian knot with their *entweder oder*; to left or to right does not matter to them so long as they can extricate themselves somehow and hurry on again . . . whither? That they do not know themselves. She would break into the middle of a talk either with an anecdote or with a practical observation—though its practical bearings were of the lowest order. Convinced that no one among us was gifted with so much practical ability as she, instead of concealing her business abilities through coquetry, she coquettishly displayed them. It must be said, moreover, that she never showed any real practical good sense. Fussing about, discussing prices and cooks, furniture and materials, is something very different from business capacity. Everything in her house was at sixes and sevens, because everything was subordinated to her monomania; she was for ever on the *qui vive*, watching her husband's face, and she put his caprices before all the real necessities of life, and even before the health and education of the children.

Herwegh naturally struggled to get away from home, and sought with us peace and harmony; he saw in us a sort of ideal family in which he loved everything, worshipped everything, the children as much as us. He dreamed of going with us somewhere far away and thence calmly watching the fifth act of the dark European tragedy. And for all that, except for having the same or very similar understanding of things in general, there was very little resemblance between us. Herwegh somehow brought everything in the world back to himself, he devoted himself for his own ends, sought attention with timidity and vanity, was diffident and at the same time persuaded of his superiority. All this taken together made him coquettish and capricious, sometimes he was intentionally melancholy, attentive or inattentive. He was in perpetual need of some one who would be guide, friend, confidant and slave all at once, precisely as Emma was, who would put up with coldness and upbraiding when his services were not needed, and who would be ready at the first beck to rush back again and do what he was ordered with smiling obedience.

I, too, sought love and friendship, sought sympathy and even applause, and tried to win them, but I have never had a trace of this feminine feline playing at *dépit* and scenes of explanation, this everlasting thirst foi attention and petting. Possibly the unrestrained truthfulness, excessive self-confidence, and healthy simplicity of my behaviour—my *laisser aller*—also arises frorr vanity, perhaps through them I call down misfortune or my head, but so it is. In laughter and in sorrow, in love and in public interests, I yielded myself sincerely, and could rejoice and grieve with no thought of myself With strong nerves and muscles, I stood independen and self-reliant, and was ready to give a helping hand to another, though I never asked for help or support as a charity for myself. With such opposite temperament it could hardly be expected that there should not be sometimes unpleasant encounters between Herwegh and me. But, in the first place, he was much more on hi guard with me than with others; in the second, he com pletely disarmed me by the mournful recognition that he was in fault; he did not justify himself, but in the nam of friendship begged indulgence for the weakness which he himself recognised and censured. I played the part of a sort of guardian, defended him from others and gave him lectures which he received submissively. His submissiveness was extremely distasteful to Emma—she was jealously resentful of it.

The year 1849 had come.

II

THE YEAR 1849

Delirium of the Heart

LITTLE by little, in 1849, I began to notice various changes in Herwegh. His moody character became more and more moody; he had attacks of insufferable melancholy and weakness. His wife's father lost his fortune for good and all; the remnants that were saved were needed for other members of the family . . . poverty knocked more rudely at the poet's door. . . . He could not think of it without shuddering and losing every trace of manliness. Emma struggled her utmost, borrowed right and left, obtained goods on credit and sold her things—and all that he might not notice the true position of affairs. She not only denied herself necessaries, but even had no underclothes made for the children that he might dine at the Provençal Frères and buy himself rubbish. He took money from her, not knowing how she had obtained it, and not wishing to know. I reproached her for this, told her that she was ruining him, and hinted the same to him—he persistently refused to understand, while she lost her temper, and everything went on as before.

Though he was ludicrously afraid of poverty, yet that was not the cause of his depression. In his lamentations about himself one note was continually recurring, and I grew sick of hearing it; in the end, it annoyed me to hear Herwegh's everlasting repetition of complaints of his own weakness, accompanied with reproaches for my not needing kindness and caresses, while he was fading and perishing without a helping hand, while he was so lonely and unhappy that he longed to die, while, though he had a deep respect for Emma, his sensitive, differently attuned soul shrank from her harsh, rough contact and even from her 'loud voice.' Then followed passionate protestations of his affection for me. . . . Through this feverish and nervous condition I began to discern a feeling that alarmed me for him as much as for myself. It seemed to me that his affection for Natalie was assuming a more passionate character. There was nothing for me to do, I remained silent, and began sorrowfully to foresee that in this way we were rapidly making for great trouble, and that something in our life would be shattered.

. . . Everything was shattered.

The everlasting talk of despair, the everlasting entreaty for attention, for a warm word, and dependence upon it, and the complaining and complaining—all this had an immense effect on a woman whose hardly-won serenity had just been destroyed, and who was suffering from the profoundly tragic surroundings in which we were living.

'There is an element left out in you,' Natalie said to me, 'and the lack of it goes very well with your character; you don't understand the yearning for the tender care of a mother, a friend, a sister, which so frets Herwegh. I understand it because I feel it myself. He is a big child, while you are a grown-up man; he can be distressed or made happy by a trifle. A harsh word is almost death to him, he must be spared. . . . On the other hand, with what infinite gratitude he thanks one for the smallest attention, for warmth, for sympathy! . . .'

Could it be? . . . But no, he would himself have told me before speaking to her . . . and I kept his secret inviolate and did not hint at it with one word. I regretted that he did not speak to me. A secret may be kept if it is entrusted to no one, but only if it is to no one. If he had spoken of his love he *could not* have been silent with a man with whom he was living in such spiritual intimacy, and about a secret so closely affecting the latter. So he had not spoken. . . . I forgot for the time the old novel entitled *Arminius*.

Towards the end of 1849 I went from Zurich to Paris to take steps about my mother's money, which was detained by the Russian Government. I parted from Herwegh when I left Geneva. On the way I met him in Berne. I found him reading to Simon[1] of Trèves fragments from *Vom andern Ufer*, from the proofs. He rushed at me as though we had not met for months. I was going on the evening of the same day. He did not leave my side for a minute, again and again repeating declarations of the most ardent and passionate affection. Why did he not find the strength then to make a straightforward and open confession? . . . I was kindly disposed to him then, everything might have happened humanely.

He saw me off to the posting-station, said good-bye and, leaning against the gate by which the posting-chaise drove out, remained there wiping his eyes. . . . This was almost the last moment when I really loved the man. . . . It was only after thinking the whole night that I came to one word which I could not get out of my head—'disaster, disaster!' 'What will come of it?'

My mother soon afterwards left Paris. I remained at Emma's, but was in reality completely alone. This solitude was essential for me; I wanted to be alone, to think what to do. A letter from Natalie, in which she spoke of her sympathy for Herwegh, gave me an opening and I made up my mind to write to her. My letter was sorrowful but calm; I begged her to look quietly and attentively into her own heart and to be open with herself and with me, I reminded her that we were too closely bound together by all the past and by all our life to leave

[1] Simon, Ludwig (1810-1872), was a lawyer of Trèves, elected in 1848 to the German National Assembly, as member for the extreme Left. In July 1849 he escaped to Switzerland; in his absence was sentenced to death at Trèves. He published in 1855 a book, *Aus dem Exil*.—(*Translator's Note*.)

anything unspoken. 'I got your letter of the 9th' (Natalie wrote, and this letter has remained, almost all the rest were burnt), 'and I, too, sit and only wonder: why is this? And I weep and weep. Perhaps it is all my fault, perhaps I don't deserve to live—but I feel just as I wrote to you on the evening when I was left alone. Blameless towards you and towards the whole world, I have had no feeling of reproach in my soul. I have grown into my love for you as I have into God's world; if I were not in it, it seems I should be nowhere! To be cast out of that world—anywhere, I must be born again. I am inseparable from it as from nature, come from it and! go back into it again. I have never for one instant felt differently. It is a wide, rich world, I know no inner world so rich; perhaps it is too large, perhaps it has too much enlarged my being and its needs—in this fullness there are minutes, and there have been from the very beginning of our life together, in which somewhere deep down in the bottom of my soul, something like a fine hair has fretted my soul imperceptibly, and then everything has been bright again. . . .' 'This unsatisfied something, this something left unused and outcast,' Natalie writes in another letter, craved other sympathy, and found it in Herwegh's affection.

This was not enough for me, and I wrote to her: 'Don't turn away from simply looking into the depths of yourself, don't try to find explanations. You won't escape the whirlpool by talking, it will carry you away just the same. There is a new note in your letters unfamiliar to me, not the note of sadness, but another. . . . Now everything is still in our hands . . . let us have the courage to go to the bottom of it. Consider that since we have put the secret which troubled our soul into words, *Herwegh will be a false note in our harmony or I shall. I am ready to go with Sasha to America*, then we shall see how things are... it will be hard for me, but

I shall try to bear it; here it will be harder still, and I cannot bear it!'

To this letter she answered with a cry of horror, the thought of separation from me had never occurred to her. 'How can you! How can you—and to part from you . . . as though that were possible . . . no, no, I long to come to you, to come to you at once. . . . I am going to pack up, and in a few days I shall be in Paris with the children!'

On the day of leaving Zurich she wrote again: 'As though after storm and shipwreck I come back to you as to my haven, with full faith, with full love. If only the state of your soul were like that in which I am now! I am happier than ever! I love you always the same, but I have learnt to know your love better, and all my accounts with life are settled—I expect nothing, I desire nothing. Misunderstandings!—I am grateful to them, they have made so much clear to me, and they will pass away and disappear like storm-clouds.'

Our meeting in Paris was not joyful, but it was filled with the feeling of deep, genuine recognition that the roots of our life had gone too deep for the storm to tear them up, that it was not easy to part us. In the long conversations of that period, one thing surprised me, and I looked out for it several times, and was every time convinced that I was right. Together with the warm affection she still retained for Herwegh, Natalie seemed to breathe more freely away from him, as though stepping out of the circle of some black magic spell; she was afraid of him, she felt that there were dark forces in his soul, she was frightened by his boundless egoism and she looked for support and protection in me.

Though he knew nothing of my correspondence with Natalie, Herwegh saw that there was something wrong from my letters. As a matter of fact, apart from everything else, I was very much displeased with him. Emma was struggling, weeping, trying to satisfy him and get him money, while he either left her letters unanswered or wrote spiteful things and kept asking for more and more money.

His letters to me which I have kept are more like ecstatic love-letters than a friendly correspondence. He tearfully reproaches me for coldness, he beseeches me not to abandon him, he cannot live without me, without the full cloudless sympathy of the past, he curses our misunderstandings and the interference of the 'frantic woman' (*i.e.*, Emma), he thirsts to begin a new life, a life far away, a life with us, and again he calls me his father, his brother, his dearest friend. To all this I wrote to him in different variations: 'Consider whether you are capable of beginning a new life, whether you are able to shake off . . . the rottenness, the corrupt civilisation'—and twice I reminded him of Aleko,[1] to whom the old Gypsy says: 'Leave us, proud man, you want freedom for yourself alone.' He answered this with tears and reproaches, but did not speak out. His letters of 1850 and our first conversations at Nice make up a terrible indictment . . . of what? Of deceit, of treachery, of lying? . . . No. And that would be nothing new—but of that weak-spirited doubleness of which I have so many times accused the Western European. Going many times over all the details of our mournful drama, I am always brought up short with amazement at how this man never once, never by one word, never by one straightforward impulse of the heart, betrayed himself. How could he, feeling the impossibility of being open with me, try to enter into closer and closer intimacy with me, and touch in his talk on those sacred places of the soul which can only be touched without sacrilege in perfect and mutual openness?

[1] Aleko, the hero of Pushkin's poem, 'The Gypsies.'—(*Translator's Note*.)

The moment when he guessed my doubt—and not only kept silent, but assured me more and more warmly of his affection, and at the same time worked more and more intensely by his despair on the woman whose heart was shaken—the moment when he began passively deceiving me by his silence while beseeching her (as I afterwards learned) not to deprive him of my affection by an incautious word—that moment was the beginning of crime.

Crime! . . . Yes . . . and all the calamities that follow come as the simple, inevitable consequence of it—they come unchecked by deaths, unchecked by penitence, because they are not the punishment but the consequence. . . . Consequences come upon a generation through the terrible immutability of what has once been done. Atonement, repentance may reconcile a man to himself and to others, penitence may redeem him, but the consequences of his action go their own terrible way. To escape from them, religion has invented paradise—and its antechamber the monastery.

I was turned out of Paris, and almost at the same time Emma was also. We decided to spend a year or two in Nice—it was then Italy—and Emma went there also. Within a short time, that is, towards winter, my mother was to come to Nice, and with her Herwegh.

Why did I go with Natalie to that town? This question has occurred to me and to others, but it is really a petty one. Apart from the fact that wherever I had gone Herwegh could have come too, was it possible to achieve anything but mortification by geographical and other external measures?

Within a fortnight or three weeks of his arrival, Herwegh assumed the airs of a Werther—in the last stages of despair—and so conspicuously that a Russian doctor, who was passing through Nice, was convinced that he was becoming definitely insane. His wife used to appear with tear-stained eyes—he treated her outrageously. She would come for hours together to weep in Natalie's room, and both were convinced that to-day or to-morrow he would fling himself into the sea or shoot himself. Natalie's pale cheeks and anxious expression, and her anxious preoccupation, even when she was with the children, showed me clearly what was passing within her.

Not a word had been said yet, but already through the external calm there was the gleam of something sinister coming nearer and nearer—like two glittering points continually disappearing and appearing again at the edge of the forest that show that a wild beast is there. Everything was moving rapidly to a climax. It was delayed by the birth of Olga.

III

THE YEAR 1851

I

BEFORE the New Year Natalie brought a water-colour she had ordered from the painter Guyot,[1] to show me.

It was a sketch of our verandah, with part of the house and the yard, with the children playing in the yard and Tata's goat lying there—Natalie herself was in the background, on the verandah. I thought that the sketch was meant for me, but Natalie said that she meant to give it to Herwegh for a New Year's present. . . . I was vexed. 'Do you like it?' asked Natalie. 'I like it so much,' I said, 'that if Herwegh will allow it, I will order a copy to be made for myself.'

From my pallor and my voice, Natalie saw that these words were both a challenge and the sign of a violent storm within. She glanced at me, there were tears in her eyes. 'Take it for yourself,' she said.

'Nothing would induce me, anything so mean . . .'

We said no more. We kept the New Year at my mother's. I was in a state of acute irritability; I sat beside Vogt and, filling his glass and mine over and over again, I kept making biting and sarcastic jokes. Vogt was rolling with laughter. Herwegh looked mournfully from under his brows. At last he understood. After drinking to the New Year, he raised his glass and said that the only thing he hoped was, 'that the coming year might be no worse than the last, that he desired this with all his heart, but did not expect it. On the contrary, he had a foreboding that all, all would fall into ruins.'

[1] Guyot, Antoine Patrice (b. 1787), a genre painter, well known in his day.—(*Translator's Note*.)

I said nothing.

Next morning I took up my old novel, *Who is to Blame?* and read over Lubinka's diary and the last chapters. Could this be a prophecy of my fate, just as Onyegin's duel foreshadowed Pushkin's fate? . . . But an inner voice said to me: 'You are a queer sort of Krutsifersky—and, indeed, he is a queer sort of Beltov! Where is his noble sincerity, where is my tearful self-sacrifice?' And in the midst of my conviction of Natalie's passing infatuation, I was even more convinced that I should fight it out with him, that he would not drive me out of her heart.

What happened was what I expected—Natalie herself invited explanation. After the scene over the sketch, and the New Year's party at my mother's, it was impossible to put it off. The conversation was painful. *We were both no longer on the high level on which we had been the year before*. She was confused, afraid of my going away, afraid of his going away, longed to go away herself for a year to Russia and was afraid to go. I saw her wavering and saw that he with his egoism would destroy her . . . while she would not have the strength to withstand. I was beginning to hate him for his silence.

Once more I repeated 'I put my fate in your hands. Once more I beseech you to weigh everything, to think of the value of everything. . . . I am still ready to accept any decision—I am ready to wait a day, a week, only the decision must be final. I feel,' I said, 'that I have reached the limit of my strength—I can still behave decently—but I feel, too, that I shan't be able to for long.'

'You are not going away, you are not going away,' she said, bursting into tears, 'I could not survive that.' On her tongue such words were not to be taken lightly. '*He must go.*'

LAST SCENE WITH HERWEGH

'Natalie, don't be in a hurry—don't be in a hurry to take the final decision because it is final . . . wait a little . . . think—as much as you like, but give me a definite answer. These ebbs and flows are more than I can stand . . . they are making me stupid. I am growing petty, I shall go off my head. . . . Ask anything you like of me, but it must be once for all. . . .'

At that point my mother and Kolya drove up to invite us to Mentone; when we went out to take our seats in the carriage, it appeared that there was one place too few. I motioned Herwegh to the seat. Herwegh, by no means distinguished by such delicacy as a rule, would not take it. I looked at him, slammed the carriage door and said to the coachman, 'Off!' We were left alone, the two of us, on the seashore in front of the house. I felt as though there were a stone on my heart; he was silent, pale as a sheet, and avoided my eyes. Why did not I begin speaking openly or shove him off the rock into the sea? A sort of nervous impotence prevented me. He said something to me about the sufferings of a poet and life being so horribly organised that a poet brings trouble everywhere. He suffers himself and makes every one near him suffer. . . . I asked him whether he had read George Sand's *Horace*. He did not remember. I advised him to read it. He went to Visconti's for the book.

I never saw him again.

When, between six and seven, we all assembled for dinner, he was not there. His wife came in—her eyes swollen with tears: she announced that her husband was ill—we all looked at each other—I felt quite capable of sticking into her the knife I had in my hand. He shut himself up in his rooms on the top storey. By this *étalage* he did for himself—I was free as regards him.

At last all the others had gone, and the children were in bed—*we were left alone*. Natalie sat in the window crying. I walked about the room, the blood throbbing in my temples; I could scarcely breathe.

'He is going,' she said at last.

'I imagine that is not necessary—it is I must go.'

'For God's sake . . .'

'I am going.'

'Alexandr, Alexandr, don't say what you may regret—listen to me—save us all. You alone can do it. He is crushed, he is utterly despondent. You know yourself what you have been to him, his frantic love—his frantic affection and the consciousness that he has caused you grief—and worse . . . he wants to go away, to vanish, but you must not complicate things—or he is not a step from suicide.'

'Do you believe that?'

'I am certain of it.'

'And it is he who says so?'

'He and Emma. He has cleaned his pistol.'

I burst into a roar of laughter and asked: 'Is it his Baden one—he 'd have to clean it, it must have fallen in the mud. You can tell Emma, though, that I will answer for his life. I'll insure it for any sum you like.'

'Mind that you do not regret your laughter,' said Natalie, shaking her head gloomily.

'If you like I'll go and persuade him . . .'

'What will it all lead to?'

'The consequences,' I said, 'are hard to foresee and still harder to avert.'

'My God! My God!—the children, the poor children, what will become of them!'

'You ought to have thought of them before!' I said.

And that, of course, was the most cruel thing of all that I said to her. I was too much worked up to understand the meaning of what I said in a humane way. I felt something convulsive in my chest and in my head, and was, perhaps, capable of bloody acts as well as cruel

REMORSE 51

words. She was utterly crushed—a silence followed. Half an hour passed, I wanted to drink my cup of bitterness to the dregs, and put several questions to her—she answered. I felt myself torn to shreds, savage impulses of revenge, of jealousy, of wounded *amour-propre*, made me drunk; no punishment, no gibbet could have had terrors for me, my life was not worth a farthing. That is what makes mad and dreadful deeds possible. I did not say a word—I stood in front of the big table in the drawing-room, with my arms folded—probably my face was utterly distorted.

The silence went on. All at once I glanced at her and was frightened—her face was covered with a deathly pallor, a bluish pallor, her lips were white, her mouth half-opened and twitching—not uttering a word, she gazed at me with vacant, frantic eyes. That look of infinite suffering, of mute agony instantly stilled the turmoil of passion; I felt sorry for her, tears trickled down my cheeks, I was ready to fall at her feet, to entreat her forgiveness. . . . I sat down on the sofa beside her, took her hand, put my head on her shoulder and tried to comfort her in a soft, gentle voice.

My conscience tormented me, I felt I had been an inquisitor, a torturer. . . . Was this what was wanted? Was this a friend's help, was this sympathy? And so with all my culture, with all my humanity, in a fit of fury and jealousy I could torture an unhappy woman, could play the part of a Bluebeard?

A few minutes passed before she said anything, before she could say anything·—then suddenly she threw herself on my neck sobbing. I let her sink on the sofa; utterly worn out, she could only say: 'Don't be afraid, dear, these are good tears, tears of tenderness; no, no, I will never be parted from you.'

Her agitation and spasmodic sobbing was too much, she closed her eyes, she was fainting; I poured eau de

Cologne on her head, moistened her temples; she grew calm, opened her eyes, pressed my hand, and sank into semi-consciousness which lasted more than an hour: I remained on my knees beside her; when she opened her eyes, she met my calm, mournful look, the tears were still rolling down my cheeks—she smiled to me. . . .

This was the crisis. From that minute the stifling fumes that weighed on her began to lift, the poison acted less freely.

'Alexandr,' she said, recovering herself a little, 'finish what you have done, swear to me—I must have it, I can't live without it—swear that it shall all end without bloodshed—think of the children . . . of what will become of them without you and without me.'

'I promise to do everything possible to prevent a collision, to sacrifice a great deal—but for that I must have one thing, that he should leave to-morrow—go at least to Genoa.'

'That's as you like . . . and we will begin a new life and let all that is past be past.'

I embraced her warmly.

Next morning Emma came to my room—she was dishevelled, with tear-stained eyes, looking very ugly, in a blouse with a cord round her waist. She approached me with tragic deliberation—at any other time I should have burst out laughing at this German melodrama. . . . now I was in no mood for laughing. I received her standing and made no attempt to conceal that her visit was unpleasant to me.

'What do you want?' I asked.

'I have come from *him* to you.'

'Your husband,' I said, 'might come himself if he wants anything—or perhaps he has already shot himself?'

She folded her arms across her bosom.

'And this is you speaking—you, his friend . . . I don't know you! Surely you must understand the tragedy of what is taking place before your eyes . . . his tender constitution will not survive separation from her, nor a rupture with you—yes, yes, with you . . . he is weeping over the sorrow he has caused you—he begged me to tell you that his life is in your hands, he begs you to kill him . . .'

'This is a farce,' I said, interrupting her speech. 'Come, who invites people to murder like this, and through his wife too? This persisting in vulgar melodramatic tricks is disgusting to me. I am not a German.'

'Herr Herzen!'

'Madame Herwegh, why do you undertake such difficult commissions? You could hardly expect to hear anything pleasant from me.'

'This is a fatal calamity,' she said, after a pause; 'it has struck you and me alike . . . but look at the difference between your anger and my devotion . . .'

'Madam,' I said, 'our parts have not been alike; I beg you not to compare them, for fear you should have to blush.'

'Never,' she said defiantly, 'you do not know what you are saying.' And then she added: 'I will take him away, he must not remain in this position—your will shall be done. But you are no longer in my eyes the man I have so much respected and looked upon as Georg's best friend. No, if you were that man, you would have parted with Natalie, let her go, let him go; I would have remained with you and the children here.'

I laughed aloud. She flushed crimson, and with a voice shaking with anger and indignation, asked me: 'What does that mean?'

'Why do you jest about serious matters?' I said to her; 'but that's enough. Here is my ultimatum: go at once to Natalie, yourself alone, talk to her—if she wants to go, let her go—I shall not hinder any one or anything except (excuse me), except your staying here;

I can manage the housekeeping myself somehow—but listen. . . . If she does not want to go, this is the last night I will spend under the same roof as your husband, we shall not both be here another night alive!'

An hour later Emma came back and gloomily announced to me, in a tone as though to say: 'See the fruits of your wickedness!'

'Natalie is not going—she has destroyed a great being from *amour-propre*—I will save him —'

'And so?'

'And so we are going in a day or two . . .'

'A day or two? What do you mean? To-morrow morning! Have you forgotten the alternative?' (Repeating this, I did not really break my promise to Natalie, I was absolutely certain she would take him away.)

'I don't know you—how bitterly I've been mistaken in you!' observed the crazy woman, and she went out again.

Her diplomatic task this time was an easy one—she came back ten minutes later saying that he agreed to everything, both to going away and to a duel, but at the same time he had told her to tell me that he had taken a vow not to lift his pistol to my breast—but was ready to accept death at my hands.

'You see how he keeps on joking with you—why, even the French king was put to death simply by a public executioner, and not by a friend. And so you will set off to-morrow?'

'I really don't know how to manage. We have nothing ready.'

'Everything can be got ready before night.'

'We must get a *visa* for our passports.'

I rang the bell; Rocca, our cook, came in. I told him that Madame Emma begged him to take their passports at once and to get a *visa* for Genoa.

'But we have nothing for the journey.'

A BOURGEOIS DEPARTURE

'Do you need much to get to Genoa?'

'Six hundred francs.'

'Allow me to hand it you.'

'We owe bills to the shops here.'

'Approximately?'

'Five hundred francs.'

'Don't worry yourself, and *bon voyage*.'

This tone she could not endure, *amour-propre* was almost her leading passion.

'Why,' she said, 'why this behaviour to *me*? Me you have no right to hate or to despise.'

'So him I have?'

'No,' she said, choking with tears, 'no, I only meant to say that I liked you sincerely as a sister, that I don't like to leave you without shaking hands with you. I respect you, you may be right, but you are a cruel man. If you knew what I have been through!'

'But why have you been all your life a slave?' I said to her, giving her my hand; at that minute I was not capable of sympathy. 'You deserve your fate.'

She went away hiding her face.

At ten o'clock next morning, in a hired coach, upon which various boxes and hampers were loaded, the poet set off—*mit Weib und Kind*—for Genoa. I was standing at the open window; he managed to whisk into the carriage so rapidly that I did not catch sight of him. She held out her hand to the cook and the maid, and took her seat beside him. Anything more ignominious than this bourgeois departure I cannot imagine. Natalie was distressed. We went out alone together into the country; the walk was a dismal one, the blood was still streaming from fresh, raw wounds. On returning home, the first person that met me was Herwegh's son Horace, a boy of nine, a mischievous and thievish little fellow.

'Where have you come from?'

'From Mentone.'

'What has happened?'

'Here is a note from Maman for you.'

'Lieber Herzen,' she wrote, as if nothing had happened between us, 'we are stopping for a couple of days at Mentone, the room at the hotel is small—Horace is in Georg's way—allow us to leave him with you for a few days.'

This lack of tact amazed me. At the same time Emma wrote to Karl Vogt to come that they might consult him—so outsiders were to be mixed up in our affairs! I asked Vogt to take Horace and to say that we had no room.

'Yet,' she sent word to me through Vogt, 'we still have the upper rooms for another three months, and I can make use of them.' That was perfectly true—only it was I who paid the rent for those rooms. Yes, in this tragedy, as in Shakespeare, the coarse laughter, oaths, and petty cheating of the market-place are side by side with strains that tear the heart, with the moan of ebbing life, of dying faith, of dimming thought.

Emma had a maid-servant, a handsome and very honourable French girl from Provence, called Jeannette; she remained behind for a couple of days, and was to go with their luggage by steamer to Genoa. Next morning Jeannette softly opened my study door and asked me whether she might come in and speak to me alone. This had never happened before; I thought that she was wanting to ask for money, and was prepared to give it her. Blushing up to her ears, the good Provençale gave me, with tears in her eyes, various unpaid bills of Emma's, and added: 'Madame told me, but I really cannot do it without asking your leave—you see, she told me to buy a lot of different things in the shops and have them put down on these bills—I couldn't do it without telling you.'

'You did quite right to tell me. What did she tell you to buy?'

'Here is the list.'

On the list were several pieces of linen, several dozen handkerchiefs, and a complete outfit of children's underclothes.

They say that Caesar could read, write, and dictate at the same moment: this is somewhat the same versatility —to be able to think of thrifty means of obtaining linen and children's stockings while lives are being ruined, and men are feeling the cold blade of Saturn's scythe. The Germans are a glorious people!

We were again alone, but this was not the past over again—everything bore the traces of the storm. Faith and doubt, weariness and irritation, the feeling of annoyance and indignation were a torture, but what was most fretting of all was that the thread of life was broken, that precious carelessness which had made life so easy was gone, nothing was left sacred. Since what had been had been, nothing was impossible. Thoughts of the past terrified me for the future. How many times we came in to dinner alone in the evening and, both scarcely touching anything and not uttering a word, got up from the table wiping away a tear, and seeing kind Rocca, with an angry face, shake his head as he carried away the dishes.

Idle days, sleepless nights . . . misery—misery. I drank spirits of all sorts, cognac, old Bellet, drank at night alone and drank by day with Engelson—and that in the climate of Nice. The Russian weakness of drowning sorrow in drink is by no means so bad as is said. Heavy sleep is better than heavy sleeplessness, and the headache of the morning after is better than deadly gloom on an empty stomach.

Herwegh sent me a letter. I sent it back without reading it. He took to writing to Natalie, letter after letter. He wrote once more to me—I sent the letter back. I looked on gloomily at this. That time should have been a time of thorough testing, of peace and of freedom from external influences. What sort of peace, what sort of freedom could there be with letters coming from a man who posed as being frantic and threatened not only suicide but the most fearful crimes? Thus, for instance, he wrote that he had moments of frenzy when he longed to cut his children's throats, to fling their corpses out of the window and to appear before us bathed in their blood. In another, he wrote that he should come to kill himself at my feet, and say: 'See to what you have brought the man who loved you so!' Side by side with this, he kept imploring Natalie to reconcile him with me, to take everything on herself, and to suggest that he should come as Sasha's tutor.

A dozen times he wrote of his loaded pistol; Natalie still believed it all. He only asked her blessing on his death. I persuaded her to write to him that she at last agreed, that she was convinced there was nothing for it but death. He answered that her words came *too late*, that he was now in a different mood and felt he had not strength enough to do it, but that, forsaken by all, he would go away to Egypt. This letter did him great damage in Natalie's eyes.

After that, Orsini came from Genoa, and he told us, laughing, how the husband and wife had tried to commit suicide. . . . Learning that Herwegh was in Genoa, Orsini went to see them and met him walking along the sea-front. Learning from him that his wife was at home, Orsini went to see her. She immediately explained to him that she had made up her mind to starve herself to death, that this form of suicide had been selected for him by himself, but that she wished to share his fate, and she besought Orsini not to desert Horace and Ada.

Orsini was petrified with astonishment.

'We have touched nothing for thirty hours,' Emma

went on; 'do persuade him to eat something, save the great poet for humanity,' and she sobbed.

Orsini went out on to the verandah and at once returned with the joyful tidings that Herwegh was standing in the corner eating *salmis*. Emma, overjoyed, rang the bell and ordered a basin of soup. At that moment her husband came in gloomily, without a word of the *salmis*, but the tell-tale basin was standing there. 'Georg,' said Emma, 'I was so delighted, hearing from Orsini that you were eating, that I, too, decided to ask for soup.'

'I felt so sick, I took a little piece of *salmis*—but that's of no consequence; death by starvation is most painful, I shall poison myself.'

His wife raised her eyes to the ceiling and glanced at Orsini as though to say: 'You see, there is no saving him.' He, too, had some soup.

Orsini is dead, but there are several witnesses of his story living, for instance, Karl Vogt, Mordini, and Charles Edmond. These antics made it very hard for Natalie. She was humiliated through him, I was humiliated through him, and she felt this poignantly.

In the spring Herwegh went away to Zurich and sent his wife to Nice (another outrageous indelicacy). I longed, after all that had happened, to rest. I took advantage of my Swiss naturalisation and went to Paris and Switzerland with Engelson.

Natalie's letters were calm, her soul seemed to be more at ease.

On the way home I met Sazonov in Geneva. Over a bottle of wine, he asked me, with the most absolute nonchalance, how things were going now between my wife and me.

'As always.'

'Well, I know the whole story, and I am asking you from friendly sympathy.'

I looked at him with a shudder of horror; he noticed nothing. What was the meaning of it? I had reckoned on its all being a secret, and here, all at once, a man speaks to me of it over a glass of wine as though it were the most ordinary everyday affair.

'What have you heard, and from whom?'

'I have heard the whole story from Herwegh himself —and I tell you openly, I don't think you are right at all. Why don't you let your wife go, or else leave her yourself?—upon my soul, it's such weakness—you could begin a new fresh life . . .'

'But what makes you imagine that she wants to go? You can't believe that I am able to *let* her go or to prevent her.'

'You coerce her morally, of course, not physically, by your words, your distress. I am very glad, though, to find you much more serene than I expected—and I don't care to be open by halves with you. Herwegh left your house, in the first place, because he's a coward, and is simply terrified of you, and in the second, because your wife promised him to come to Switzerland as soon as you were calmer.'

'That's a foul lie!' I shouted.

'That's what he told me, I give you my word of honour on it.'

When I got home to the hotel, I flung myself, sick and shattered, on the bed, without undressing, in a state bordering on madness or death—did I believe it or not? I do not know, but I cannot say that I entirely disbelieved what Sazonov had told me.

And so, I repeated to myself, this is how our poetical life is ending, in deceit, and incidentally in a European scandal . . . ha, ha, ha! They pity me, they spare me from compassion, they give me time to rest, like a soldier who is taken half-way through the flogging to the hospital, when his pulse is weak, and zealously tended that he may have the other half when he is stronger. I was insulted, outraged, humiliated.

In that state of mind I wrote at night a letter—my letter must have borne traces of frenzy, despair, and distrust. I repent, I bitterly repent that insult from afar—that wicked letter.

Natalie answered in words of black gloom. 'I were better dead,' she said; 'your faith is shattered, every word now will call back all the past to you. What am I to do, and how can I ever convince you? I weep and weep.'

Herwegh had lied.

Her following letters were briefly mournful; she was sorry for me, she wanted to heal my wounds, and what must she herself have been suffering! . . . Why did that man turn up to repeat me that lie . . . and why was there no other there to stop my letter, written in a fit of criminal fury?

2

TURIN. OCEANO NOX

On the night between the 7th and 8th of July, between one and two in the morning, I was sitting on the step of the Carignano Palace in Turin; the square was completely empty, at a little distance from me a beggar was dozing, and a sentinel was walking slowly up and down, whistling a tune from some opera and jingling with his gun. . . . It was a hot, soft night, saturated with the scent of the scirocco.

I felt extraordinarily happy, as I had not for ages; I felt again that I was still young and full of energy, that I had friends and convictions, that I was as full of love as I had been some thirteen years before. My heart was beating as I had not felt it for years; it was beating as on that March day in 1838, when I stood wrapped in my cloak under the lamp-post waiting for Ketscher in Povarsky Street.

Now, too, I was awaiting a meeting, a meeting with the same woman, and awaited it perhaps with even more love, though sad and gloomy notes were mingled with it; but on that night they were hardly audible. After the frantic crisis of bitterness and despair that had come over me on my way through Geneva, I felt better. Natalie's gentle letters, filled with sadness, tears, pain, and love, had worked my healing. She wrote that she was coming from Nice to Turin to meet me, that she longed to spend a few days in Turin. She was right: we needed to look into each other once more alone, to wash the blood from each other's wounds, to wipe away our tears and to find out once for all whether there was still happiness for us together, and all that in solitude, without the children even, and in another place too, not in the surroundings where the furniture, the very walls, might at the wrong moment bring reminder, whisper some half-forgotten word.

The posting-chaise was to arrive between one and two from the direction of the Col di Tenda; I was waiting for it at the gloomy Carignano Palace—it was to turn the corner not far from it.

I had arrived on the morning of the same day from Paris, through Mont Cenis to the Hotel Feder. I was given a large, lofty, rather handsomely furnished sitting-room and bedroom. I liked its holiday air, it was in keeping. I ordered a little supper for us and went to wander about the town, waiting for the night.

When the chaise drove up to the posting-station, Natalie recognised me. 'You here!' she said, nodding to me at the window. I opened the door, and she threw herself on my neck with such rapturous joy, with such an expression of love and thankfulness, that words from her letter flashed like lightning into my mind: 'I come back

RECONCILIATION 63

like a ship to its own haven, after storms, shipwrecks, and misfortunes—broken but saved.'

One glance, two or three words, were enough . . . all was explained and understood; I took her little travelling-bag, threw it on a stick over my back, gave her my arm, and we walked gaily along the empty streets to the hotel. There every one was asleep except the porter. On the table (laid for supper) stood two unlighted candles, bread, fruit, and a decanter of wine. I did not want to wake any one; we lighted the candles and, sitting down to an empty table, glanced at each other and at once both thought of our days at Vladimir.

She had on a white muslin dress or blouse, put on for the journey on account of the blazing heat, and at that first interview, when I came from exile, she had been in white, too, and her wedding dress had been white. Though her face wore deep imprints of violent agitations, anxieties, sufferings, and reflections, its expression recalled her features at that time.

And we ourselves were the same, only now we gave each other our hands, not as conceited young creatures, self-confident and proud in our faith in ourselves, in our faith in each other, and in our fate being somehow exceptional, but like veterans tempered in the struggle for life, who had tested not only our strength, but our weakness too, and had only just come safely from terrible blows and irretrievable mistakes. . . . Starting on the road anew, we shared the painful burden of the past together, with no settling of accounts.

We had to move forward with a humbler step for that burden, but our aching hearts still kept safe within all that was needed for settled mature happiness. Through our horror and dull agony we had seen the more clearly how inseparably years and circumstances, children and life in foreign lands, had welded us together.

At this meeting all was over, the broken threads grew

together more firmly than ever, as sometimes parts of a broken bone will grow together, not without leaving a scar. The tears of sorrow, not yet dry in our eyes, united us by a new bond—the feeling of deep compassion for each other. I saw her conflict, her agony, I saw how exhausted she was. She saw me weak, unhappy, humiliated and humiliating others, ready for sacrifice and ready for crime.

We had paid too dear a price for each other not to know what we were worth, and what we had cost each other. 'In Turin,' I wrote at the beginning of 1852, 'was our second wedding; it meant perhaps something deeper and more significant than the first, it was accompanied with full consciousness of all the responsibility which we took up anew in regard to each other, still in sight of terrible events. . . .'

Love by some miracle survived the blow which might have destroyed it.

The last dark clouds passed further and further away, for hours we talked . . . as though we had been separated for years; it was not till long after bright streaks of daylight had filtered through the shutters that we got up from the empty table. . . .

Three days later we drove home together through the Riviera to Nice. We caught a glimpse of Genoa, a glimpse of Mentone, where we had so often been, and in such a different frame of mind, a glimpse of Monaco, thrusting its velvety grass and velvety sand into the sea; they all greeted us gaily, like old friends after a separation; and here were the little vineyards, the rose-bushes, the orange-trees, and the sea lying stretched before the house, and the children playing on the beach. . . . Now they had seen us and rushed to meet us, we were at home.

I am thankful to destiny for those days and for the four months which followed them. They made a glorious ending to personal life for me. I thank her, the

THE IRREVOCABLE PAST

old heathen, for crowning the doomed victims with the rich wreath of autumn flowers and strewing their path, if only for the time, with her poppy of forgetfulness and fragrance!

The differences that parted us had vanished, the barriers had fallen. Was not this the hand which had lain in mine through my whole life, were not these the same eyes though sometimes dimmed with tears? 'Be comforted, sister, friend, comrade, all is over—and we the same as in our young, bright, holy years!'

'After sufferings, you, perhaps, know how great, have come some minutes full of bliss; all the cherished beliefs of childhood, of youth, have not only come true, but have passed through terrible ordeals, losing neither their freshness nor their fragrance, and have blossomed with new splendour and new power. I have never been so happy as now,' she wrote to her friend in Russia.

Of course, there was a sediment left from the past which could not be touched with impunity, something broken within, some lightly slumbering fear and pain.

The past is not a proof that can be corrected, but a guillotine knife; after it has once fallen there is much that cannot grow together again, and there is always something left that cannot be set right. It remains as though cast in metal, distinct, unalterable, dark as bronze. Men as a rule forget only what is not worth remembering, or what they do not understand. If only a man could forget two or three incidents, such and such happenings, such a day, such a word, he would be strong and young and bold, but burdened with them he sinks like a key to the bottom. One need not be a Macbeth to meet the ghost of Banquo; ghosts are not criminal judges, nor pangs of conscience, but the happenings that can never be obliterated from the mind.

But one ought not to forget; that is a weakness, that is a falsity of a sort; the past has its rights, it is fact, one has to get over it and not to forget it—and we moved towards that, keeping step.

Sometimes it would happen that a trivial word, uttered by outsiders, or some object that caught the eye, would pass like a razor over the heart, and blood would flow, and the pang would be insufferable, but at the same instant I would meet eyes full of alarm, looking at me with infinite distress and saying: 'Yes, you are right, it can't be helped, but—'and I tried to chase away the gathering clouds.

Holy time of reconciliation, I think of it through my tears. . . .

No, not reconciliation, that is not the word. Words are like ready-made clothes that fit all people of the same height up to a certain point and are equally unbecoming to every one. We had no need to be reconciled, we had never quarrelled; we had suffered for each other, but we had never drifted apart. At the blackest moments a sort of indissoluble unity, of which neither doubted, and a deep respect for each other remained intact. We were more like people recovering after a high fever; the delirium had passed, we knew each other again as we looked with dim and troubled eyes. The pain we had been through was fresh in the memory, and we were still conscious of exhaustion, but we knew that all the trouble was over and that we were safely on shore again.

An idea, that had several times occurred to Natalie before, absorbed her more and more now. She wanted to write the story of her heart. She was dissatisfied with the beginning and burnt the pages; only one long letter and one brief page have remained. . . . From these one can judge what has been lost. . . . Reading them almost terrifies one, one feels that one is touching a warm and suffering heart, one seems to hear the whisper of those unvoiced secrets, for ever hidden, and scarcely awakening into consciousness. In those lines one can trace the anguish of struggle leading up to new strength of spirit and of pain leading up to thought. If this work had not been cruelly interrupted, it would have been a precious document, filling the gap left by the evasive silence of woman and the haughty patronage of her by man. But the most senseless blow broke over our heads and shattered everything for ever.

Dans une mer sans fond, par une nuit sans lune, sous l'aveugle océan à jamais enfouis. V. HUGO.

So ended the summer 1851. We were quite alone. My mother, with Kolya and Spielmann, had gone to Paris to stay with Marya Kasparovna. We spent our days quietly with the children. It seemed as though all our troubles were behind us.

In November we received a letter from my mother to tell us she was setting off immediately, then another from Marseilles to say that next day, the 15th of November, they would take the steamer and come to us. During her absence we had moved into another house, also on the sea, in the suburb of St. Hélène. In this house, which had a large garden, there was a room for my mother; we decorated it with flowers, our cook went with Sasha to get Chinese lanterns, and we hung them about the walls and trees. Everything was ready. From three o'clock in the afternoon the children watched from the verandah; at last, between five and six, a dark coil of smoke could be discerned on the horizon and a few minutes later the steamer, too, could be seen, a motionless point growing larger and larger. All was bustle in the house. François ran down to the harbour, I got into the carriage and drove there.

When I reached the harbour the steamer had already

arrived, boats were waiting for the permission of quarantine authorities for the passengers to land. One of them came up to the landing-stage. Francis was standing in it.

'How is this?' I asked, 'you are back again already?'

He did not answer. I glanced at him and my heart sank; his face was livid, and he was trembling all over.

'What is it?' I asked, 'are you ill?'

'No,' he answered, avoiding my eyes, 'but our people have not come.'

'Haven't come?'

'Something happened with the steamer, so some of the passengers haven't come.'

I hastily got into a boat and told them to push off at once.

On the steamer I was met with a sort of ominous consideration and complete silence. The captain himself was waiting for me; all this was so unusual that I felt something awful was coming. The captain told me that between the island of Hyères and the mainland the steamer on which my mother was sailing had run into another vessel and sunk to the bottom, that most of the passengers had been picked up by him and by another steamer that was passing by. 'I have only two young girls of your party,' he said, and he led me to the upper deck—every one stepped aside with the same gloomy silence. I followed senselessly without even asking a question. My mother's niece, who had been staying with her, a tall slender girl, was lying on deck with wet and dishevelled hair; beside her was the maid who looked after Kolya. Seeing me, the young girl tried to sit up, to say something, but could not; she turned away sobbing.

'What has happened? Where are they?' I asked, taking the maid's hand with a sick dread.

'We know nothing,' she answered. 'The steamer

sank, we were pulled out of the water half dead. An Englishwoman gave us her clothes to change into.'

The captain looked mournfully at me, shook my hand and said: 'You must not despair; go to Hyères, perhaps you will find some of them there.'

Leaving Engelson and François to look after the girls, I drove home in a sort of stupefaction; everything in my head was confused and shuddering, I only wished that our house had been a thousand miles away. But soon I caught a gleam between the trees, and more and more; it was the lanterns lighted by the children. At our gate stood our servants, Tata, and Natalie, with Olga in her arms.

'What, you alone?' Natalie asked me calmly. 'Why, you might have brought Kolya, at least.'

'They are not there,' I said, 'something happened to their steamer. They had to change on to another, this one did not take them all. Luise is here.'

'They are not here!' cried Natalie, 'and only now I see you, your eyes are dim, your face is working. For God's sake, what has happened?'

'I am going to look for them in Hyères.'

She shook her head and added: 'Not here, not here!' Then without a word she pressed her forehead against my shoulder. We walked up the avenue without saying a word. I led her into the dining-room; as we passed, I whispered to Rocca: 'For God's sake, the lanterns'; he understood me and rushed to put them out. In the dining-room everything was ready—a bottle of wine in ice, a nosegay of flowers before my mother's place, new toys before Kolya's.

The terrible news quickly spread about the town, and our house began to be filled with friends, such as Vogt, Tessier, Hoetsky and Orsini, and even complete strangers; some wanted to find out what had happened, others to show their sympathy, others to give all sorts of advice, mostly foolish. But I will not be ungrateful; the sympathy shown me then in Nice touched me deeply. In face of these senseless blows of destiny, men wake up and feel their common bonds.

I decided to go to Hyères that same night. Natalie wanted to go with me; I persuaded her to remain behind; besides, there had been an abrupt change in the weather, the mistral was blowing cold as ice, and it was raining heavily. I had to get a permit to go to France across the Var bridge; I went to Léon Pilet, the French Consul; he was at the opera; I went to his box with Hoetsky. Pilet, who had already heard something of what had happened, said to me: 'I have no right to give you permission, but there are circumstances in which it would be a crime to refuse. I give you on my own responsibility a permit to cross the frontier. Will you go for it to the Consulate in half an hour's time?'

At the entrance to the theatre about a dozen of the people who had been with us were waiting for me. I told them that Léon Pilet would give the permit.

'You go home and don't trouble about anything,' they said to me on all sides; 'the rest shall be done; we will take the permit, we will get the *visa* at the office, we will order the post-horses.'

My landlord, who was present, ran to get a carriage; an hotel-keeper offered his free of charge.

At eleven o'clock in the evening I set off in the pouring rain. It was an awful night; the squalls of wind were sometimes so violent that the horses stopped; the sea that had buried them only that day beat and roared almost unseen in the darkness. We mounted the Esterel, the rain changed into snow, the horses stumbled and almost fell on the slippery ice. Several times the driver, exhausted by his efforts, tried to warm himself; I offered him my flask of brandy and, promising him double fares, besought him to make haste.

DESPAIR

What for? Did I believe in the possibility of finding any of them, of any one being saved? It was hard to suppose it after all I had heard—but to find out, to look at the very spot, to find something, some rag, to see an eyewitness even. . . . One needed to be convinced that there was no hope. I needed to be doing something, to be away from home, to come to myself.

While they were changing horses at Esterel, I got out of the carriage; my heart ached, and I almost sobbed as I looked round. It was near the very tavern where we had spent a night in 1847. I remembered the huge trees which formed a canopy over it; the same view lay stretched before it, only then it had been lighted up by the rising sun, while now it was hidden behind grey clouds, unlike Italy, and in places was white with snow.

I vividly recalled that time with every minute detail; I remembered how our hostess had regaled us with a hare, the highness of which was disguised by a terrible quantity of garlic, how bats had flown about the bedroom, how with the help of our Luise I drove them out with a towel, and how for the first time we felt the breath of the warm southern air. . . .

At the time I wrote: 'From Avignon one feels and sees the south. For a man who has always lived in the north, the first contact with a southern landscape is filled with solemn joy, one feels younger, one longs to sing, dance and weep; everything is so brilliant, so light, so gay, so luxuriant. After Avignon we had to cross the Maritime Alps. We went up the Esterel by moonlight; when we began to go down again the sun was rising, the mountain chains stood out from the morning mist, the rays of the sun threw a dazzling red light upon the snowy peaks; around was vivid green, flowers, sharply-cut shadows, immense trees and gloomy rocks, covered here and there with poor and rough vegetation; the air was intoxicating, extraordinarily limpid, refreshing, and resonant, our words and the notes of the birds sounded louder than usual, and all at once at a little curve in the road there was a fringe of brilliance round the mountains, and there, quivering with the flash of silver, lay the Mediterranean.'[1]

And now, after four years, I was in the same place again.

We could not reach Hyères before night; I went at once to the Commissaire of Police; with him and a brigadier of gendarmes I went first to the Commissaire of the Port. He had all sorts of things that had been saved; I found nothing among them. Then we went to the hospital. One of the victims was dying; the others told me they had seen an elderly woman, a child of five, and with him a young man with a fair bushy beard . . . that they had seen them at the very last minute, and that therefore they, too, had gone to the bottom like every one else. But here again one asked oneself how was it these people were alive, though they too, like Luise and the maid, had no clear idea how they were saved.

The bodies that had been found were lying in the crypt of a nunnery. We went there from the hospital; the Sisters of Mercy met us and conducted us, lighting our way with church candles. In the crypt stood a row of closed boxes, each containing one body. The Commissaire ordered them to be opened; it appeared that they were nailed up. The brigadier sent a gendarme for a chisel and told him to break open one lid after the other.

This examination of the bodies was insufferably painful. The Commissaire had a little book in his hand, and in an official tone he asked at the opening of each box: 'Do you testify in our presence that this body is not known to you?' I nodded. The Commissaire made a mark with his pencil and, turning to the gendarme, ordered him to close it again. We passed on to the next. The gendarme lifted the lid; with a sort

[1] *Letters from France and Italy*.

IDENTIFYING THE DEAD

of terror I glanced at the dead and was, as it were, relieved when I met unfamiliar features, though in reality it was still more horrible to think that all three were lost without a trace, lying forsaken at the bottom of the sea, tossed by the waves. A body without a grave, without a tomb, is more dreadful than any burial, and we had not even our dead.

I found no one. One body impressed me; a beautiful woman of twenty, in Provençal holiday dress; her bosom was bare (she had had a baby in her arms, carried away, of course, by the waves) and a stream of milk was still trickling from her bosom. Her face was utterly unchanged, the brown sunburn made her look as though living.

The brigadier could not help saying: 'What a beauty!' The Commissaire made no comment; the gendarme, as he covered her, observed to the brigadier: 'I knew her, she was a peasant woman living not far from the town, she was going to Grasse to her husband. Well, he 'll have to wait.'

My mother, my Kolya, and our good Spielmann had vanished without a trace. Nothing was left of them; among the articles saved there was not a scrap belonging to them. There could be no doubt of their death. All the saved were either in Hyères or on the steamer which had brought Luise. The captain had made up the tale to comfort me. I was told in Hyères of an elderly man who had lost his whole family, and would not stay in the hospital, but went off somewhere on foot, with no money, in a state bordering on madness; and of two English girls who had been sent to the English Consul—they had lost father, mother, and brother.

It was approaching daybreak; I ordered the horses. Before setting off, the waiter took me to a part of the shore that jutted out into the sea, and showed me from there the place of the shipwreck. The sea was still boiling and tossing, grey and muddy-looking from the storm of the previous day; in the distance, in one place, there was a peculiar patch, as though of a thicker, transparent liquid. 'The steamer was taking a cargo of oil, you see it is floating, that's where the accident happened.' That floating patch was all.

'And is it deep there?'

'It must be one hundred and eighty metres.'

I stood a little; the morning was very cold, particularly by the sea. The mistral was still blowing, the sky was covered with the clouds of a Russian autumn. Farewell! . . . A hundred and eighty metres deep, in a floating patch of oil.

> 'Nul ne sait votre sort, pauvres têtes perdues,
> Vous roulerez à travers les sombres étendues,
> Heurtant de vos fronts des écueils inconnus. . . .'

I came back with a terrible certainty. Natalie, who had only just recovered, had not the strength to bear this blow. From the day of the death of my mother and Kolya, she never recovered her health again. The horror, the pain remained—it entered into her blood. Sometimes in the evening or the night, she would say to me, as though imploring my help: 'Kolya, Kolya is always with me; poor Kolya, how frightened he must have been, how cold he was! and then the fishes, the crabs!' She would take out his little glove, which had been in the maid's pocket—and a silence would follow, that silence in which life flows away as though a sluice had been raised. At the sight of these agonies, which passed into nervous illness, at the sight of her glittering eyes and increasing thinness, I for the first time doubted whether I should save her. . . . The days dragged by in an anguish of uncertainty, something like the existence men lead between sentence and execution, when a man at once hopes and knows for certain that he will not escape the axe.

IV

THE YEAR 1852

I

AGAIN the new year had come; we met it about Natalie's bedside—at last her strength had failed, and she had been obliged to lie up.

The Engelsons, Vogt, and a couple of intimate friends were with us. We were all melancholy. The 2nd of December in Paris weighed like a stone on our hearts. . . . Everything—public and private—was rushing to ruin, and was already so far on its way that there was no stopping nor turning back; one could but wait, dully, miserably, till the headlong rush ended in destruction.

The usual healths were drunk. At twelve o'clock we forced a smile; within was death and horror, we were all ashamed to add any wishes for the new year. To glance forward was more terrible than to look back.

The symptoms became more definite; pleurisy in the left lung set in.

She spent a terrible fortnight between life and death, but for the time life conquered. Convalescence followed and with it a last ray of hope shed its pale radiance over our troubled life.

The powers of her spirit came back first . . . there were marvellous moments—the last chords of a music that was to be hushed for ever.

A few days after the crisis of the illness, I went early in the morning into my study and fell asleep upon the sofa. I must have slept soundly, for I did not hear the servant come in. When I woke up I found a letter on the table. Herwegh's handwriting. What excuse had he for writing, and how dared he write to me after all that had passed? I had given him no pretext whatever. I picked up the letter in order to send it back, but seeing on the envelope the words, 'Containing an honourable challenge,' I opened it. The letter was revolting, infamous. He said that by my *calumnies* I had bewildered Natalie, that I had taken advantage of her weakness and my influence over her, that she had *betrayed him*. In conclusion, he made charges against her, and said that fate had decided between me and him: 'it drowns in the sea your progeny (*votre progéniture*) and your mother. You wanted to end this in blood, while I supposed it was possible to end it humanely. Now I am ready and demand satisfaction.' I never read this letter again, and only once opened it afterwards. In 1853, on Natalie's birthday, the 23rd of October, I burnt it without reading it.

This letter was the first insult I had ever received in my life. I leaped up like a wounded beast, with a sort of moan of fury. Why was not that wretch in Nice . . . why was a dying woman lying the other side of the passage?

After sousing my head two or three times in cold water, I went in to Engelson (after my mother's death he had her rooms), and after waiting till his wife had gone out, I told him that I had received a letter from Herwegh.

'So you have actually received it?' said Engelson.

'Why, did you know—did you expect it?'

'Yes,' he said, 'I heard about it yesterday.'

'From whom?'

'From Karl Vogt.'

I clutched at my head, it seemed to me I was going mad. Our silence had been so complete that neither my mother nor Marya Kasparovna Reihel had once spoken to me about what had happened. I was more intimate with Engelson than with other people—but to him I had only once, as we were walking in the environs of Paris, spoken of it in a brief answer to a question he put to me about the cause of my rupture with Herwegh. I had been overwhelmed in Geneva when I heard from Sazonov of the scoundrel's gossip—but how could I have imagined that near me, close at hand, the other side of the door, every one knew, every one was talking of what I regarded as a secret buried between few persons . . . that they even knew of letters which I had not yet received.

We went in to Vogt. He told me that two days previously Emma had shown him a letter from her husband, in which he said he would send me a *terrible letter*, that he would fling me down 'from the height' on which Natalie set me, 'that he would cover us with disgrace, if he had to pass over the dead bodies of children, and bring us all, and himself too, into the prisoner's dock of the criminal court.' Finally, he wrote to his wife (and she had shown all this to Vogt, to Charles Edmond, and to Orsini), 'you alone are pure and innocent, you ought to be the avenging angel,' namely, I suppose, to cut our throats. There were people who said he had been driven out of his mind by love, by his rupture with me, by the wound to his *amour-propre*. That is nonsense. The man never took one *step* that was dangerous or incautious, the madness was only in *words*, he raged in literature. His vanity was stung, silence was for him harder to bear than any scandal, the peace that had returned to our life gave him no rest. A petty bourgeois, like George Sand's Horace, he talked to revenge himself upon the woman whom he loved and the man whom he had called brother and father, and, a bourgeois German, he threatened in melodramatic phrases, composed in pseudo-Schilleresque style.

At the very time when he was writing this letter to me and a string of insane letters to his wife, at that very time he was living with, and at the expense of, a former mistress of Louis Napoleon's, a dissolute woman, who was notorious in Zurich. With her he spent his days and nights, at her expense he lived in luxury, drove about in her carriage and feasted in big hotels . . . no, that is not madness! . . .

'What do you intend to do?' Engelson asked me at last.

'Go and kill him like a dog. That he is a fearful coward you know and every one knows—the chances are all in my favour.'

'But how can you go . . . ?'

'That's the whole point. Write to him meanwhile that it is not for him to demand satisfaction of me, but for me to punish him, and that I will myself choose the means and the time to do it, that I will not leave a sick woman for that, and that I spit on his rudeness.'

To that effect I wrote to Sazonov, and asked whether he would help in the matter. Engelson, Sazonov, and Vogt received my proposition with eagerness. My letter was a great mistake, and gave him a pretext for saying afterwards that I had accepted his challenge, and that I had refused it later on.

To refuse a challenge is a difficult thing and requires much strength of mind or much weakness.

The feudal duel has a firm standing in modern society, betraying that it is not altogether so modern as it seems. Rarely does any one venture to attack this sacred relic set up by aristocratic honour and military *amour-propre*—and, indeed, it is rare for any one to be in a position so independent as to be able to insult the bloody idol with impunity and to accept the charge of cowardice.

To prove the absurdity of the duel is not worth while—in theory no one justifies it except a few bullies and fencing masters, but in practice every one gives in to it in order to prove—the devil knows to whom—his courage.

The worst thing about the duel is that it justifies any

blackguard, either by giving him an honourable death, or by making him an honourable murderer.

A man is charged with cheating at cards—he insists on a duel, as though one cannot cheat at cards without being afraid of a pistol. And how shameful to put the card-sharper on a level with the man who denounces him!

A duel may sometimes be preferred as the means of escaping the gallows or the guillotine, although the logic is not clear even then, and I do not understand why a man under penalty of general contempt is bound not to fear his antagonist's sword, though he may be afraid of the knife of the guillotine.

The death penalty has this advantage, that it is preceded by a trial, which may condemn a man to death, but cannot deprive him of the right of showing up his enemy, dead or alive. In a duel everything remains secret and concealed. It is an institution belonging to that pugnacious period when blood was still so fresh on men's hands that the wearing of deadly weapons was looked on as a sign of nobility and exercise in the art of killing as an official duty.

So long as the world is governed by military men duels will not be abolished; but we may boldly demand that the choice should be left to us when we should bow the head to an idol we do not believe in, and when show ourselves free men in our full stature and—after battling with the gods and the powers of this world—dare to challenge the bloody, mediaeval ordeal. . . . How many men have passed with proud and triumphant faces through all the hardships of life, prison, poverty, sacrifice and toil, the tortures of the Inquisition, and I do not know what, and have succumbed to the impudent challenge of some trivial scoundrel? There must be no more such victims. The principle that regulates a man's actions should lie within himself in his own reason;

if it lies without himself, he is a slave, however valiant he may be.

I neither accepted nor refused the challenge; the chastisement of Herwegh was for me a moral necessity, a physical necessity—I tried to think of some sure means of revenge and one which could not redound to his glory. But whether by a duel or whether by a knife I attained it, was a matter of complete indifference to me. He himself suggested the solution. He wrote to his wife—and she, as she always did, showed the letter to every one she knew—that in spite of everything I was a head and shoulders above all the rabble round me, that I was influenced for harm by men like Vogt, Engelson, Golovin (!), that if he could see me for one minute, all would be set right—'he (*i.e.*, I) alone can understand me'; and this was written after his letter to me!

And for this reason the poet concluded, 'What I should like best of all is that Herzen would accept a duel without witnesses. I am convinced that from the first word we should fall into each other's arms, and all would be forgotten.'

And so a duel was proposed as a means for a theatrical reconciliation. If I could at that time have got away for five days or a week, I should certainly have set off to Zurich and gone to him to carry out his desire—and he would not have been left alive.

A few days after receiving Herwegh's letter, Orsini came in to me one morning at nine o'clock. Orsini, through a sort of physiological absurdity, was passionately devoted to Emma; what there was in common between this handsome, ardent young Southerner and the ugly, lymphatic German woman, I never could imagine. His early arrival surprised me. He very simply and directly said to me that the news of Herwegh's letter had revolted his whole circle, and that many common acquaintances had offered to form a court of honour. Then he began to defend Emma, saying that she was not in fault except in her senseless love for her husband and her slavish submission to him, that he himself had seen how much she had felt it all. 'You ought,' he said, 'to hold out a hand to her, you ought to punish the guilty, but you ought also to rehabilitate an innocent woman.'

I gave a resolute and unconditional refusal. Orsini was too clear-sighted not to see that I should not change my mind, and so did not insist.

Among other things, speaking of a court of honour, he told me that he had already written about the whole story to Mazzini and asked his opinion. The court of honour was never held, but I received later on a letter that amounted to a verdict on Herwegh, signed by names that were dear to me—and among others the heroic martyr Pisacane, Mordini, Orsini, Bertani, Medici, Mezzacapo, Cosenz, etc. Was not that horrible again? Parties were formed, verdicts were passed, Mazzini was written to—and all this without my knowledge, and all this concerning events at which a week before no one had dared to hint in my presence. After seeing Orsini out, I took a sheet of paper and wrote a letter to Mazzini. Here I was confronted with a sort of Court of Wehm—and a self-invited court. I wrote to him that Orsini had told me of his letter, and that, fearing that he might not have presented the cause quite correctly, since he had never heard a word about it from me, I wanted to tell my story and to ask advice. Mazzini at once replied. 'It would have been better,' he wrote,' to bury the whole thing in silence, but I doubt whether that is possible for you now, and therefore you had better come boldly forward to the attack and leave us to form a court.' That I believed in the possibility of such a court was, perhaps, my last illusion.

I was mistaken and paid dearly for my mistake.

Together with Mazzini's letter I received a letter

from Haug, to whom Mazzini, knowing that he was an intimate friend of mine, had shown Orsini's letter and mine. After my first meeting with Haug in Paris, he had served under Garibaldi and distinguished himself in battle near Rome. There was much that was good in the man and a vast deal that was immature and absurd. He had slept the unbroken sleep of an Austrian lieutenant in his barracks, till he was suddenly awakened by the alarm bell of the Hungarian rising and the Vienna barricades. He snatched up a weapon, not to slay the insurgent people, but to take his place in its ranks. The transition had been too violent and left, as it were, traces of angularity and incompleteness.

A dreamy and rather impetuous man, generous and devoted, proud to the point of arrogance, a Bursch and a Cadet, a student and a lieutenant, he had a real affection for me. Haug wrote that he was going to Nice, and besought me to take no steps without him. 'You have left your country and have come to us as a brother; do not imagine that we will permit any fellow-countryman of ours to go unpunished after adding calumny to all his previous treachery, and then covering it all up with his insolent challenge. No, we have a very different conception of our mutual responsibility. It is enough that a Russian poet[1] has been killed by the bullet of a western adventurer—a Russian revolutionist shall not be!'

In reply I wrote a long letter to Haug. This was the first time I had told the story. I told him everything that had happened—and waited for him to come. . . .

And meanwhile, in the bedroom close by, a great life was feebly flickering out in a desperate struggle with

1 Pushkin was killed in a duel by G. C. Dantès, a man who began his career as a page of the Duchesse de Berry, was by her recommended to Nicholas 1., and was adopted by the Dutch ambassador to Russia. After killing Pushkin he was expelled from Russia. Later on he became a chamberlain of Napoleon 111.— (*Translator's Note.*)

bodily weakness and terrible forebodings. I spent day and night beside the sick-bed—she liked me to give her her medicine and to prepare her orangeade; at night I kept up the fire, and when she slept quietly I had hopes again of saving her. But there were moments of insufferable misery. I felt her thin, feverish hand, I saw her gloomy, anxious eyes fixed upon me with entreaty, with yearning and the terrible words: 'The children will be left alone—they will be orphans—all will be lost, you are only waiting . . . for the children's sake drop it all, don't defend yourself from the mud . . . let me, me, defend you—you shall come out clean, if only I can get a little stronger physically—but no, no, strength will not come. Do not leave the children!' And for the hundredth time I repeated my promise.

In one of these conversations Natalie suddenly said to me: 'Has he written to you?'[1]

'Yes.'

'Show me the letter.'

'What for?'

'I want to see what he could write to you . . .'

I was almost glad that she had spoken of the letter; I passionately longed to know whether there was a grain of truth in one of the charges he made against her . . . I could never have brought myself to ask, but now that she had herself spoken of the letter, I could not overcome my desire, I was horrified at the thought that the doubt would always remain, and, perhaps, grow stronger when her lips would be closed for ever. . . .

'I am not going to show you the letter, but tell me, did you say something like this . . .?'

'How can you imagine such a thing!'

[1] Rumours of what had happened had reached her, and I imagine that this was not accidental. There was a hint in reference to his letter in a letter from Marya Kasparovna Reihel, who had heard it all in Paris from N. Melgunov.—(*Author's Note.*)

'He writes it.'

'It 's almost incredible—he writes that with his own hand. . .?'

I folded the letter back at the passage and showed her—she glanced at it, was silent for a little and then said mournfully: 'How vile!'

From that moment her contempt passed into hatred, and never in one word or one hint did she forgive him or express pity for him.

A few days after this conversation she wrote him the following letter:

'Your persecution and your infamous conduct force me once more to repeat, and in the presence of witnesses, what I have written to you several times already; yes, my infatuation was immense and blind, but your character, treacherous, Jewish in the worst sense, your unbridled egoism, have been displayed in all their hideous nakedness when you were leaving here and since, while Alexandr's goodness and devotion have been greater every day. My unhappy infatuation has only been a new pedestal on which to raise my love for him. You have tried to cover that pedestal with mud, but you can do nothing to break our union, which is stronger and firmer now than ever it was. Your charges, your slanders against a woman only fill Alexandr with contempt for you, you dishonour yourself by this baseness. What has become of your everlasting protestations of religious respect for my will, of your love for the children? It is not long since you swore that you would rather vanish off the face of the earth than cause Alexandr a moment's distress. Have I not always told you that I could not for one day survive parting with him, that if he left me, even if he died—I would remain alone to the end of my life . . .?

'As for my promise to see you again some day, it is true that I made it—I was sorry for you then, I wanted

A LAST REQUEST

our parting to be humane—you have made it impossible for me to keep that promise.

'From the time you went away you began torturing me, demanding first one promise, then another. You meant to vanish for years, to go away to Egypt, if only you could take with you the smallest hope. When you saw that that did not answer, you suggested one absurd thing after another—impossible, ludicrous—and ended by threatening me with *publicity*, tried to estrange me completely from Alexandr, tried to make him kill you, fight you, and finally threatened to commit terrible crimes. These threats had no more effect on me, you had repeated them too often. I tell you again what I wrote in my last letter: "I remain in my home—my home is Alexandr and my children," and if I could not remain as mother and wife, I would remain as nurse and servant. There is no bridge between me and you. You have made even the past loathsome to me.

'Natalie Herzen.'

'Nice, *February* 18, 1852.'

A few days later the letter returned from Zurich. Herwegh sent it back unopened; the letter had been sent registered with three seals, and was returned with the receipt in the same envelope.

'If that 's it,' observed Natalie, 'it shall be read to him.'

She sent for Haug, Tessier, Engelson, Orsini, and Vogt, and said to them:

'You know how I long to justify Alexandr, but what can I do, chained to my bed? I may not get over this illness—let me die in peace, trusting that you will carry out my last request. That man has sent me back my letter; I want one of you to read it to him, and in the presence of witnesses.'

Haug took her hand and said: 'Your letter shall be read to him, I stake my life on that!'

That simple vigorous action affected us all—and the sceptical Vogt went out as much stirred as the fanatical Orsini, who preserved a fervent respect for Natalie to the end of his days. The last time I saw him before he went away to Paris—at the end of 1857—he spoke with tenderness of Natalie, and perhaps with secret reproach. Of us two, Orsini certainly is not the one who could be accused of moral inconsistency—of dualism of words and deeds!

Once, late in the evening, or rather night, I had been having a long and melancholy discussion with Engelson. At last he went to his room, and I went upstairs. Natalie was sleeping quietly; I stayed a few minutes in her bedroom and went out into the garden. Engelson's window was open. Standing disconsolately at the window he was smoking a cigar. 'Such is fate, it seems,' he said and came towards me. 'Why aren't you asleep, why have you come?' he asked, and there was a nervous quiver in his voice. Then he caught hold of my hand and went on. 'Do you believe in my boundless love for you, do you believe there is no one in the world dearer to me than you?—leave Herwegh to me—there is no need of a court, or of Haug—Haug's a German—give me the right to avenge you, I am a Russian . . . I've thought over a complete plan; I need your confidence, your blessing.' He stood with a pale face before me, his arms folded, in the light of the coming dawn. I was deeply touched and felt ready to fall on his neck with tears. 'Do you believe or not that I would sooner perish, be wiped off the face of the earth, than compromise a business in which so much is involved that is sacred to me? But without your confidence my hands are tied. Tell me openly: yes or no? If it's no—good-bye and the devil take it all, and the devil take you and me too. I shall go away to-morrow, and you will not hear of me again.'

'I believe in your friendship and in your sincerity, but I am afraid of your imagination and your nerves, and I have no great faith in your practical ability. You are nearer to me than any of the others here, but I must own, I fancy that you may do harm and get yourself into trouble.'

'So you think General Haug has practical talents?'

'I don't say that, but I believe Haug is a more practical man, just as I think Orsini is more practical than Haug...'

Engelson would hear no more—he began dancing about on one leg, singing, and at last recovering himself, said to me: 'There you are, there you are, putting your foot in it.' He put his hand on my shoulder and added in an undertone: 'It's with Orsini that I thought out the whole plan, with the most practical man on earth. Come, give us your blessing, father.'

'But will you give me your word not to attempt anything without telling me?'

'Yes.'

'Tell me your plan, then.'

'I can't do that, at any rate I can't do that now.'

A silence followed. What he meant to do it was not difficult to guess.

'Good-night,' I said, 'let me think a little,' and I could not help adding: 'What possessed you to tell me about it?'

Engelson understood me.

'My damned weakness, but nobody will ever know that I've told you.'

'But I know,' said I in answer, and we parted.

Anxiety over Engelson and fear of some catastrophe which would be a fatal shock to Natalie in her weak state compelled me to prevent his scheme from being carried out. Orsini shook his head, and looked at it regretfully . . . and so instead of punishing I saved

Herwegh, though, of course, it was not for his sake nor for my own. There was not a trace of sentimentality or magnanimity about it.

And, indeed, how are magnanimity and sympathy possible with this hero turned inside out? Emma, alarmed by something, quarrelled with Vogt for speaking impertinently of her Georg, and besought Charles Edmond to write to the latter, advising him to stay quietly at Zurich and abandon every sort of provocation —or it would be the worse for him. I do not know what Charles Edmond wrote, his task was not an easy one. But Herwegh's answer was remarkable. First, he said it was not for the Vogts nor for Charles Edmond to judge him, then that it was I who had broken the bond between him and me, and so the whole responsibility fell upon me. After going into everything and defending himself even in the ambiguous part he had played, he concluded thus: 'I don't even know whether this can be called treachery. Those cads are still talking about money— to put a stop to that paltry accusation once for all, I may say openly that Mr. Herzen did not with his few thousand francs pay too high a price for the moments of distraction and enjoyment which we spent together in that oppressive time!' *'C'est grand, c'est sublime,'* said Charles Edmond, *'mais c'est niederträchtig.'* To which Hoetsky replied that the stick was the only answer to such letters, and that he would give it him the next time they met. Herwegh relapsed into silence.

2

DEATH

With the coming of spring Natalie was better; she would sit up for the greater part of the day in an easy-chair, was able to do her hair for the first time during her illness and was soon able to listen without exhaustion when I read aloud to her.

We were planning, as soon as she should be a little better, to go to Seville or Cadiz. She was eager to get strong, eager to live, eager to go to Italy.

After the return of the letter there was complete silence, as though both husband and wife felt in their conscience that they had reached a limit rarely reached, had overstepped it, and desisted.

Natalie had not yet gone downstairs and was in no haste to do so: she meant to go down for the first time on the 25th of March, my birthday. She was having a white merino blouse made for that day, and I had ordered an ermine cloak from Paris. Two days before, Natalie herself wrote or dictated to me the list of the guests she wanted to invite besides the Engelsons, Orsini, Vogt, Mordini, and Paccelli and his wife.

Two days before my birthday, Olga developed a cold and cough, there was influenza in the town. Natalie got up twice in the night and went across her room to the nursery. It was a warm night, but stormy. She woke up in the morning with an acute attack of influenza —she had an agonising cough and towards evening fever.

There could be no question of her getting up next day; a feverish night was followed by terrible prostration and aggravated symptoms. All the faint reviving hopes to which we clung so desperately were shattered. The unnatural sound of the cough had a sinister menace.

Natalie would not hear of putting off our visitors. Anxious and melancholy, at two o'clock we sat down to table without her.

Madame Paccelli brought with her a song her husband had composed for my birthday. She was a silent, melancholy and very kind-hearted woman. It seemed as though some sorrow weighed upon her—either the curse of poverty was too great a burden, or perhaps life had promised her something more than everlasting music-lessons and the devotion of a feeble, colourless man, conscious of his inferiority to her.

In our house she met with more homeliness and a warmer welcome than with her other pupils, and she came to love Natalie with southern fervour.

After lunch she sat a little with the invalid, and came away from her, pale as a sheet. The guests begged her to sing the song she had brought with her; she sat down at the piano, struck a few chords, began singing and all at once, with a frightened look at me, burst into tears, let her head fall on the instrument and sobbed spasmodically. So ended our fête.

Almost without saying a word, the guests dispersed, with a weight like a stone on their hearts.

I went upstairs. The same fearful cough continued. It was the prelude to the funeral.

And there were two of them.

Within two months from my birthday Madame Paccelli was buried too. She had set off for Mentone or Roccabrunn on a donkey. The donkeys in Italy are accustomed to ascend the mountains at night without missing their footing. On this occasion the donkey stumbled in broad daylight—the hapless woman fell off, rolled on to the sharp rocks and died on the spot in terrible agonies. . . . I was in Lugano when I received the news. So she was no more. *Nur zu*—what grotesque absurdity was to come next . . .?

After that all is clouded over . . . there comes a blank gloomy night indistinct in my memory, it is useless or impossible to describe it . . . a time of pain, anxiety, sleeplessness, the stupefying consciousness of terror, of moral impotence and horrible physical strength. . . .

Everything in the house seemed to have collapsed. There was a peculiar disorder and chaos, a hurry and

A TEUTONIC GEM

bustle, the servants were run off their legs; and together with the approach of death, there came fresh scandal, fresh nastiness. . . . Fate did not gild the pill for me, nor did men spare me either; his shoulders are broad, they seemed to say, let him bear it.

Three days before Natalie's end, Orsini brought me a note for her from Emma. She besought Natalie 'to forgive her for all that had been done against her and against all of us.' I told Orsini that it was out of the question to give the patient the note, but that I fully appreciated the feeling that had led Emma to write these lines and that I accepted them. I did more: on one of the last peaceful moments, I said quietly to Natalie: 'Emma asks your forgiveness.' She smiled ironically and did not answer a word. She knew the woman better than I did.

In the evening I heard a loud conversation in the billiard-room, which was where our intimate friends usually gathered. I went in and found a heated conversation going on. Vogt was exclaiming, Orsini was urging something and was paler than usual. The argument stopped at my entrance.

'What is it?' I asked, feeling certain that some fresh meanness was in question.

'Why,' Engelson answered, ' what's the use of making a secret of it? but it's so charming, such a Teutonic gem, that I should be ready to stand on my head if it had happened at any other time. . . . The chivalrous Emma has commissioned Orsini to tell you that, since you forgive her, she suggests that in proof of it you should give her back the I.O.U. for ten thousand francs which she gave you when you paid off their creditors. *Stupendisch theuer, stupendisch theuer.*'

Orsini, embarrassed, added: 'I think she has gone out of her mind.'

I took out her note and, giving it to Orsini, said to

him: 'Tell the woman that she asks too high a price—that, if I did value her feeling of repentance, it was not at ten thousand francs!'

Orsini did not take the note.

Through such filth I was dragged beside her death-bed: what was this? madness or vice, depravity or density?

On the evening of the 29th of April, Marya Kasparovna arrived. Natalie had been expecting her from day to day. She had several times begged her to come, fearing that Madame Engelson would take the charge of the children into her hands. Every hour she looked for her coming, and when we got a letter from her she sent Haug and Sasha to meet her at the bridge over the Var. But in spite of this, seeing Marya Kasparovna was terribly agitating for her. I remember the faint cry, almost a moan, with which she said 'Masha,' and could say nothing more.

The illness had found Natalie half-way through her pregnancy, Bonfils and Vogt thought that her condition had assisted her recovery from the pleurisy.

Marya Kasparovna's arrival brought on the birth, which was easier than had been expected; the baby was born alive, but her strength was exhausted. A terrible prostration followed. The baby was born towards morning. Towards evening she told us to give her the little one and call the children. The doctor had prescribed absolute quiet. I besought her not to do this. She looked at me gently.

'You, too, heed what they say, Alexandr,' she said; 'mind that you are not very sorry later on for robbing me of this moment. I am a little easier just now. I want to show baby to the children myself.' I called the children.

Not having the strength to hold the little one, she laid him beside her, and with a bright and joyous face said to Sasha and Tata: 'Here is another little brother. You must love him.' The children rushed with delight to kiss her and the baby. I remembered that a few days before Natalie had repeated, looking at the children:

> 'And may the young life sport and play
> About the entrance to the grave.'

Overwhelmed with grief, I looked at this apotheosis of the dying mother. When the children had gone I besought her to rest and not to speak. She tried to rest and could not: tears trickled down her cheeks. 'Remember your promise. . . . Ah, how terrible to think that they will be left alone, quite alone . . . and in a foreign land! . . . But can it be that there is no hope?'

She fixed on me a glance of entreaty and despair. These transitions from terrible hopelessness to illusive dreams of recovery tore my heart inexpressibly those last few days. At the moments when I had least faith, she would take my hand and say: 'No, Alexandr, it can't be so, it's too stupid, we have a life before us if only this weakness would pass.'

The rays of hope slipped away, they faded of themselves and were replaced by unutterably gloomy, quiet despair.

'When I am not here,' she would say, 'everything will be arranged somehow; now I can't imagine how you'll live without me, it seems I am so necessary to the children, but when one thinks—they will grow up just the same even without me, and everything will go on as though it had always been so.' She added a few words more about the children, about Sasha's health, said how glad she was that he had grown stronger in Nice, and that Vogt, too, agreed that he had. 'Look after Tata, you must be very careful with her—she has a deep and reserved character. Ah,' she added, 'if only I could live till my Natalie[1] comes! . . . Well, are the children asleep?' she asked a little later.

'Yes,' I said.

There was the sound of a child's voice in the distance.

'That is Olenka,' she said, and smiled (for the last time). 'See what she wants.'

Towards night she became terribly restless, without speaking she motioned that her pillow was uncomfortable. But however I arranged it, she was still restless, and with distress and even vexation kept changing the position of her head; then she fell into a heavy sleep.

In the middle of the night she made a movement with her hand as though she wanted to drink; I gave her a spoonful of orange juice mixed with sugar and water, but her teeth were firmly clenched; she was unconscious. I was numb with horror. It was daybreak. I drew back the curtain and, with a sort of senseless feeling of despair, saw that not only her lips but even her teeth had turned black.

Why was it, why this awful unconsciousness, why this black colour?

Dr. Bonfils and Karl Vogt had been sitting all night in the drawing-room. I went and told Vogt what I had seen. He avoided my eyes and went upstairs without answering. No answer was needed. Her pulse was scarcely beating.

About midday she came to herself and sent for the children, but did not utter a word.

She thought that it was dark in the room. It was the second time this had happened in the daylight. She asked me why there were no candles (two candles were burning on the table). I lighted another candle, but not noticing it, she said that it was dark: 'Oh, my dear, how my head aches!' she said, and two or three words more.

[1] Natalie Kutchkov-Ogaryov is meant.—(*Translator's Note*.)

She took my hand—and already hers was not like a living hand—and covered her face with it. I said something to her. She answered indistinctly, consciousness was lost again and never came back. . . .

In that condition she remained till the following morning, from midday or one o'clock on the 1st of May till seven o'clock on the morning of the 2nd. I longed for one more word . . . one word . . . or for the end to come! Those awful, cruel nineteen hours!

At moments she returned to half-consciousness, said distinctly that she wanted to take off the flannel, the dressing-jacket, asked for a handkerchief, but nothing more.

Several times I began to speak: it seemed to me that she heard but could not utter a word, a look of bitter pain seemed to pass over her face. Twice she pressed my hand, not convulsively but intentionally. At six o'clock in the morning I asked the doctor how long it would go on. 'Not more than an hour.'

I went into the garden to call Sasha. I wanted him to keep his mother's last minutes in his memory for ever. As I went upstairs with him, I told him what a sorrow was in store for us. He had no suspicion of the truth.

Pale and almost fainting, he went into the room with me.

'Let us kneel here side by side,' I said to him, pointing to a rug by the side of the bed. The sweat of death covered her face, her hand spasmodically caught at her dressing-jacket, as though trying to take it off. A few moans, a few sounds that reminded me of Vadim's death agony—then those, too, ceased.

The doctor took her hand and let it drop, it fell like a stone.

The boy was sobbing. I do not fully remember what happened for the first moment. I rushed away into the hall, met Charles Edmond, tried to say something to him, but, instead of words, a sound such as I had never heard broke from me. I stood before the window and, stupefied, with no clear understanding, stared at the senselessly moving, sparkling sea.

Then suddenly I remembered the words: 'Look after Tata.' I felt alarmed that the child might be frightened. I had forbidden their speaking to her before, but could I rely upon it? I had her fetched and, shutting myself up with her in the study, sat her on my knee and, preparing her little by little, told her at last that Mother was dead. She trembled all over, her face flushed in patches, tears came into her eyes. . . . I led her upstairs. There already everything was changed. Natalie was lying as though alive on a bed decked with flowers, beside the baby, who had died the same night. The room was draped with white and full of flowers. The taste of the Italians, artistic in everything, knows how to bring something soothing into the heartrending sorrow of death. The frightened child was impressed by the beautiful surroundings. 'Mamma is here,' she said; but when I lifted her up and she touched the cold face with her lips, she broke into hysterical weeping.

I could bear no more, I went out. . . .

An hour and a half later I was sitting alone again by the same window and again staring blankly at the sea and the sky. The door opened and Tata came in. She came up to me and, caressing me, said in a frightened whisper: 'Daddy, I was good, wasn't I? I didn't cry very much.' I looked at the motherless child in deep distress. Yes,' I thought, 'you will need to be good. You will know no mother's petting, no mother's love, nothing can take their place. There will be a gap in your heart, you will not experience the best, purest devotion, the only disinterested devotion in the world.

DEATH

You will feel it yourself, perhaps, but no one will fed it for you. What is a father's love compared with a mother's anguish of love?'

Natalie lay all surrounded with flowers. The blinds had been let down. I sat on the chair, the same chair as usual, beside the bed; all was stillness except the splash of the sea under the window. It seemed as though a faint, faint breath were rising from her lips.

Gently grief and distress sank into calm, as though suffering had passed away without a trace, effaced by the careless serenity of the tomb that knows not what it stands for. And I watched and watched all night. What if she really should wake?

She did not wake; it was not sleep, it was death.

And so it was true.

On the floor and down the staircase masses of orange-red geranium had been flung. That fragrance even now makes me tremble like an electric shock, and I recall all the details, every minute, and see the room draped in white, with the veiled looking-glass; beside her, also covered with flowers, the yellow body of the baby, who had fallen asleep without awakening; and her cold, terribly cold brow. . . . I go with rapid steps, with no thought, no aim, into the garden. Our Francois is lying on the grass sobbing like a child. I try to say something to him and have no voice, I run back there again. A lady I do not know, dressed all in black, and followed by two children, softly opens the door—she asks leave to repeat a Catholic prayer—I am ready to pray with her myself. She kneels down before the bed and the children kneel beside her, she murmurs a prayer in Latin. The children softly repeat it after her. Then she says to me: 'They, too, have no mother, and their father is far away. You were at the burial of their grandmother.' They were Garibaldi's children.

Within twenty-four hours crowds of exiles had

gathered in the courtyard and the garden. They had come to follow her to the grave.

Vogt and I laid her in the coffin, and it was carried out. I walked firmly after it, holding Sasha by the hand and thinking: this is how men look at the crowd when they are led out to be hanged. Two Frenchmen (one of them, I remember, was the Comte de Voguet) in the street pointed with hatred and derision at the absence of a priest. Tessier rebuked them. I was panic-stricken, and made a sign to him with my hand; silence was essential. An immense wreath of small dark-red roses lay on the coffin. We each picked a rose; it was like a drop of blood on every one.

As we went up the hillside, the moon rose and there was a gleam on the sea that had had its share in killing her. We buried her on the hillside that stands out in sight of Esterel on the one hand and Corniche on the other. There was a garden all round. And so she was still among flowers as on her bed. . . .

A fortnight later Haug recalled her last wish and his promise, and he and Tessier prepared to go to Zurich.

It was time for Marya Kasparovna to return to Paris. Every one insisted that I should let Tata and Olga go with her, and myself go with Sasha to Genoa.

It made my heart ache to part from them, but I had no confidence in myself. Perhaps, I thought, it really will be better for them; well, if it is better for them, so let it be. I only begged her not to take the children before the 9th of May, I wanted to spend with them the fourteenth anniversary of my wedding.

The day after that I saw them as far as the bridge over the Var. Haug went with them as far as Paris. We watched the customs-house authorities, the gendarmes and police of all sorts worrying the passengers.

Haug lost his stick, a present from me, hunted for it and was vexed. Tata was crying. The conductor, in a uniform jacket, sat down beside the driver. The diligence drove off along the Draguignan road, and we, Tessier, Sasha, and I, went back across the bridge, got into the carriage and drove to the place where I lived.

A home I had no longer. With the departure of the children the last trace of family life vanished. Everything assumed a bachelor air. Engelson and his wife went away two days later. Half of the rooms were shut up. Tessier and Edmond moved into the house. The feminine element was excluded. Only Sasha's age and features reminded one that there had been something else . . . recalled some one absent.

Five days after the funeral Herwegh wrote to his wife: 'This news has grieved me deeply. I am full of gloomy thoughts. Send me by the first post *I Sepolcri* of Hugo Foscolo.' And in a following letter: 'Now has come the time for reconciliation with Herzen. The cause of our quarrel exists no longer . . . if only I could see him face to face—he is the only man capable of understanding me!'

Yes, I did understand him.

3

APPENDIX

Haug and Tessier went one morning to the hotel in Zurich where the Herweghs were staying. They asked whether he was at home, and, on the waiter's answering that he was, asked to be taken straight up to him without being announced. On seeing them, Herwegh, trembling and white as a sheet, got up and without a word leaned against a chair.

'He was a terrible sight—the look of horror so distorted his face,' Tessier told me.

'We have come to you,' Haug said to him, 'to carry

out the wishes of our dead friend. On her deathbed she wrote to you—you sent the letter back with the seal unbroken, on the pretext that it was written under compulsion. She herself commissioned Tessier and me to bear witness that she wrote that letter herself, of her free will, and then to read it aloud to you.'

'I don't want—I won't . . .'

'Sit down and listen,' said Haug, raising his voice.

They sat down, Haug broke open the letter and took out of it *a note in Herwegh's handwriting*.

When the letter, which had purposely been registered, was sent back again, I gave it into Engelson's keeping. The latter observed to me that two of the seals had been tampered with.

'You may be sure,' he said to me,' that that scoundrel has read the letter and that is just why he has sent it back.' He took the letter to the candle and showed me that there were two sheets of paper instead of one inside it. 'Who sealed up the letter?' 'I did.' 'Was there nothing but the letter in it?' 'Nothing.'

Then Engelson took a similar sheet of notepaper, a similar envelope, put three seals on it and ran to the chemist's shop; there he weighed both the letters— the one that had been sent back weighed half as much again as the other. He came home prancing about and singing and cried out to me, 'I was right! I was right!'

Haug took out the note, read the letter aloud, then glanced at the note, which began with abuse and up-braiding, handed it to Tessier and asked Herwegh:

'Is that your handwriting?'

'Yes, yes, I wrote it.'

'Then you did open the letter?'

'I am not bound to account to you for my actions.'

Haug tore his note into bits and, flinging them in his face, said: 'What a blackguard you are!'

HERWEGH'S COWARDICE

Herwegh, panic-stricken, snatched at the bell-rope and began pulling it with all his might.

'What are you about? are you crazy?' said Haug and seized him by the arm. Herwegh, pulling himself away from him, dashed to the door, opened it and shouted, 'Murder! Murder!' ('*Mord! Mord!*').

At the violent ringing of the bell and this shout, there was a general rush up the stairs to his room—waiters and visitors from rooms in the same passage appeared on the scene.

'Police! police! murder!' Herwegh was by now shouting in the corridor.

Haug went up to him and, giving him a sound smack on the cheek, said to him: 'There, you scoundrel (*Schuft*), that is for sending for the police.'

Tessier, meanwhile, went back into the room, wrote down their names and addresses and handed them to Herwegh without a word. A crowd of spectators had gathered on the stairs. Haug first apologised to the hotel-keeper, then went away with Tessier.

Herwegh rushed off to the Commissaire of Police, begging for the protection of the law against the persons who had been sent to murder him, and kept asking whether he could not take proceedings against them for the slap in the face.

The Commissaire of Police, in the presence of the hotel-keeper, inquired into the details of the case and expressed doubts whether persons who had come in this way in broad daylight to the hotel, without concealing their names and addresses, were really hired assassins. As regards legal proceedings, he imagined that it would be very easy to take them and thought it almost certain that Haug would be condemned to a small fine and a brief term of imprisonment.

'But what is inconvenient in your case,' he added, 'is

that to secure the conviction of that gentleman you will have publicly to prove that he really did give you a slap in the face; it seems to me that it would be more to your advantage to drop it—God knows what revelations it might lead to.'

The Commissaire's logic gained the day.

I was staying at the time at Lugano. Thinking things over, I felt very uneasy: I was certain that Herwegh would not challenge Haug or Tessier, but I was not at all certain that Haug would quietly leave Zurich and do nothing further. A challenge on Haug's part [1] would be quite out of keeping with the character I wanted to give to the business. Tessier, on whose good feeling and intelligence I could thoroughly rely, was altogether too much of a Frenchman.

Haug was capriciously obstinate and childishly irritable. He was continually having tiffs or being huffy, first with Hoetsky, then with Engelson, then with Orsini and the Italians, whom he succeeded in setting against him in the end—and Orsini, shaking his head a little with his characteristic smile, used to say very funnily: '*Oh il general, il general Aug!*'

Karl Vogt, with his clear, practical view of everything, was the only person who had any influence over Haug. He treated him aggressively, pelted him with gibes, shouted at him—and Haug obeyed him.

'What secret have you discovered,' I once asked Vogt, 'for subduing our Bengal general?'

'*Vous l'avez dit*,' answered Vogt. 'You have put your finger on the secret. I subdue him just because he is a general and believes he is. A general knows what discipline means—he cannot oppose a higher authority—you forget that I am a Vicar of the Empire.'

Vogt was perfectly right. A few days later Engelson, not thinking what he was saying and that he was speaking

[1] He did actually send one.—(*Author's Note.*)

AN INSULT TO GERMANY

in Haug's presence, said: 'Only a German could be such a blackguard.'

Haug was offended. Engelson assured him that he had not meant it, that the silly phrase was a slip of the tongue. Haug observed that what mattered was not his saying it in his presence, but his having such an opinion of Germans. And he walked out of the room.

Early next morning he went to Vogt, found him in bed, woke him and told him of the insult paid to Germany, begging him to be his second and to take a challenge to Engelson.

'Why, do you think that I have gone out of my mind as well as you?' Vogt asked him.

'I am not in the habit of accepting insults.'

'He did not insult you. One says all sorts of things— besides, he apologised.'

'He insulted Germany—and he shall see that he cannot with impunity insult a great nation in my presence.'

'But why are you the exclusive representative of Germany?' Vogt shouted at him. 'Am not I a German? Have not I the right to defend her as much as you—more than you?'

'No doubt, and if you take it on yourself, I will give way to you.'

'Good—but entrusting it to me, I hope you will not interfere. You sit quiet here, and I will go and find out whether Engelson really has that opinion, or whether it was just a phrase dropped by chance—and meanwhile, we will tear up your challenge.'

Half an hour later Vogt came in to me—I knew nothing of what had happened the day before. Vogt walked in, laughing aloud as usual, and asked me: 'Is Engelson walking about freely here or not? I have shut our general up at home. Only fancy, he wanted to fight Engelson on account of the damned Germans, of whom Engelson spoke rudely; I persuaded him that the privilege is mine. Half the business is settled; now you must smooth down Engelson if he is not in a state of delirium.'

Engelson had no suspicion that Haug was so angry—at first he wanted to have a personal explanation with him and was ready to accept the challenge, then gave way, and we sent for Haug. The Vicar of the Empire laid aside his medusae and his *salpi* for that morning, and stayed on till Haug and Engelson were engaged in a perfectly friendly discussion over a bottle of wine and cutlets *à la Milanaise.*

In Lucerne, where I went from Lugano, I found a new problem awaiting me. On the very day of my arrival, Tessier told me that Haug had written an article in regard to the slap in the face and had described the whole affair in it; that he wished to publish this note and that Tessier had only succeeded in preventing him by urging that he could not publish such a thing without my consent. Haug, who had no doubt whatever of my consent, was induced to await my coming.

'Do everything you can to prevent this unlucky article being published,' Tessier said to me; 'it will ruin everything—it will make an everlasting laughing-stock of you and all of us and the memory so precious to us.'

In the evening Haug gave me his manuscript. Tessier was right. I could never have risen again from such a blow. Everything was stated with an ardent enthusiastic affection for me and for Natalie, and it was all funny, *funny to me* —at that time of tears and despair. The whole article was written in the style of Don Carlos in prose. The man who was capable of writing such a thing was bound to have a high opinion of his work and, of course, could not relinquish it without a struggle. My task was not an easy one. It had all been written for my sake, from affection, in all good faith, honesty, and sincerity, and, instead of showing gratitude, I had to poison for him the idea which had taken such deep root in his mind and had gained such a hold upon him.

I could make no compromise. After hours of reflection, I made up my mind to write him a long letter; I thanked him for his affection, but besought him not to publish the article. 'If it really is necessary to publish anything about this dreadful business, that melancholy right belongs to me alone.'

I sealed up this letter and sent it to Haug at seven o'clock in the morning. Haug answered me: 'I don't agree with you; I have set up a monument to you and to her, I have raised you to an unassailable pinnacle, and if any one dared to hint a word against you I would make him hold his tongue. But you have the right to decide in your own affair and, of course, if you want to write it I give way to you.'

He was morose and abrupt in his manner all day. In the evening the awful thought occurred to me: 'If I die he will set up that monument,' and so, as I said good-bye, I embraced him, saying: 'Haug, don't be angry with me; really, no one can be a better judge than I in such a thing.'

'But I am not angry, I am only hurt.'

'Well, if you are not angry, leave me your manuscript, make me a present of it.'

'With the greatest pleasure.'

It is interesting that from that time Haug retained a literary grudge against me, and later on, in London, on my observing that he wrote in too elaborate and figurative a style to Garibaldi and Murchison, Haug answered smiling: 'I know that you are a polemical writer, you have the style of cold reason—but feeling and poetry have a different language.'

And once more I thanked my stars that I had not only taken his manuscript from him, but on my departure for England had burnt it.

The news of the slap in the face had spread far and wide, and suddenly an article appeared in a Zurich paper signed by Herwegh. He said that the 'celebrated' slap in the face had never been given, but that on the contrary he had pushed Haug away so that his back had rubbed against the wall—which apart from everything else was hardly credible to people who knew the muscular and alert Haug and the frail and awkward leader of the Baden expedition. He said further that it was all part of an intrigue with far-reaching ramifications contrived by Baron Herzen on Russian gold, and that the men who had visited him were in my pay.

Haug and Tessier at once published in the same newspaper a grave, concise, restrained, and dignified account of the incident.

I added to their explanation that I had never had any one in my pay except my servants and Herwegh, who had lived for the two previous years at my expense and was the only person of my acquaintance in Europe who owed me a considerable sum of money. This weapon, so alien to me, I used in defence of my slandered friends.

To this Herwegh retorted in the same paper that 'he had never needed to borrow money from me, and did not owe me a farthing.' (His wife had always borrowed for him.)

At the same time a doctor wrote to me from Zurich that Herwegh had commissioned him to challenge me.

I answered through Haug that now, as before, I looked upon Herwegh as a man not entitled to satisfaction. That his punishment had begun, and that I should continue to go my own way. One cannot help observing that of the only two persons (apart from Emma) who took Herwegh's side—this doctor and Richard Wagner, the musician of the future—neither had any respect for Herwegh personally. The doctor who sent the challenge added: 'As for the rights and wrongs of the case, I know nothing about it and wish, to have nothing to do with it. 'And in Zurich he had said to his friends:' I am afraid that he will not go through with it, but wants to get up a scene of some sort, only I will not let him trifle with me and make a fool of me. I have told him I shall take a second loaded pistol in my pocket. That is for him!'

As for Richard Wagner, he complained to me by letter that Haug had been too rough and ready, and said that he could not pass a severe judgment on a man 'whom he loves and pities, that he needs considerate treatment, and that he may still be redeemed from his trivial effeminate life, his eccentric dissoluteness, may rally his forces and show himself in a different aspect.'

Loathsome as it was to make a scandal about money, together with all the other horrors, yet I saw that by that I should deal him a blow which all the bourgeois world, that is, the whole public opinion of Switzerland and Germany, would understand and take to heart.

The I.O.U. for ten thousand francs, which Madame Herwegh had given me and had afterwards tried to redeem for a few words of belated penitence, was in my hands. I gave it to a notary.

With the newspaper in one hand, and the I.O.U. in the other, the notary went to Herwegh demanding an explanation.

'You see,' he said,' that is not my signature.'

Then the notary showed him his wife's letter, in which she wrote that she was borrowing the money for him and with his knowledge.

'I know nothing about it and never authorised her to do so; but you must address yourself to my wife in Nice. I have nothing to do with it.'

'So you really do not remember authorising your wife . . .?'

'I don't remember it.'

'That is a great pity; it puts quite a different complexion on this simple money claim, and your creditor may prosecute your wife for obtaining money under false pretences . . .'

On this occasion the poet showed no alarm, but valiantly replied that that was not his business. The notary laid his answer before Emma. I did not pursue the matter. They never paid the money, of course.

'Now,' said Haug, 'now to London. . . . We could not leave that blackguard like that.' A few days later we were looking out at the London fog from the fourth storey of Morley's Hotel.

With my move to London in the autumn of 1852 the most painful part of my life ends—and with it I break off my story.

(*Finished in* 1858.)

To-day is the 2nd of May 1863 . . . the eleventh anniversary. Where are those who stood at the graveside? Not one of them is here . . . some are gone for ever, others are very far away—and not only geographically.

Orsini's head has rolled bleeding from the scaffold.

The body of Engelson—who died an enemy—lies at rest in a Channel island.

Tessier du Mothe, the chemist-naturalist, has remained the same gentle and good-natured fellow, but is calling up spirits and turning tables.

Charles Edmond, the friend of Prince Napoleon, is librarian in the Palais du Luxembourg.

Karl Vogt has remained more unchanged, more true to himself than any.

Haug I saw a year ago. He quarrelled with me over some trifle in 1854, left London without saying good-bye and broke off all relations. I learnt by chance that he was in London. I sent word to him 'that the tenth anniversary of her burial had come, that it was shameful to keep up ill-feeling on no serious grounds, that we were bound together by sacred memories, and that if he had forgotten I still remembered with what readiness he had held out the hand of friendship to me.'

Knowing his character, I took the first step and went to him. He was touched and glad to see me, but for all that the meeting was more melancholy than any parting.

At first we talked of persons and of incidents and recalled details of the past. Then a pause followed. It was obvious to us that we had nothing to say to each other, that we had become complete strangers. I made an effort to keep up the conversation. Haug did his utmost; various incidents of his trip in Asia Minor served our turn. They, too, were exhausted at last, and it was difficult again.

'Oh dear,' I said suddenly, taking out my watch' ' it 's five o'clock and I have an engagement. I must leave you.' It was a fib. I had no engagement at all. Haug, too, seemed to feel as though a weight had rolled off his back.

'Is it really five o'clock? I am going to dine to-day at Clapham.'

'It will take you an hour to get there, I will not keep you. Good-bye.'

And going out into the street, I was on the point of bursting into "laughter"?—no, tears.

Two days later he came to lunch with me. It was the same thing again. He was meaning to leave London the next day—so he said; he remained a good deal longer, but we had had enough and we did not try to see each other again.

ADDENDA TO SECTION THREE
Extracts from a Diary

Feb. 2, 1863.—The moments are rare when it occurs to me to put down anything in this book—some fresh pain, trouble, anxiety. This book might be called—if it were not zu *Deutsch* —a book of lamentations.

The Polish rebellion, the fate of the Russian officers, illness, dissensions, misunderstandings all about one—separation, and the old phrase comes back into my mind again, 'What an endless capacity for suffering is given man and what a tiny capacity for enjoyment!'

Moreover, happiness, harmony—all that flies away, scarcely leaves a trace, merely touches the present moment—while grief, sickness, the expectation of trouble, all that drags on and on, cuts more deeply, like a plough, and leaves deep furrows.

Sept. 24, 1863, *Genoa, Hotel Feder. Can luoghi io vi ritrovi.* —I have come to Italy by the same route by which I came in 1847. Then I went down from Esterel to Cannes and to Nice on a most exquisite autumn day. I went there again in to1851, on the way to Hyères, twenty-four hours after the awful news of the loss of my mother, my son, and Spielmann. And that is already twelve years ago. I longed to look once more at these parts, yet was afraid to be again in the same surroundings. Nature, that ages slowly, remains the same, but man changes. The first time that I came here, I was looking for a full life with a rich setting.

The Alps were before us, there were no clouds above us and, light-hearted and full of courage, I pushed on ahead.

The second time I came stunned with grief. Before me was the wrecked ship, behind me my wrecked life. Now I am going to my children, expecting nothing for

EXTRACTS FROM A DIARY

myself personally, except leisure for thought, free from anxiety, with harmony and peace about me, the *noli me tangere* of weariness and age.

Between Toulon and Nice we left the railway and drove to Hyères. Everything has been wiped away in twelve years. I could not even find the hotel at which I stayed then. The Napoleonic mania for reconstruction has passed over this too. . . . Then there was no body, no rag, now no house, no place. . . .

Loss more complete there could not be. *Fu . . . e non è!*

We made a triumphal entry into Nice. The railway was not yet finished; we sat on the roof of the diligence, the evening darkened, and the moon rose, it had been a day like summer! Towards morning the mistral blew with passing spurts of rain, and we heard the dreary murmur of the sea.

That sound always upsets me, and it was never more hateful than at that moment when, after twelve years, I came back for the first time to visit her grave.

But what a lovely place! Her body is not lowered into the darkness underground, but lifted up into the mountain . . . in the distance stretch the Alps, below there is the sea. . . . One broken string has ruined all the melody . . . but such a string—with it the knot that held all together is severed and the web is unravelled.

I was vexed with myself in the graveyard, the earth was cold, the stones were cold . . . only then I saw the painful effect of the absence of a tombstone. Without a form, a sign, a written word, a material symbol, in fact, one loses hold.

The cornice of Italy! Again I passed along it. It saw me last when, with hopes renewed, we were going home from Turin in 1851. And those beautiful *cari luoghi* called back the past more vividly than the graveyard, her bright image floated against the background of the dark blue sea and the mountains—and with it I fell asleep, and for a brief space all the dreadful happenings of the past were blotted out.

In Nice I visited both our houses. There was no one living in either of them, and I could wander through the rooms. Inside almost everything remained as of old . . . the shutters were closed, there was thick grey dust and the air was close. It seemed as though we had left it a few days before. I looked at these dumb witnesses of dreadful things and thought: Why had I summoned them as witnesses of the past? And I longed to escape from them, to get away, though I feared no testimony, no accusation—I feared my memories.

In the room where she died I opened the shutters. The familiar view of the sea, the shore, and the church . . . she sketched it several times. . . . The bedstead was standing in the same place—the mattresses had been taken off it and piled up beside it on the floor—the funeral might have been yesterday. The cook who lived with us came, and the gardener of Sue's house, and I met the maid who was with us then. I saw simple-hearted genuine delight on their faces. The two misfortunes that had befallen us while they were with me had made a close bond between us. In their affection for me there was an element of sympathy, of pity. The faces were the same, only a little older.

Yes, it all happened here!

Steamer Aunis, Sept. 27, 1863, Civita Vecchia.—We stopped before the wall of a fortress. . . . Everything is sullen and ugly except the sky. . . . French soldiers saunter up and down—a lad absolutely naked swims up to the steamer and sitting in a little boat reminds me of the boy in Flandrin's[1] picture. I cannot land on the Papal shore—I remain on deck. Towards night we

---

[1] The French painter.—(*Note to Russian edition*.)

sail into Naples; I go to my children, as to the great winter holiday. It will not be long before my 31st of December. May she who is absent be there in them, and may the flowers of their young life surround me once more. And again to work, again to the road which every day grows stonier, but which we tread together[1] as we did when we set off in 1833—thirty years ago! Amen.

Zurich, Nov. 27, 1868.—Two years . . . another two years . . . and the same chaos . . . Zurich . . . here began the tragedy that ended in the funeral of the 2nd of May. Here were written the first letters full of doubt, of terror, of concealed hope. Here he lived for years.

I looked at this town, as Ulysses looked at the rocks on which he left his blood and fragments of torn flesh. And strange to say, I like meeting these blood-stained rocks. I recall that time of unbroken pain—the few minutes of intense passion and the serene figure of a child—his untroubled eyes in the midst of grief and confusion, and I look with love at the garden, at the avenue along which I used to walk with him.

Why did no one guess how much love was left in me, how much, how much, was lavished upon me? Even *she* forgot it for the time, and only fully understood it afterwards. And Natalie, what an infinite pity that she never understood that side!

Only the strong acknowledges his fault, only the strong is humble, only the strong forgives—and indeed only the strong laughs, though often his laughter is equal to tears.

[1] With Ogaryov is meant.—(*Note to Russian edition.*)

SELECTIONS FROM CORRESPONDENCE RELATING TO SECTION THREE

A Letter to Richard Wagner[1]

DEAR SIR,—Allow me to thank you for your letter of June 30. It is another proof of the universal condemnation of the person in question, which will overwhelm him in the end. I appreciate with all my heart your magnanimous desire to champion the man. And I can give you no better proof of my deep respect for you than by expressing my own opinion with perfect frankness. I do not in the least share your hopes: there is a degree of degradation from which a man can never rise, for he must have destroyed everything human in himself before he could sink to such depths. Believe me, I thoroughly understand that passion is a law to itself, and that no one can be held responsible for the fatal consequences of the tragic conflicts it involves. Unfortunately, the misdeeds of this man are of quite a different character—mean, utterly plebeian, vulgar, cynical, and cowardly. To inspire respect passion must be coupled with power, with irresistible force—then and only then it escapes censure. It must be what it really is, *i.e.* tempestuous, overwhelming. It burns and sweeps all before it, it kills but does not poison drop by drop—does not scheme for a year to deceive a friend and for another year to take vengeance on the woman by slander. Passion will face death, but will not face being ignominiously kicked out of the house. I have come to know you through your fine work on the *chef d' œuvre* of the future. You have well grasped the bond uniting all the arts, which ought to be combined in a harmonious concrete whole. I appeal to your aesthetic sense. How can you justify

[1] Originally written in French. Wagner's letter to Herzen has not been preserved.—(*Note to Russian edition,*)

an existence devoid of every religious feeling, how can you dream of a future of serenity and self-restraint for a creature destitute of all manliness, of all chivalrous and generous feeling, a man without a trace of a conscience? A man, no—a hetaira of the male sex, who has sold his youth for francs to an unsexed woman, a worthy accomplice of all his infamies—a creature who for the sake of comfort has betrayed his convictions, whose part in the German revolution was a flight from the field of battle, without accounting for the money entrusted to him— such a creature has no future. Every day he was warmly pressing his friend's hand, calling him in his letters his one support, his one defence, longing for the moment to pour out his soul to him, for ever talking enthusiastically of friendship, and at the same time betraying his friend! That creature has not passed through a tragedy—he has simply behaved like a blackguard.

A man who brought his wife into his friend's house in order to sully it—with the sole object of keeping his family at the friend's expense, at his expense paying his debts—is not a Werther but a Robert Macaire.[1]

In any case, the second part of the story surpasses the first. I am not speaking of the slanders he has circulated —secretly, but in such a way that they are known in Russia—nor of the coarse brutality of leaving his ex-wife in Nice to spy upon me, to insult me, to drive me out of the town. A year after he has allowed himself to be turned out of the house, he sends me a mean challenge. Knowing little of the etiquette of affairs of honour, he sends me a challenge by post, without mentioning even his seconds. Then he returns my wife's letter as though unopened, *after tampering with the seal*. The disgusting challenge, in which, among other things, he gibes at the

[1] The leading figure in *L'Auberge des Adrets*, by Frédéric Lemaître, is the typical French version of the highwayman.—(*Translator's Note*.)

unhappy death of my son, does not explain in what way I have wronged him. There was no possibility of understanding for what insult he desired satisfaction. It was not a *cartel*, but an equivalent of a slap in the face. Unhappily, I was then by the bedside of a dying woman, a woman of the loftiest soul, saintly in her regrets, who had come to understand the sort of man she had to deal with—such was the woman whose end was hastened by the filthy attacks of this depraved man.

A duel between him and me? Never! What would it prove? We are not equals. I am his judge. I might be his executioner, but not his opponent. A duel is no expiation, no punishment; a duel is rehabilitation of honour, but I want to establish his dishonour. As a socialist and a revolutionary, I have appealed to the only authority I recognise. I had the spirit, the courage to submit the affair to the judgment of my friends the democrats. I showed the letters, I told the facts. My appeal roused a general outburst of condemnation. Herwegh's moral death has been decreed. Despised by all decent men, excommunicated from the body of democrats, he will be forced to hide his ignominious existence in some remote corner of the world. For he will find no peace in France, Italy, Switzerland.

I swear, and my friends swear it also—every day brings us fresh proofs—that all representatives of the militant revolution stand by us.—Receive, etc.

A. Herzen.

Letter from Haug to Herzen[1]

My unhappy Alexandr!—Do nothing to avenge your outraged honour till you have seen me. I shall be in Nice in a few days. I have only just seen your letter to Mazzini of February the 6th. What fatal consequences

[1] Originally written in French.—(*Note to Russian edition.*)

have followed the fact that my last letter, written in December, did not reach you!

My heart is as desolate as a graveyard. Nothing but crosses and tombstones. The best of humanity are turning to dust before my eyes, happiness has vanished for ever, I see with a curse the holiest hopes of human love at its highest defiled by the grotesque images of abject scoundrels.

My poor, unhappy Iskander, I suffer as you do, more bitterly than you do, for I have the highest esteem for Madame Herzen.

You don't know that one evening Mazzini sent me the brief sentence: '*on vous aura écrit que Herzen a perdu sa femme.*' This was at the very moment when France was dying. One thing on the top of another. An angel at the deathbed of a nation. Only later I heard that the calamity had overtaken your mother. Poor woman!

For a year you kept silent. By your silence and by the laconic way in which you returned my letter to Madame Herzen, you gave rise to a prolonged hideous uncertainty. It has been a burning poison. You don't know to what a point my soul, perhaps from excess of enthusiasm, has grown into your life. When, late one night, near La Madeleine, you told me that Natalie was your bliss, your heaven, I came to love that heaven, with which, perhaps, I was in love before. Natalie was for me the incarnation of the spirit of the East, you were its representative. You yourself said to me once, Alexandr, 'Haug, you are a pure-hearted man.' Yes, I am. And I am faithful to my feeling. You are my religion. I have never consciously profaned it.

Your distress comes as an agony into my life. I will heal it. The dream of our age, the solidarity of nations, would become . . . [*word illegible*] if those who dream of it would carry it out in action instead of talking of it. You are right in refusing to fight. Already one of the greatest sons of the East has been struck by a scoundrel's bullet. And where was the expiation, where was the justice of destiny? Solidarity ought to have another side. Darkness is dispelled, but the light is too glaring. There must be the true light which will make the blind see. The truth of a better future . . . [*word illegible*]. My greetings to the angel of your life, Natalie. She is a saint of humanity. She must be a saint, for every one loves her. And Mazzini says, '*la femme c'est l'ange perdu.*' Good-bye.

Herzen's answer to Haug

Dear Haug,—Your letter of March the 10th gave me great pleasure. I have been so unhappy of late, I feel so shattered, so insulted in all that was holiest and most precious to me, and there are moments when my strength fails me, I am overcome by utter despair, I feel impotent, humiliated. . . . Your letter found me at such a moment, it revived me again—I thank you.

Yes, I accept your brotherly sympathy, I press your outstretched hand, not that you should fight my battles, but only support me in this painful struggle that I may end it as I should wish.

But before bringing you into the thick of this sad and distressing business, I must make you acquainted with a few facts. I will tell you them. It is very painful to me, but it is unavoidable. When I have told my story, judge and act according to the dictates of your heart.

You reminded, me in your letter of a conversation we had walking by the Madeleine at night. Ah, how grateful I am to you for that! That conversation does not only lighten my burden, but serves me as a kind of proof and testimony, in any case, as regards you. Yes, I opened my heart and soul to you that night. That rarely happens with me, I never talk of my feelings, I am, as it were, ashamed—my feelings are for myself alone. And so I told you then that only one woman has played a part in my life, and that that part was an immense one, that I have loved only one woman, and that love was living unchanged in my heart. A deep affection bound us together as children and survived all the ups and downs of a stormy life; I will add now that that love gives me the strength to bear the tortures of my present position. Yes, our love has worked a miracle—a far greater one than that of lasting fourteen years—it has survived the shock that might have destroyed it. We have never been so united as since this misfortune has befallen us. It has welded us more closely together. The humiliations I am suffering on her account, the fact that I have taken half the blame upon myself, have been fresh foundations for our love.

We are no longer the same people, and that is why nothing has changed between us.

Hand in hand, we proudly entered upon life; we thought that we should pass with head erect before admiring multitudes. What was there to fear after twelve years of union, of love? . . . A filthy encounter, a pestilential breath which we could not withstand has humbled us. Now we are moving away from life in a lowlier spirit, crushed by an awful memory, we are approaching the grave, weary and downcast, but hand in hand as before. Neither of us is innocent, nor guilty; one who has the strength to forgive shares the responsibility for the past. If any man despises us, let him hold aloof, let him forget us. Our union, so humanly holy, has been desecrated by that creature. But you, you who love us so much, must pause, you must ponder more deeply what I am saying to you and discern the true image of our indissoluble union under the dirt and disgrace with which it has been covered.

I pass to the facts. When we met that creature

for the second time he was very unhappy. Reviled by friends of his own party—he was accused of cowardice in connection with the Baden expedition, and even of dishonesty—he was no better off in his private life: tied for the sake of money to a woman whom he did not love, but who made him feel his indebtedness to her, depraved and spoiled by a passionate thirst for trivial enjoyments, he was not capable of undertaking anything new. He was alone, there were people who thought highly of his talents, but there was not one who respected him personally. I held out a hand to him. At the bottom of that embittered soul I descried earnest thought, poetical talent which dazzled me. He became passionately attached to me, he never left my side. No other man has said so much of his affection for me, he was jealous over me, tried to keep my friends from me, called me his brother, his twin soul, his one friend and support; he wrote to me that if I were to take it into my head to cast him off, he would cling to me because he could not exist without me. He reproached me for coldness and shed tears, recalling our first meeting.

I will show you his letters, which I have fortunately kept.

This passionate, ardent affection for me and boundless love for my children was what first drew him and Natalie together. She abandoned herself to her liking for him without a second thought, and he had plenty of time to draw his nets closer and closer round a woman who fell into the snare more naively than one who would have struggled against it. There was nothing to restrain chat utterly depraved creature; he found nothing in his heart to make him feel all the baseness and vileness of such an outrage. Neither regard for the children, nor respect for the house that had given him a shelter, nor respect for himself—why, you know he still persisted in his declarations of love to me.

Do you know what it means to have doubts and not to dare to put them into words, to suspect and not to have the courage to confess it? I am not going to give you the inner history of that awful time, we will talk of that in the future. To-day I will only say that that struggle has aged me, I wasted in it what was left of life and energy. No, I said to myself, this is impossible: how could they conceal the truth from me, from me, their true and faithful friend, how could they put me in the degrading position of a spectator, how could I have deserved such contempt? On the other side I saw that every explanation was avoided. In Paris, in December, I began to express my suspicions more boldly. I was alone in Paris. Natalie was left in Zurich, where the creature was staying at my mother's. In her letters Natalie protested, spoke of the indissoluble ties that held us together, and finally came herself to Paris.

While I was in Paris I had the opportunity of studying that creature's character more closely. There had always been something in him that revolted me, the selfish injustice, the harsh coarseness of his behaviour to others, especially to his wife, whom he exploited, demanding money. My letters to him from Paris were full of amazement at his behaviour; with my habitual frankness I blamed him without reserve. His letters became more and more tender, he talked of nothing but our leading a pure and serious life together, which should serve as an example and foundation for the future, far from the crowd and full of harmony. I answered him: 'You will bring with you into that life the corroding egoistic element that will poison it,' and quoted the lines of Pushkin:

> 'Leave us, proud man!
> . . . .
> Freedom you want, but only for yourself;
> Your very voice strikes terror to our hearts.
> Fearful and kindly are we gypsy folk,
> You are bold and evil—go away from us!'

When I was turned out of Paris in July 1850, I went to Nice.

This was a great blunder, I ought to have gone to London. All this time the creature was living at my mother's in Zurich. At the end of August she brought him to Nice. Two days before his arrival, Madame Herwegh, foreseeing misunderstandings, borrowed ten thousand francs from me for two years. They were without means. I offered them a storey in the house which I had taken, accepting, from motives of delicacy, a nominal rent, ostensibly to cover the cost of it. And so the whole family, women and children, established themselves at my expense. He knew all this, allowing his wife to act as she thought best, and now she has the effrontery to reproach me with having reminded her of this when she was leaving.

At Nice I grasped the full extent of the catastrophe. Natalie was struggling between two feelings. She was trying to forget herself, she was afraid to face the truth. I was shattered, wounded, profoundly unhappy. And looking at this abject, pitiful creature, who avoided any explanation, who oppressed his wife, who was beginning to envy me my fortune, I often repeated the words which Hamlet said to his mother.

But an inner voice told me that this was not so. I saw it with my own eyes but I did not believe it. That saved me, saved Natalie, saved the children. It was time to put an end to it all, in any case to the falsity of the position. The idea of playing the part of judge and injured husband never entered my head.

Never in my life have I stooped to a degrading inconsistency between my principles and my actions. *I* demanded the truth; that I was entitled to.

After two or three feverish conversations Natalie told me all. (You will see later on the abominable use to which the creature put this word 'all.')

No one without my iron health could have lived through the agonies I endured listening to her, and the four or five sleepless nights that followed our first conversation.

On one of those nights we were sitting together on the sofa; there was death in my heart; thoughts of suicide for the first time floated before my mind; I wanted to drink the cup to the bitter dregs. I put one or two questions to her. She answered. A silence followed. I was annihilated, I was overwhelmed by a rush of rage, shame and anguish, and, I confess it to you, I had an impulse to kill Natalie. With a feeling of gladness I dwelt on the thought. . . .

The silence continued. At last I raised my eyes and looked at her. Her face was awful, terribly pale, bluish; her lips were blanched, her features were working; she said nothing but looked fixedly at me with dim, questioning eyes. Her appearance affected me so much, that forgetting everything I took her hand, and letting my head fall on her shoulder, began comforting her in a voice full of tenderness which came from my heart. This was the real crisis for Natalie. She flung herself sobbing on my neck; I laid her on the sofa; she was almost unconscious, and only had the strength to say: 'Don't be afraid, these are good tears, it's my admiration for you, it 's my tenderness. No, no,' she kept saying, 'I will never leave you, if only you can put up with me and forget what has happened.' Her soul, spellbound by a morbid passion, awakened and revived with the energy and force of former days. She came back Mike a ship returning to its haven after a storm, half-wrecked but triumphant at its escape' (her own words in a letter to me).

In her infatuation she had not seen whither she was drifting. She was going to meet death, while he was still seeking 'a brilliant future' in the words of Madame

Herwegh, who, I swear on my honour, was already drawing up a plan for the division of my property.

After that scene I knew that Natalie would remain, but that she was still under the influence of the creature's threats, under the influence of the past. I had to take action. I suggested that I should leave Nice the following day and let them settle things as they thought best. Natalie would not hear of my going. Then I insisted that the creature should leave the house. As Natalie was terribly afraid of a duel or some bloody encounter, she asked me in token of my reconciliation and forgiveness to promise her that I would not do anything to provoke it. I promised, but on condition that he left the house. This is what the creature calls 'using pressure' and 'taking a base advantage of my position.' Of course I used influence, but only by devotion, by love.

Prevention and persuasion are very different things. At this moment, for instance, I am influencing you. I must tell you too that all this time the creature remained in hiding in his room on the first storey and did not come down to the dining-room or the drawing-room. But he sent me his wife, who came with the most monstrous proposition, made in a naively disgusting form, to which no woman but a Berlin German would demean herself. She proposed that I should let Natalie go with the creature while she would remain with me. I repeated for the last time that I was ready to go if Natalie wished it; she ran off to Natalie at once. She knows her answer and can tell it you, I know the result. At first the creature refused to go, then went through a farce of suicide, then told me through his wife, that he was ready for a duel to the death, but nothing would induce him to fire at 'the friend' whom he was conscious of having wronged.

But soon his timid, lymphatic temperament got the

upper hand and, in a very bourgeois style, with his luggage, governess and children, he went on to Mentone and then to Geneva.

There was something so humiliating and ludicrous in this male Hagar with his Berlin Ishmael, cast out from the house which had sheltered them, that I took no further action. I was absorbed by a very different question. I wanted to reach a clear understanding of the true state of Natalie's heart. The step she had just brought herself to was the inevitable compensation for the insult I had suffered. Passion might gain the ascendant. What motives were guiding her now? Was it renunciation, self-sacrifice, devotion without love? And if so, would she have the strength to hold out and, finally, had I the right to accept such a sacrifice? After the first weeks during which our conversations were often passionate and gloomy, I grasped that it was a perfectly natural return to the love which had been her guiding thread throughout her life, she was coming back to her normal condition, her momentary passion had been a casual incident; as soon as she had thrown off the yoke of a capricious, exacting creature who worked upon her only by threats, she felt more free, more youthful in soul.

The creature's mean behaviour destroyed the last vestiges of her unhappy attachment. In his first letter to Natalie he begged her not to justify herself by throwing the blame on him, to take it all on herself. Then followed threats of scandal, murder and amazing suggestions such as that she should rehabilitate him in my opinion and take him as a tutor to my children. Natalie felt that she must not drive him to despair and asked my sanction to write to him at times. I told her that I looked at it very differently, but she might act as she thought best. The correspondence, which all passed through my hands, led to all the horrors that followed.

Natalie gave him a promise to meet him a year later on condition that he should not misuse the privilege of writing to her—that only increased his epistolary incontinence. Natalie took back her promise and at last, in August or November, broke off all correspondence with him. She despised him, was ashamed of him.

Only one thing was wanted to complete the meanness of his behaviour—that was to make it public; and he spread abroad the whole story. He did his share and his wife did hers. But they did not merely publish it abroad, they added slander. No one ventured to mention the man's name in my hearing; I held my peace, respecting the obligation of silence which has no sacredness for the plebeian soul.

All of a sudden, in July, I learned in Geneva from Sazonov that the creature had told him the whole story. This unexpected intelligence distressed me and I returned to Turin, depressed and gloomy. Natalie, seeing from my letters how unhappy I was, came from Nice to meet me and reached Turin the same day as I did. This sign of affection touched me. There, for the last time, we talked it all over. We came to understand each other better than ever. Yes, we were the same, with one terrible memory, one deep scar added. Those days in Turin brought back to me our glorious youth; they reminded me of our life together at Vladimir. Yes, it was a second wedding, a wedding of more significance, perhaps, than the first. It was accompanied by deep consciousness, full understanding of all the responsibility we were taking up anew, and for this we were indebted to the past which had almost ruined us and covered us with disgrace. I leave it to Natalie to give you the inner account of our reconciliation and the full harmony of our home life, which lasted until the terrible blow that fell upon us. On November 16th my mother, my second son and his tutor—one of my friends—

perished in the Mediterranean. This blow shattered Natalie's health. Exhaustion and weakness passed into acute illness. She was attacked by pleurisy: on the 2nd or 3rd of January, she was so much worse that the doctors doubted whether she would recover. And the wretch seized this moment to send me a mean challenge. Through his wife, whom he made live in Nice, he knew everything that was happening to us. I should not have opened his letter, except that he wrote on the envelope 'an honourable challenge.'

Inside, instead of a challenge, I found a dirty letter, revolting in its cynicism, full of charges against Natalie and the basest disclosures. He covered the vileness of this by saying, 'You have been told all,' as though I would ever have cared to demean myself or Natalie by the repetition of all the revolting details. I spoke of this letter to my friend Engelson (he was the first person after Sazonov to whom I spoke of this business). What was my amazement when I saw that he too was fully informed of all that had taken place. Monsieur and Madame H. had initiated all their acquaintances into the sad details of our breach with them, forgetting that he had played the part of a traitor and she of a go-between. I was amazed and scandalised. What duel could suppress these slanders! Natalie and I, by keeping it all absolutely secret, had given them full opportunity for circulating their vile calumnies. Next day it was public property that I had received a challenge. The creature had told his wife, and a few days later Madame Reihel informed my wife from Paris that she had just heard it from Madame Kolatchek.

After the intervention of the Baden heroine it would have been too absurd to play a melodramatic part in this mournful drama. A duel would be unthinkable, it would have set nothing right, it would have been a trap, he was the only man who could have been rehabilitated by a duel. As for me, I did not think about my honour, I wanted to chastise the wretch, to revenge myself on him; the defence of my honour was of very little interest to me. I may say frankly that my past, beginning with five years of exile on the borders of Siberia and ending with our banishment from Paris, gave me, if not certain rights, at any rate a confidence in myself. If my honour could depend upon a traitor whose past was as well known as my own, I should prefer to lose it.

To refuse a duel is not an easy thing to do. Remember, I am writing to you two months after the challenge. I passed through a regular mental illness before I succeeded in recovering my sense of honour by a firm, resolute decision to rise superior to this man, who is devoid of every feeling of dignity and generosity, to rise superior to time-honoured conventions, and obstinately to refuse this miscreant the honour of fighting. I was conscious that I was taking my stand against a monstrous and merciless force. This unjust, haughty, inhuman force is all-powerful where honour is concerned, it dominates even the most independent natures, they submit to its decrees and abandon their own convictions simply to show that they have the courage to face a pistol. I take my stand against despotism, because I feel myself pure, guiltless, because I feel myself strong enough to appeal to my friends and to lay it all before them. My refusal had another, more serious significance: I wanted my action to be a definite and solemn recognition of the freedom of woman. I wanted to leave it to woman to defend her own honour in complete independence. Only the weak-minded, the immature and the feeble need to be defended, and in this case the woman is strong, and if she acts alone she is stronger still. This man, revenging himself upon her for not persisting in wrongdoing, for not becoming his slave, thought to crush her with his cynicism. He will be himself crushed by the grandeur of her repentance. . . . Not a month ago that woman spoke, and public opinion, amazed, went over to her side. Before that, I alone was pitied and the slanderous charges, rapidly circulated during the previous twelve months by the efforts of Madame H., were continually repeated, but now Natalie stands confronting them all, lovely in her energy and determination.

That was the beginning of my triumph.

I am finishing, dear Haug. The details, the letters of my friends, the creature's insolent and stupid behaviour, his refusal, for instance, to receive my answer through my second, his asking for a secret duel, his return of a certain letter—all that you will learn from my friends, who have surrounded me with so much warmth and devotion and given me the strength to bear my humiliating position.

What they will tell you will not differ in any material point from my story; all you will learn from them is the depths of degradation to which a plebeian, mean, coarse and abject soul can sink. For what does all this parade of eloquence amount to, what is the object of all these letters, all these words? Why did not he simply come, pistol in hand, why did he run away from the house, why did he not try (he wrote twenty times about it) to kill Natalie or me, why in the last resort did he not kill himself? He had neither the energy nor the daring for that. It is easier to spread calumnies, to bully his wife—and that is what he does. One must put an end to it and punish the wretch. For that, I need the help and the advice of my friends, and above all the conviction that should I, by the irony of fate, perish in the conflict, my friends will set an awe-inspiring example of justice and solidarity,—Your devoted

A. HERZEN.

Letter of Herzen to his Wife

Geneva, a Café, *June* 28, 1851.

Judge for yourself what I am feeling, and the state I am in.

He has told Sazonov all about it. . . . Details that took my breath away. He told him that 'he was sorry for me, but that what was done could not be undone, that you had begged him to keep silent, that in a few months' time, *when I was calmer*, you would leave me. . . .'

Dear! I will not add a word. Sazonov said he had heard you were ill and asked what it was. I was numb with horror while he talked. I insist upon an answer from you to this last point. It is all beyond the wildest dreams. Sazonov knows absolutely all about it. . . . I insist on having the truth. . . . Answer me at once; I shall weigh every word. My heart is breaking. . . . And you call this consistent development.

To-morrow I am going to Freiburg. I have never sunk so low as this before. Address your answer to this to Turin, *poste restante*.

Can it be really you that they are talking about? My God, my God, what I have suffered for my love. . . . What more is there? . . . Answer, answer to Turin!

Letters of Natalie Herzen to her Husband

July 3, 1851.—My dear, my dear, if only I had wings, how I would fly to you! It is more than I can bear. . . . I can't tell you how I have felt since your last letter, and I don't know how to say anything. All I know, dear, is that I love you with all the power of loving there is in me, that nothing but death can tear me from you. These latter days have shown it to me more clearly than ever. And—I, too, will be open—I will say more. My love for you makes me afraid: it is too beautiful, it is timid, dear, it has too vivid a memory of the anguish of not being understood, not valued, not wanted, not loved in the same way. . . . Well, so be it! My fate is settled once for all; to live and to die for you. . . . The children . . . they too are you. You can make of it what you like.

I embrace you, Alexandr! Be well and calm.

July 4.—Alexandr, my Alexandr, let us suffer together! Darling, how hard it is! How sorry I am for you, for you, dear! and what can I do? If only I could hold you in my arms . . . and to die with you if you don't care to live or don't believe me, if I can do nothing for you. . . . I think now that education is all nonsense: the children have good natures and that will save them. . . . Life is hard, dear, insufferable, when I know that you are so unhappy. Yesterday I could not bear to have people about me, so I drove in the evening to the Engelsons and spent a long time on the way. . . . It was awful coming back to the house without you. No, I can't stay like this, I shall come to you in Turin on the 7th or before, so as to be there on the 8th: inquire for me at the Hotel Feder. My chest and all my bones feel as though they were broken, but my brain won't stop working. . . . It is awful to think that there are two more days before the 7th and two days on the journey. . . . If I am not in Turin on the 8th, it will be because something has kept me here —don't wait for me, but come here; I am writing that I may be there, perhaps, for fear we may miss each other.

I have just spoken to Rocca. I sent him to book a seat in the post-chaise that goes on Sunday afternoon at half-past four; so that by Tuesday morning we may meet in the hotel. . . .

My heart throbs and throbs and throbs still, I can hardly breathe. . . . Oh, if I could comfort you, dear, set your heart at rest! . . .

I embrace you, I embrace you.

July 7.—Yesterday I received the letter in which you write that you will not reach Turin before the 10th; I have put off going till to-morrow; two extra days without the children and without you would be awful.

I don't know what to say to your reproaches, dear, after all that I have said already. It seems to me after them that it is of no use for me to go . . . on your account. . . . Tata is inconsolable since she has heard that I am going. 'Father is big and can come alone, or take me, take me with you.' I say, 'The mountains are high and dangerous for children to go over them'—'I would rather die with you than be left without you'—and all that was said so quietly, in secret from the rest. What sufferings life has in store for such a nature! . . . It 's silly but it breaks my heart to listen to her, yet I can't help it, this time I must be selfish; not on your account, I shall come for my own sake; I must see you and hear you, my dear, my heart is so heavy. Tata may have much happiness before her in her life, but for me the sun is going down and time is ebbing.'

And so till we meet, Alexandr. . . . Why am I going? Your last letter was so cold. . . .

Letter of Herzen to his Son

June 28 (1851).

Greetings, Sasha! Do you often think of me, my little dear? Do think of me: it will make me gladder and happier. I may come sooner than I expected—perhaps about the tenth. I would give a great deal to be with you all now, to look at you and Tata asleep.

Good-bye, dear.

I shall be in Freiburg on the 30th of June, and shall stay there five days; if I leave by the 6th I shall be in Turin by the 8th.

Tell me how you met the Colonel.[1]

Letter from Herzen to M. K. Reihel

GENEVA, *June* 29 (1851), *morning*.

This evening I am going to Freiburg, and so I shall be there to-morrow; I shall stay there not more than four or five days; so that when you get this letter, you can send on other letters *poste restante*, Turin.

When I stepped on Swiss soil I felt that I was really free; unless the whole country were occupied by a foreign army there is no danger here; moreover, a Swiss subject cannot actually be expelled from Piedmont —so that everything is right on that score. As to other things, what am I to say to you? I have grown older. That I have told you before, that you have seen for yourself; at times I seem to fall back into the old rut, but there is no limpidity, the water is dull, troubled, muddy, and it is not at all amusing. But you, Marya Kasparovna, were very kind in the way you met me and saw me off. Give me your hand, we are old friends; mind that prolonged absence and other interests do not cool your helpful affection for us (don't be angry— human nature is weak and changeable, nothing in it is quite secure). Perhaps life will bring us together again —anything may happen, for everything comes by chance.

[1] Engelson is meant.—(*Note to Russian edition*.)

Most likely you have already sent off an answer to Bernacki,

Good-bye; give my love to Reihel. Was Maurice pleased with the toys?[1]

The colonel has set off gloomily from Lyons: he suffers much, for he loves much; he is consumed by an inward fire and no palm baths will put it out.

Once more good-bye. Give my greetings to Bernacki.

Letter from Herzen to his Wife

June 29-30, 1851.

I embrace the children. I will write to them from Freiburg, but I have no time now. I have to go off somewhere. I went to bed late and overslept myself to-day.

My love to mother and every one.

Why have the books that were returned been paid for? Golovin was to have asked for them from Turin.

Letter from Herzen to his Son

Freiburg , *July* 2 (1851).

Dear Sasha,—Yesterday I went with the local treasurer to Morat, and from there with the prefect to the village which has adopted us: Burg or in the French Châtel. A little village; the inhabitants came to meet us, and the elder made me a speech in broken German, which I answered as best I could; then they brought me an immense glass of wine and the schoolmaster made a speech. The elder apologised for not having made preparations for my reception, and especially for no guns having been fired. They are all kind, simple people, they were very much pleased with me, and

---

[1] Reihel's son by his first wife.—(*Note to Russian edition*.)

invited me to come with all my family next year. Goodbye, dear; I kiss Tata, Kolya, Olenka.

Kiss Granny's hand for me.

Letter from Herzen to his Wife

GENEVA, *July* 5 (1851), *Saturday*.

I arrived here an hour ago—here I am already nearer to you, darling; I don't know how things will go in Piedmont; I think of leaving the day after to-morrow at eleven o'clock in the evening, or if I can't get a seat, on the 8th; so by the 10th I shall be in Turin and by the 13th I may be at home; but that is not certain yet.

There has been a tremendous holiday here; I was really touched by the grandeur of the reception of the federal banner and of the deputation from Argau. Yes, say what you like, it is a republic.

I cannot write: frightfully tired; at one o'clock in the night I got into the diligence and travelled without stopping till I arrived here at four in the afternoon. But fatigue is good for me, only my hand won't write, and my thoughts won't hang together.

I have found out everything about education in Vevey —if necessary we might be there. Moreover we have never once thought of the Italian Switzerland, *i.e.* Ticino; they say Lugano is a very charming town, and until there is a European war life there is possible.

Good-bye, dear; I feel rather better, but all that depends on a dream, on memory, on nothing.

I kiss the children.

Chambéry is all nonsense.

Letter from Herzen to his Wife

July 1851.

Here is something more for the colonel. Sazonov's uncle has sent him the decision of the Senate and the

Tsar concerning him. The Senate has sentenced him to penal servitude for disobedience to the Imperial command, but the Imperial Council has mitigated the sentence, and the Tsar has confirmed that . . . *Risum teneatis*, 'To condemn him, Sazonov, to perpetual exile from the borders of the Empire'—there's a punishment for an emigrant! His uncle has sent him 6000 francs and he is going to London.

The Germans who saw Bakunin at Prague said that the latter part of the time he was chained to the wall!

A Postscript to his Son

TURIN, *July* 10, 1851.

Mother has written you so much that she has crowded me into the margin. But soon we shall be talking, dear; I think we may set off in three days' time.

Letter from Natalie Herzen to her daughter Natalie

TURIN, *July* 13, 1851.

Tatotchka, my darling, my birdie, my little star, my little flower, my joy! I am hastening to you. Soon I shall see you and how happy we shall be together! I' ll tell you how I travelled over mountains and valleys. And meanwhile, till I come, my little one, be well and merry and good. Kiss Olya as I kiss you. Hug Puponka.   YOUR MOTHER.

Herzen's Postscript to the above Letter

Here we are travelling and travelling; the carriage creaks, the horses snort, the whip clacks, we go on and on, and soon we shall arrive. François will run and open the gate, Rocca will fry and bake. And Tata—

she will run and scream and throw herself—flop!—on her daddy's neck.

Look after Hoetsky,[1] and see that he does not get into mischief. Make a low bow for me to Alexandra Christianovna and press her hand warmly.

Letter from Herzen to his Son

TURIN, *July* 13, 1851.

Perhaps, dear Sasha, we may be in time to arrive on Tuesday, and on Wednesday you may almost certainly expect us by the diligence coming from Geneva, I believe it stops at the Hotel York. Did you get the telegraph? Show Kolya how to play with it—it is a very ingenious toy, and I think it will greatly amuse him.

I read with great pleasure in Engelson's letter that he is satisfied with your conduct. But you are in your thirteenth year, and if we were poor people you would have to be earning your own living and helping your family. You can see for yourself that the children of the poor are much more sensible and steady, especially in everything practical: they are less timid and more cautious. What they gain through necessity we must acquire by will.

P. S.—Your letters of the 11th have just come.

[1] In Vol. III. this name has been transliterated as Hoetsky, on the assumption that it was Russian. Apparently it is Polish, and should be Choecki, but I retain the approximately phonetic spelling to avoid confusion.—(*Translator's Note.*)

SECTION FOUR

ENGLAND

(1852-1855)

Chapter 1

The Fogs of London

WHEN at daybreak on the 25th of August 1852 I passed along a wet plank on to the shore of England and looked at its dirty white cliffs, I was very far indeed from imagining that years would pass before I should leave those chalk cliffs.

Entirely under the influence of the ideas with which I was leaving Italy, stunned and sick, bewildered by a series of blows which had followed one on the other with such brutal rapidity, I could not see clearly what I was doing. It seemed as though I had needed to be brought again and again into concrete contact with familiar truths in order that I might grasp again what I had known before or ought to have known.

I had been false to my own logic and forgotten how different the man of to-day is in opinions and in actions, how noisily he begins and how humbly he carries out his programme, how good are his desires and how feeble his muscles.

Two months had been filled with unnecessary meetings, fruitless seeking, painful and quite useless conversations, and I was still expecting something . . . expecting something. But my realistic nature could not remain for long in that world of phantoms. I began little by little to grasp that the edifice I was raising had no foundation, that it would inevitably crumble into ruins.

I was humiliated, my pride was outraged, I was angry with myself. My conscience tormented me for the sacrilegious desecration of my grief, for the year wasted in petty agitation, and I was conscious of a terrible inexpressible weariness. . . . How I needed then a friend who, without judging and condemning, could have received my confession and have shared my unhappiness! but the wilderness about me grew more and more desolate, there was no one near to me, not one . . . and perhaps that was for the best.

I had not meant to stay more than a month in London, but little by little I began to understand that I had absolutely nowhere to go and no reason to go anywhere. Nowhere could I have found the same hermit-like seclusion as in London.

Having made up my mind to remain there, I began by taking a house in one of the remotest parts of the town, beyond Regent's Park, near Primrose Hill.

The little girls remained in Paris, only Sasha was with me. As the fashion is here, the house was divided into three storeys. The whole middle storey consisted of an immense, cold, uncomfortable drawing-room. I changed it into my study. The owner of the house was a sculptor and had piled up the whole room with all sorts of statuettes and models; a bust of Lola Montes [1] was always before my eyes, together with Queen Victoria.

When on the second or third day after moving there, having unpacked and settled in, I went into that room in the morning, sat down in a big armchair and spent some two hours in complete stillness, disturbed by no

[1] Lola Montes was born in 1818 at Montrose in Scotland, of an officer called Gilbert and a Creole, and died in New York in 1861. An adventuress whose audacity has rarely been equalled, she was the mistress of the King of Bavaria (and of many other men). Her life, which was spent in roaming over the world as an actress, was a series of scandalous adventures. Her skill in wielding a horse-whip was never contested by those with whom she quarrelled.—(*Translator's Note.*)

one, I felt myself somehow free, for the first time after years and years.

My heart was not the lighter for this freedom, but yet I looked gladly out of window at the gloomy trees in the park, dimly showing through the smoky fog, and was thankful to them for the peace.

For whole mornings together I used now to sit utterly alone, often doing nothing, not even reading; Sasha would sometimes run in, but he did not interfere with my solitude.

Haug, who lived with me, never without extreme necessity came in before dinner, and we dined between six and seven. In this leisure I went, fact by fact, over the whole past, myself and the words and letters of others. I found mistakes to the right, mistakes to the left, vacillation, weakness, uncertainty in action and over-readiness to be influenced by others. And in the course of this analysis, by degrees, a revolution took place within me . . . there were bitter moments and more than once tears rolled down my cheeks; but there were other moments, not of gladness but of courage: I was conscious of power in myself. I no longer relied on any one else, but my confidence in myself grew stronger, I grew more independent of every one.

The emptiness around me strengthened me, gave me time to collect myself, I grew apart from others, that is, I did not seek real intimacy with them; I avoided no one, but I no longer cared for people—I saw that I had no ties that rested on really deep feelings. I was a stranger among strangers; I had more sympathy for some than for others, but was in no close intimacy with any. It had been so in the past, too, but I had not noticed it, being continually absorbed by my own thoughts; now the masquerade was over, the dominoes had been removed, the garlands were taken from the heads, the masks from the faces, and I saw features very

THE FOGS OF LONDON

different from those I had imagined. What was I to do? I could help showing that I liked many people less, that is, knew them better, but I could not help feeling it; and, as I have said, these discoveries did not rob me of my courage, but rather strengthened it.

London life was very favourable for such a change. There is no town in the world which is more adapted for training one away from people and training one into solitude than London. The manner of life, the distances, the climate, the very multitude of the population in which the individual is lost, all this together with the absence of Continental diversions conduces to the same effect. One who knows how to live alone has nothing to fear from the dulness of London. The life here, like the atmosphere here, is bad for the weak, for the frail, for one who seeks a prop outside himself, for one who seeks cordiality, sympathy, attention; the moral lungs here must be as strong as the physical lungs, whose task it is to get rid of the sulphuric acid in the smoky fog. The masses are saved by the struggle for daily bread, the commercial classes by their absorption in heaping up wealth, and all by the fuss and hurry of business; but nervous and romantic temperaments, fond of living among their fellows, of intellectual sloth and emotional idleness, are bored to death and fall into despair.

Wandering lonely about London, through its stony lanes and through its stifling passages, sometimes not seeing a step before me for the thick, opaline fog, and running against flying shadows—I lived through a great deal.

In the evening when my son had gone to bed, I usually went out for a walk; I scarcely ever went to see any one; I read the newspapers and stared in taverns at the alien race, and stood on the bridges across the Thames.

On the one hand, the stalactites of the Houses of Parliament would loom through the darkness ready to vanish again, on the other, the inverted bowl of Saint Paul's . . . and street-lamps . . . street-lamps without end in both directions. One city, full-fed, lay sleeping, while the other, hungry, was not yet awake—the streets were empty, nothing could be heard but the even tread of the policeman with his lantern. I used to sit and look, and my soul would grow quieter and more peaceful. And so through all this I came to love this dreadful ant-heap, where every night a hundred thousand men know not where they will lay their heads, and the police often find women and children dead of hunger beside hotels where one cannot dine for less than two pounds.

But such violent transitions, however rapid, are not achieved all at once, especially at forty. A long time passed while I was coming to terms with my new ideas. Though I had made up my mind to work, for a long time I did nothing, or did not what I meant to do.

The idea with which I had come to London, to seek the judgment of my own people, was a sound and right one. I repeat that even now with full and deliberate conviction. To whom, indeed, are we to appeal for judgment, for the establishment of the truth, for the unmasking of falsehood?

It is not for us to go suing for justice to our enemies, who judge by other principles, by laws which we do not recognise.

One can settle one's quarrels for oneself; no doubt one can. To take the law in one's own hands is to snatch back by force what has been taken by force, and so restore the balance; revenge is just as sound and simple a human feeling as gratitude; but neither revenge nor taking the law into one's own hands explains anything. It may happen that a clear explanation is what matters most to a man. The establishment of the truth may be more precious for him than revenge. My own error lay not in the main proposition, it lay in the underlying assumption; to win the judgment of one's own people one must first of all have one's own people. Where were mine . . . ?

I had had my own people once in Russia. But I was so completely cut off in a foreign land; I had at all costs to get into communication with my own people; I longed to tell them of the weight that lay on my heart. Letters could not get in, but books would get through of themselves; writing letters was useless—I would print; and little by little I set to work upon *My Past and Thoughts*, and upon founding a Russian printing-press.

Chapter 2
THE MOUNTAIN HEIGHTS—THE CENTRAL EUROPEAN COMMITTEE—MAZZINI—LEDRU-ROLLIN—KOSSUTH

IN London I made haste to see Mazzini, not only because he had taken the warmest and most active interest in the misfortunes which had befallen my family, but also because I was charged with a special commission to him from his friends. Medici, Pisacane, Mezzacapo, Cosenz, Bertani and the rest were dissatisfied with the direction of affairs given from London; they said that Mazzini did not understand the new position, and they complained of the revolutionary sycophants who, to curry favour, supported his idea that everything was ready for a rising and only waiting for a signal. They wanted internal changes in the party, they thought it essential to introduce a far more military element and to have strategists at the head of the movement, instead of lawyers and journalists. With this object they wished Mazzini to associate himself more closely with generals of genius, such as Ulloa,[1] who with old Pepe[2] stood in dissatisfied aloofness.

They commissioned me to tell all this to Mazzini, partly because they knew he had confidence in me, and partly because my position outside the Italian parties freed my hands.

[1] There were two Neapolitan brothers of this name, both military men; probably Girolamo (1810-1880), an artillery general who published several works on military science, is the one to whom Herzen is referring here.

[2] There were two Neapolitan brothers, Italian generals, of this name?Florestano (1780-1851), and Guglielmo (1782-1855), of whom the latter is the more famous. He defeated the Austrians in 1821, fled from Naples, was sentenced to death in his absence, returned in 1848, and was a prominent military leader in the war of independence, assisting Manin, defending Venice, etc. He wrote Memoirs, and a *Histoire des Revolutions et Guerres d'ltalie en 1847-1848.*—(*Translator's Notes.*)

Mazzini received me as an old friend. At last the conversation turned on the message given me by his friends. At first he listened to me very attentively, though he did not disguise the fact that he was not quite pleased at opposition; but when from general propositions I came down to details and personal questions, then he suddenly cut me short.

'That is not so at all, there is not a word of sense in it!'

'It is not six weeks, though,' I observed, 'since I left Genoa, and I have spent the last two years in Italy and can myself confirm a great deal of what I have said, speaking in the name of your friends.'

'It is just because you have been in Genoa that you say that. What is Genoa? What could you hear there? The opinion of one group of the exiles! I know that they think that, but I know too that they are mistaken. Genoa is a very important centre, but it is only one point and I know the whole of Italy; I know the needs of every little spot from Abruzzi to Vorarlberg. Our friends in Genoa are out of touch with the whole peninsula, they cannot judge what it wants, they cannot judge the state of mind of the public.'

I made two or three more attempts, but by now he was *en garde*, beginning to get angry and answering impatiently. I ceased speaking, with a feeling of sadness; I had not noticed such intolerance in him in old days.

'I am very grateful to you,' he said, after a moment's thought. 'I ought to know our friends' opinion; I am ready to weigh everything, to consider everything, but whether I agree or not is a different matter; a great responsibility lies upon me, not only before God and my conscience, but before the Italian people.'

My mediation was a failure.

Mazzini was already planning his 3rd of February 1853; the question was settled in his mind, and his friends did not agree with him.

'Do you know Ledru-Rollin, and Kossuth?' he asked.

'No.'

'Would you like to make their acquaintance?'

'Very much.'

'You ought to see them. I will write you a few words to both. Tell them what you have seen, how you have left our friends. Ledru-Rollin,' he went on, taking up the pen and beginning a note, 'is the most charming man in the world, but a Frenchman *jusqu'au bout des ongles*. He firmly believes that Europe will never move without a revolution in France. *Le peuple initiateur!* . . . But where is French initiative now? Though even in the past the ideas which moved France came from Italy or from England. You will see that Italy will begin the new era of revolution! What do you think?'

'I must own that I do not think so.'

'Why,' he said smiling, 'will it be the Slav world?'

'I didn't say that; I do not know on what Ledru-Rollin bases his convictions, but it is very probable that no revolution will succeed in Europe while France is in the state of prostration in which we see her.'

'So you are still under the influence of the prestige of France?'

'The prestige of her geographical position, her formidable army and her natural support by Russia, Austria and Prussia.'[1]

'France is asleep, we will awaken her.'

There was nothing left for me to say but, 'God grant that your words may come true!'

Which of us was right at that moment was shown

[1] This conversation took place in the year 1852.—(*Author's Note.*)

by Garibaldi. In a former chapter I have spoken of my meeting with him in the West India Docks on his American ship, *The Commonwealth*.

There at lunch with him, in the presence of Orsini, Haug and me, Garibaldi, speaking with great affection of Mazzini, gave his candid opinion of the attempt of the 3rd of February 1853 (we met in the spring of 1854), and spoke of the necessity of uniting all the Italian groups in one fighting party. And on the evening of the same day, we met at the house of an acquaintance; Garibaldi was not in good spirits, Mazzini took out of his pocket a number of the *Italia del Popolo*, and showed him an article in it. Garibaldi read it through and said: 'Yes, it is smartly written, but a very mischievous article. I tell you plainly, the journalist or the writer ought to be severely punished for such an article. To do all he can to increase the breach between us and Piedmont when we only have one army, the army of the King of Sardinia! It is a recklessness and unnecessary insolence that borders upon crime.'

Mazzini defended the paper, Garibaldi became still more depressed.

When leaving his ship, he had said it would be too late to go back to the docks and that he would sleep at a hotel, and I had invited him to come home with me instead. He had consented. Besieged on all sides by an indomitable legion of ladies, Garibaldi succeeded by a series of marches and countermarches in extricating himself from the throng and, reaching me, whispered in my ear: 'How long are you staying?'

'Let us go at once if you like.'

'Please do.'

We took leave; on the way home he said to me: 'How sorry I am, how terribly sorry that Peppo[1] is so carried away and with the noblest and purest inten-

[1] The diminutive of Giuseppe.—(*Author's Note*.)

tions makes such mistakes! It was more than I could stand just now; he is pleased at having trained his followers to irritate Piedmont. Why, if the king goes over altogether to the reactionaries, free speech will be silenced in Italy and the last support of the movement will be lost. The republic, the republic! I have been a republican all my life, but it is not a question of a republic now. I know the Italian masses better than Mazzini, I have lived with them and lived their life. Mazzini knows the educated classes of Italy and sways their intellects; but out of them there is no making an army to drive out the Austrians and the Pope; for the mass, for the Italian people, the only banner is "Unity and the expulsion of foreigners!" And how is that to be attained by estranging the one powerful kingdom in Italy which, for one reason or another, wishes to stand by Italy, and is afraid to do so; instead of inviting its co-operation, they repel it and insult it. On the day when the *young man* believes that he has more in common with the archdukes than with us, the progress of Italy will be delayed for a generation or two.'

Next day was Sunday; he went for a walk with my son, had his daguerrotype taken at Caldesi's and brought it me for a present, and then stayed to dinner.

In the middle of dinner, I was called out to see an Italian who had been sent by Mazzini and had been looking for Garibaldi all day; I asked him to sit down to the table with us.

The Italian seemed anxious to speak to him alone, I suggested they should go into my study. In the course of the conversation Garibaldi twice over repeated what he had said to me on the way home.

In aim he was completely at one with Mazzini, but differed from him in the method of achieving it. That Garibaldi understood the masses of the people better

GARIBALDI

I am absolutely convinced. Mazzini, like a mediaeval monk, had a deep understanding of one side of life, but invented the others; he lived a great deal in thought and passion, not in the everyday world; from his early years till his hair was grey, he had lived in the juntas of the Carbonari, and in a circle of persecuted republicans and Liberal writers; he was in relations with Greek revolutionary clubs and Spanish *exaltados*, he conspired with the genuine Cavaignac and the impostor Ramorino,[1] with the Swiss James Fazy, with the Polish democracy, with the Moldo-Wallachians. . . . From his study the enthusiastic Konarski set off with his blessing, went to Russia and was lost. All that is so, but he was never in touch with the people, with that *solo interprete della legge divina*, with that thick layer that goes down to the foundations, that is, reaches the fields and the plough, and includes the wild shepherds of Calabria, the *facchinos* and the boatmen; while Garibaldi, not only in Italy but everywhere, lived among them, knew their strength and their weakness, their griefs and their joys: he knew them on the field of battle and on the stormy ocean, he could become a legendary figure like Bem,[2] and inspired more faith than his patron, San Giuseppe. . . .

Only Mazzini did not believe in him.

[1] Ramorino, Girolamo, a Genoese, was one of the leaders in the Polish rising of 1831. In 1849 he was in command of a division of Lombard fugitives.

[2] Bem, Joseph (1795-1850), a Polish leader of the Hungarian revolt against Austria, took an active part in the Polish rebellion against Russia in 1830. In 1848 he took command of an Hungarian army and defeated the famous Ban Jellachich, a victory he announced in the three words, 'Bem Ban Bum' (Bem has beaten the Ban). He was defeated later on by greatly superior forces at Schässburg and again at Temesvar, and made his escape into Turkey, where he became a Mahomedan and a general in the Turkish army. He died at Aleppo, after suppressing a rising of the Arabs against the Christians there. — (*Translator's Notes*.)

And Garibaldi as he went away said: 'I am going with a heavy heart, I have no influence over him, and again he will undertake something before the time is ripe!'

Garibaldi guessed right. Before a year was over, there were again two or three unsuccessful outbreaks; Orsini was arrested by the Piedmont gendarmes on Piedmont soil, almost with a weapon in his hands, one of the centres of the movement was discovered in Rome, and the marvellous organisation of which I have spoken was broken up. The panic-stricken governments strengthened their police: the brutal coward, the King of Naples, resorted to torture again.

Then Garibaldi could stand it no longer, and published the famous letter in which he said: 'None but madmen or enemies of the Italian cause can take part in these unfortunate risings.'

Perhaps that letter ought not to have been published. Mazzini was crushed and unhappy. Garibaldi had dealt him a blow . . . but that his letter was perfectly consistent with what he had said to me and before me —of that there can be no doubt.

Next day I went to see Ledru-Rollin; he received me very graciously. His colossal, imposing figure, which did not gain by scrutiny *en détail,* made a favourable impression as a whole. He must have been both a *bon enfant* and a *bon vivant.* His grey hair and the wrinkles on his brow showed that his anxieties had not passed over him quite without leaving a trace. He had spent his life and his fortune on the revolution and the public favour had deserted him. The strange, ambiguous part he played in April and May and his feebleness in the days of June had estranged from him a section of the Reds, without bringing him any nearer the Blues. His name which had served as a symbol, and had at one time heen on the lips of the peasants. though in a distorted form,[1] was more rarely heard. Even his party in London was gradually melting away; especially after Felix Pyat set up in London.

Settling himself comfortably on a sofa, Ledru-Rollin began to 'harangue' me: 'The revolution,' he said, 'can only radiate (*rayonner*) from France. It is clear that whatever country you belong to, you ought first of all to assist us for the sake of your own cause. The revolution can only come from Paris. I know very well that our friend Mazzini is not of that opinion. He is carried away by his patriotism. What can Italy do with Austria on her back and the soldiers of Napoleon in Rome? What we need is Paris; Paris means Rome; Warsaw, Hungary, Sicily—and happily Paris is perfectly ready—make no mistake about it, she is perfectly ready! The revolution is made. *La révolution est faite, c'est clair comme bonjour.* I don't think about that, I think of what is to follow it, of how to avoid our mistakes of the past.' He went on in this way for half an hour and, suddenly realising that he was not alone and not facing an audience, said to me in a very good-natured way: 'You see you and I are entirely at one about it.' I had not opened my lips. Ledru-Rollin went on: 'As for the material fact of the revolution, it is delayed by our lack of funds. Our means have been exhausted in this struggle which has been going on for years and years. If only I had at once a hundred thousand francs at my disposal—yes—a miserable hundred thousand francs—there would be revolution in Paris the day after to-morrow or the day after that.'

'But how is it,' I observed at last,' that such a wealthy

[1] The peasants of remote parts of France loved *le due* Roilin, and only regretted that he was influenced by the woman with whom he was connected, La Martine, saying that she led le due astray, though he himself was *bon pour le populaire*,—(*Author's Note.*)

nation, absolutely ready to rise, does not find a hundred thousand or even half a million francs?'

Ledru-Rollin coloured a little but answered without faltering: '*Pardon, pardon*, you are speaking of theoretical hypotheses, while I am speaking of facts, simple facts.'

That I could not understand.

When I was leaving, Ledru-Rollin escorted me down the stairs in the English fashion and, giving me his enormous, titanic hand, said once more: 'I hope this is not good-bye. I shall always be pleased to see you, and so *au revoir*.'

'In Paris,' I added.

'In Paris?'

'You have so convinced me that the revolution is just upon us, that I really don't know if I shall have time to see you here.'

He looked at me in perplexity, and so I made haste to add: 'Anyway I sincerely hope so. That I think you cannot doubt.'

'Otherwise you would not have been here,' he observed, and we parted.

. . . .

Kossuth I saw for the first time on my second visit. It happened like this: when I arrived I was greeted in the parlour by a military gentleman in a semi-Hungarian military costume, with the information that His Honour the Governor was not receiving.

'Here is a letter from Mazzini.'

'I will give it him at once. Kindly sit down.' He offered me a pipe and then a chair. Two or three minutes later he returned. 'His Honour the Governor extremely regrets that he cannot see you, he is just finishing his American mail. However, if you like to wait, he will be delighted to see you later.'

'And will he soon have finished his letters?'

'At five o'clock exactly.'

I glanced at my watch; it was half-past one.

'Well, I am not going to wait three hours and a half.'

'But will you not come again later?'

'I live at least three miles from Notting Hill. However,' I added, 'I have no pressing business with His Honour the Governor!'

'But His Honour the Governor will be extremely sorry.'

'Here is my address, then.'

A week passed; one evening a long gentleman with long whiskers appeared—a Hungarian colonel whom I had met in the summer at Lugano.

'I have come to you from His Honour the Governor. He is very much troubled at your not having been to see him.'

'Oh, how unfortunate! However, I did leave him my address. If I knew the right time to go I would certainly go to see Kossuth to-day or . . . ' I added inquiringly, 'what ought I to say . . . to His Honour the Governor?'

'*Zu dem Olten, zu dem Olten,*' observed the colonel, smiling; 'we always call him *der Olte* among ourselves. What a man! You will see. Such a head as his there is not in the whole world, never has been and . . . ' the colonel inwardly sang a hymn in praise of Kossuth.

'Very good, I will come to-morrow at two o'clock.'

'That is impossible. To-morrow is Wednesday. To-morrow morning the old man only receives our people, only Hungarians.'

I could not help laughing, and the colonel laughed too.

'When does your old man drink tea?' I asked.

'At eight o'clock in the evening.'

'Tell him that I will come to-morrow at eight o'clock. If that won't do you must write to me.'

'He will be delighted—I will wait for you in the reception-room.'

This time as soon as I rang the bell the long colonel met me, and a short colonel at once led me to Kossuth's study.

I found Kossuth working at a big table; he was wearing a black velvet Hungarian jacket and a little black cap: he is far better-looking than all his portraits and busts; in his youth he must have been a handsome fellow and the romantically pensive character of his face must have been terribly attractive to women. His features have not the classical correctness of Mazzini's, Saffi's or Orsini's; but—and perhaps indeed owing to this fact—he was more akin to us Northerners. Not only a strong mind but a deeply feeling heart could be seen in his mournfully gentle expression; his melancholy smile and rather impressive manner of speech put the finishing touches to his charm. He speaks extremely well, though with a distinct accent, equally persistent in his French, his German and his English. He does not elaborate his phrases nor deal in commonplaces; he thinks with one, listens, and develops his thought almost always originally, because he is much freer than the others from pedantry and the spirit of party. Perhaps a legal training may be detected in his manner of advancing arguments and objections, but what he says is earnest and well thought out.

Kossuth had had a great deal to do with the practical business of his countryside before 1848; this gave him a certain correctness of judgment. He was very well aware that in the world of events and practice it is not always possible to fly straight as the crow, that facts rarely develop along a simple logical line, but take a tacking course, zigzagging or going off at a tangent. And that is among others the reason why Kossuth is inferior to Mazzini in fiery activity, and why, on the other hand, Mazzini is continually making attempts, desperate efforts, while Kossuth makes none at all.

Mazzini's attitude towards the Italian revolution is that of a fanatic; he believes in his idea of it; he does not subject that idea to criticism, but bounds forward *ora e sempre*, like an arrow loosed from the bow. The less he takes circumstances into account the simpler and more persistent is his activity, and the purer his idea.

The revolutionary idealism of Ledru-Rollin is not complicated either; it may be all found in the speeches of the Convention and the measures of the Committee of Public Security. Kossuth brought with him from Hungary no common store of revolutionary tradition, no apocalyptic formulas of social doctrinairism, but simply the protest of his own country, which he had studied thoroughly, a new country, unknown as regards its needs, as regards its barbaric free institutions and as regards its mediaeval forms. In comparison with his comrades, Kossuth was a specialist.

The French refugees, with their unfortunate habit of judging everything wholesale and measuring everything by their own standard, made it a great reproach against Kossuth that in Marseilles he had expressed his sympathy with Socialist ideas, and, in the speech delivered in London from the balcony of the Mansion House, had spoken with deep respect of the parliamentary system.

Kossuth was perfectly right. These events occurred during his journey from Constantinople, that is, during the most triumphantly heroic episode of the dark years that followed 1848. The American ship which tore him from the uplifted claws of Austria and Russia was proudly sailing with the exile to one republic and stopped on the shores of another. There already a decree of the police-dictator of France was waiting to forbid the exile's stepping on the soil of the future empire. Now that would have been the end of it; but in those days there were still men in France not completely broken in, and crowds of workmen hastened in boats to the ship to greet Kossuth, and Kossuth very naturally spoke with them of Socialism. The scene changes. On the way, one free country begged of the other a visit from the exile. Kossuth, publicly thanking the English for his reception, did not conceal his respect for the system which made it possible. He was in both cases perfectly sincere; he did not represent any party at all; he could sympathise with the French workman and sympathise with the English constitution without becoming an Orleanist or being false to Republicanism. Kossuth knew this and well understood his position in England as regards revolutionary parties on the negative side, too; he became neither a Glückist nor a Piccinist;[1] he held himself equally aloof from Ledru-Rollin and from Louis Blanc. With Mazzini and Worcell he had ground in common, their frontiers were adjacent, their struggle was similar and, indeed, almost the same; with them he first made friends.

But Mazzini and Worcell had long been what the Spanish call *afrancisados*. Kossuth, with stubborn reluctance, gave in to them, and it is well worth noting that he yielded in proportion as his hopes of a rising in Hungary grew fainter and fainter.

From my conversation with Mazzini and Ledru-Rollin, it is evident that Mazzini looked for the revolutionary impulse from Italy, and was altogether greatly dissatisfied with France, but from that it does not follow that I am wrong in calling him *afrancisado*. His attitude was on the one hand due to a patriotism

[1] The reference is to the famous war in Paris between the admirers of Glück and his rival, an Italian composer called Piccini. —(*Translator's Note*.)

not altogether in harmony with the idea of the brotherhood of peoples and the universal republic, and on the other hand to his personal indignation with France for having in 1848 done nothing to help Italy and in 1849. everything to ruin her. But being irritated against the France of to-day does not mean being outside her influence; the French revolutionary faith has its common uniform, its ritual, its creeds; within its limits one may be a political liberal or a desperate democrat; one may without loving France love one's own country in a French fashion; all those will be variations, personal cases, but the algebraical formula will remain the same.

Kossuth's conversation with me at once took a serious turn, there was more sadness than cheerfulness in his views and his words; he certainly did not expect a revolution to-morrow. His knowledge of South-Eastern Europe was immense; he surprised me by quoting points from the treaties of Catherine with the Porte.

'What terrible mischief you did us at the time of our rebellion,' he said, 'and what terrible mischief to yourselves! What a narrow and anti-Slav policy to support Austria! You may be sure Austria will not say thank you for being saved; do you imagine she does not understand that Nicholas was not helping her, but despotic power in general?'

He knew far less about the social than about the political and military state of Russia. That is not surprising. There are but few of our own statesmen who know anything about it except generalities and casual, private, disconnected observations. He thought that the Crown peasants paid their taxes in the form of labour, and questioned me about the village commune and the power of the landowners; I told him what I knew.

On leaving Kossuth I asked myself what he had in

common with his comrades, except caring for the independence of his people. Mazzini was dreaming of freeing humanity by means of Italy, Ledru-Rollin wanted to free mankind in Paris and then sternly to dictate freedom to the whole world. Kossuth hardly troubled about humanity and was, it seemed, scarcely concerned whether a republic would shortly be proclaimed in Lisbon, or whether the Bey of Tripoli would be called a simple citizen of the one and indivisible Tripoli commonwealth.

This distinction, which struck me from the first glance, was apparent afterwards in a succession of actions. Mazzini and Ledru-Rollin, as men independent of practical considerations, did their utmost to make revolutionary attempts every two or three months, Mazzini by risings, Ledru-Rollin by the dispatch of agents. Mazzini's friends were perishing in the Austrian and Papal prisons, Ledru-Rollin's emissaries were perishing in Lambessa and Cayenne,[1] but with the fanaticism of blind believers they persisted in dispatching their Isaacs to the sacrifice. Kossuth made no attempts; Libényi,[2] who stuck a knife in the Emperor of Austria, had no connection with him.

No doubt Kossuth came to London with more sanguine hopes, and, indeed, there is no denying that he might well have had his head turned. One need but recall the continual ovation, the regal procession across seas and oceans, and the towns of America quarrelling over the honour of being the first to meet him and to conduct him within their walls. Proud London, the

[1] Lambessa, an old Roman town of North Africa, and Cayenne, the capital of French Guiana, were used as penal settlements from 1852 onward. The climate of the latter was particularly unhealthy, and numbers of the exiles perished there.

[2] Libényi was a Hungarian who attempted to assassinate the late Emperor Francis Joseph of Austria in 1853.—(*Translator's Notes*.)

city of two millions, stood waiting for him at the railway-station, the Lord Mayor's carriage was there in readiness for him; aldermen, sheriffs, Members of Parliament escorted him through a sea of surging people who greeted him, shouting and flinging up their hats. . . . And when he came out on the balcony of the Mansion House with the Lord Mayor, he was welcomed with thunders of 'Hurrah!' such as Nicholas could never wring from the crowd in London through the patronage of Wellington, the statue to Nelson, or by courting favour over race-horses.

The haughty English aristocracy, who went down to their country seats while Napoleon III. was banqueting with the Queen at Windsor or carousing with shopkeepers in the City, forgot their dignity and crowded in coaches and carriages to see the famous agitator. People of the highest rank were presented to him, the exile. *The Times* frowned on it at first, but was so scared at the clamour of public opinion that it began abusing Napoleon to smooth over its error.

Is it strange that Kossuth came back from America full of hopes? But after spending a year or two in London and seeing the direction history was taking on the Continent and the cooling of enthusiasm in England itself, he saw that a rising in Hungary was impossible and that England was a poor ally of revolution. Once again he was filled with hopes and again championed his old cause before the English people: that was at the beginning of the Crimean War.

He abandoned his seclusion then and appeared hand in hand with Worcell, that is, with democratic Poland, which besought the Allies for no more than a summons, no more than their consent, in order to risk a rebellion. No doubt this was for Poland moment—*oggi o mai*. If the restoration of Poland had been sanctioned, what might not Hungary have expected? That was why Kossuth appeared at the Polish meeting of the 29th of November 1854, and asked for a hearing. That was why he afterwards, in company with Worcell, visited the principal towns of England, promoting the agitation for the benefit of Poland. Kossuth's speeches delivered on those occasions are very remarkable both in form and matter, but this time England was not carried away by him: people flocked in crowds to the meetings, applauded his marvellous eloquence, were ready to subscribe to funds; but the movement went no further, his words did not call forth that echo in other circles, in the masses, which might have influenced Parliament or have forced the Government to change its course. The year 1854 passed; 1855 had come; Nicholas was dead. Poland had not moved, the war was confined to the shores of the Crimea; it was useless even to dream of the restoration of Polish nationalism; Austria was a bone in the throat of the Allies. Besides, all were longing for peace, all that mattered had been attained, the civilian Napoleon was covered with military glory.

Kossuth withdrew from the stage again. His articles in the *Atlas* and the lectures on the Concordat, which he gave in Edinburgh and Manchester, are rather to be reckoned as private work. Kossuth had saved neither his own fortune nor his wife's. Accustomed to the lavish luxury of Hungarian magnates, he had in a foreign land to earn his livelihood; he did this and made no secret of it.

There is something of dignity and melancholy about the whole family: one can see that great events have passed over it and have raised the diapason of all. Kossuth is to this day surrounded by a few faithful followers; at first they were his court and now they are simply his friends.

Events have left their trace on him, he has grown

much older of late, and his resignation makes one's heart ache.

The first two years we rarely met; then chance brought us together at one of the most beautiful spots not only in England but in Europe—in the Isle of Wight. We spent a month in Ventnor at the same time that he was there in 1855.

Before he went away we were all at a children's party. Kossuth's two sons, splendid and charming lads, were dancing with my children. . . . Kossuth stood in the doorway and looked mournfully at them, then with a smile towards my son said to me:

'Here is the younger generation quite ready to replace us.'

'Will they see it?'

'That is just what I was wondering. Meanwhile let them dance,' he added and watched them still more mournfully.

I fancy that then, too, we were thinking the same thing: will their fathers see it? And what will they see? Does not the revolutionary era, for which we, in the light of the dying glow of the 'nineties, were striving, for which Liberal France, Young Italy, Mazzini, Ledru-Rollin were striving, already belong to the past? Are not these men becoming the sorrowful representatives of the past, around whom a new life and new problems are springing up? Their religion, their language, their movement, their aims are all akin to us, and at the same time alien . . . the chime of the church bell on the still morning of a saint's-day and the singing of the liturgy thrill the soul even now, but yet we have no faith!

These are melancholy truths: it is hard, bitter to look some things in the face, hard sometimes to tell plainly what one sees. And is it necessary? It, too, is in its way an obsession or a disease. 'The truth, the bare truth and nothing but the truth!' All that is very fine; but is the seeing of it compatible with our life? Will it not corrode it, as too strong an acid eats away the sides of a vessel, and is not the passion for it a terrible infirmity that bitterly punishes one who cherishes it in his heart?

One memorable day for me a year ago, this thought was particularly insistent.

On the day of Worcell's death I was awaiting the sculptor in the poor room where that martyr's sufferings ended. An old servant was standing with a guttering yellow candle-end in her hand, to light up the wasted corpse that lay covered by a single sheet. As afflicted as Job, he had fallen asleep with a smile on his lips, faith was still steady in his dimming eyes, closed by a fanatic like himself, Mazzini.

I loved that old man and grieved over him, and I did not once tell him all the truth that I had in my mind. I did not want to trouble his failing spirit, he had suffered far too much, he needed the prayer for the dying and not the truth, and that is why he was so glad when Mazzini whispered vows and words of faith into his dying ear!

Appendix
(To Chapter 2)[1]

What has changed? The years '59 and '60 have widened the horizon. Persons and parties are more clearly defined, some have grown stronger, others have vanished. With strained attention, checking not only every criticism, but even the throbbing of our hearts, we have watched over those dear to us for these last two years. They have at times disappeared behind the smoke of battle, at times have stood out vividly against it, growing vaster every minute, and again have vanished in the smoke. At this moment it has passed away and we can breathe again, all those dear to us are safe!

And beyond the smoke, in the shade, apart from the noise of battle, with no share in the rejoicings of victory, with no share in the laurel wreaths, one figure stands out like a colossus.

Cursed by all parties, by the cheated plebeian, by the savage priest, by the cowardly bourgeois, and the scum of Piedmont; vilified by all the organs of all the reactions, from the papal and imperial *Moniteur* to the liberal eunuchs of Cavour, and the grand eunuch of the London money-changers, *The Times* (which cannot mention Mazzini's name without vulgar abuse), he remained not only 'unshaken in the midst of universal error,' but with joy and rapture blessing the friends and foes who were carrying out *his* thought, *his* plan. Pointing to him, as to some angel of destruction:

> 'The people mysteriously saved by him
> Reviled his sacred head,'[2]

but beside him stood not Kutuzov but Garibaldi. In

---

[1] An extract from the *Polar Star*, vol. vu., 1861.

[2] A quotation from a poem of Pushkin's on General Barclay de Tolly.—(*Translator's Note*.)

the person of her hero, her deliverer, Italy did not break with Mazzini. How was it Garibaldi did not yield him half his laurels? Why did he not openly avow that he went hand in hand with him? Why did not the abandoned triumvir of Rome urge his claims? Why did Mazzini himself beg Garibaldi not to mention him? And why did the popular leader, pure-hearted as a child, keep silence and thus falsely admit the breach?

There was something dearer to both than their persons, their names, their reputations . . . Italy!

And the vulgar world of to-day did not understand them. It could not grasp such greatness; its bookkeeping is not equal to adjusting the accounts of such a debit and credit!

Garibaldi has become more than ever a figure from Cornelius Nepos; he has the same antique grandeur on his little farm, the same, simple-hearted, pure grandeur, as a description from Homer or a Greek statue. No trace of rhetoric, of melodrama, of diplomacy. They are superfluous in the heroic epic; when it was over and everyday life began, then the King dismissed him as one dismisses the driver who has brought one to one's destination and, embarrassed at not being able to give him a tip, surpassed Austria in his colossal ingratitude; while Garibaldi did not resent it, but, with a smile on his face and fifty *scudi* in his pocket, went out from the palaces of the countries he had subdued, leaving the courtiers to reckon his expenses and decide that he had spoiled the bear's skin.

They might amuse themselves as they pleased: half of the great work was done, if Italy was welded into one and the white *cretins* had been driven out.

There were painful moments for Garibaldi. He is captivated by people; just as he was captivated by Alexandre Dumas, he is captivated by Victor Emmanuel; the King's lack of delicate feeling wounds him, the

King knows this, and, to soften him, sends pheasants killed by his own hands, flowers from his own garden, and loving notes inscribed: *'Sempre il tuo amico Vittorio.'*

For Mazzini, people do not exist, for him nothing exists but the cause and, indeed, the one cause; he himself exists, 'lives and moves,' only in it. However many pheasants and flowers the King might send him, he would not be touched. But he would at once collaborate, not only with him whom he reckons a good though foolish man, but even with his Talleyrand in miniature, whom he does not reckon a good or even a decent man. Mazzini is an ascetic, the Calvin, the Procida [1] of Italian emancipation. One-sided, for ever absorbed by one idea, for ever ready and on his guard, Mazzini keeps his vigil with the same obstinacy and patience with which he created a compact party out of scattered individuals and vague yearnings, and, after a dozen failures, called out Garibaldi and his army of half-free Italy, and preserved the living, infallible hope of its unity. Day and night, catching fish and going out hunting, lying down and getting up, Garibaldi and his followers see the thin, melancholy hand of Mazzini pointing to Rome, and they will still march thither.

I did wrong in omitting from a fragment that I have published already some pages about Mazzini; his figure has not come out so clearly without them. I dwelt particularly on his breach with Garibaldi in 1854 and on my difference of opinion with him. I did this through delicacy, but such delicacy is too petty for Mazzini, there is no need to keep anything back about such men, there is no need to spare them!

[1] Procida (Giovanni da), one of the chief instigators of the massacre on Easter Monday, 1282, of the French army of occupation in Sicily, known as the Sicilian Vespers.— (*Translator's Note.*)

After his return from Naples he wrote me a note; I hastened to him, I had a pang at my heart when I saw him, I was still expecting to find him sad and wounded in his love, his position was tragic in the extreme. I did in fact find him older physically but younger in soul; with both hands stretched out, as his habit was, he rushed towards me with the words: 'And so at last it is coming true!' There was a look of delight in his eyes, and his voice trembled.

He spent the whole evening telling me of the time that preceded the expedition to Sicily, of his relations with Victor Emmanuel, then of Naples. In the enthusiasm, in the love with which he talked of Garibaldi's victories and heroic deeds, there was as much affection for him as in his abuse of him for over-trustfulness and inability to read men.

As I listened to him, I tried to catch a single note, a single sound of wounded pride, and I could not catch it; he was sad, but sad like a mother abandoned for the time by a beloved son—she knows that the son will come back and, more than that, knows that the son is happy: that covers everything for her.

Mazzini is full of hopes, he stands closer to Garibaldi than ever. With a smile he described how Neapolitan crowds, incited by the agents of Cavour, surrounded his house, shouting: 'Death to Mazzini!' They had been persuaded, among other things, that Mazzini was a 'Bourbon republican.'

'There were several men and one young Russian with me at the time,' he told me; 'he was surprised at our going on talking as before. "Don't be uneasy," I said to soothe him, "they won't kill me, they will only shout!"'

No, there is no need to spare men like that!

January 31, 1861.

Chapter 3

I

THE EXILES IN LONDON—THE GERMANS AND THE FRENCH—PARTIES—VICTOR HUGO—FELIX PYAT—LOUIS BLANC AND ARMAND BARBÈS

'By the waters of Babylon we sat down and wept.'

IF any one from outside had conceived the idea of writing the inner history of the political exiles and refugees from the year 1848 in London, what a melancholy page he would have added to the records of to-day! What sufferings, what privations, what tears . . . and what triviality, what narrowness, what poverty of intellectual powers, of resources, of understanding, what obstinacy in quarrelling, what pettiness in wounded vanity! . . .

On the one hand, those simple-hearted men, who have accepted the cause of revolution through heart and instinct and have made for its sake the greatest sacrifice a man can make, that of voluntary poverty, form a small group of the righteous. On the other hand, there are men, actuated by disguised and ill-concealed ambition, for whom the revolution meant office, *position sociale*, and who were driven into exile without attaining such position. Then there were fanatics of all kinds, monomaniacs of every sort, men who were insane with every variety of insanity. It was due to this nervous, strained, hysterical condition that table-turning numbered so many victims among the exiles. Almost every one was turning tables—from Victor Hugo and Ledru-Rollin to Quirik Philopanti—who went further still and found out everything that men were doing a thousand years ago.

And with all that not a step forward. They were like the court clock at Versailles, which pointed to one hour, the hour at which the King died. . . . And like the clock, they had not been wound up since the death of Louis XVI. They point to one event, the end of some event. They talk about it, they think about it, they go back to it. Meeting the same men, the same groups, —in five or six months, in two or three years—one feels terrified: the same arguments are still going on, the same personalities and recriminations, only the furrows drawn by poverty and privation are deeper; jackets and overcoats are shabbier; there are more grey hairs, and everything about them is older and bonier and more gloomy . . . and still the same things being said over and over again.

The revolution has remained the philosophy of social order with them, as it was in the 'nineties, but they have not and cannot have the naive passion for the struggle which in those days gave vivid colour to the most meagre generalisations and body to the dry outlines of their political skeleton; generalisations and abstract ideas were a joyful novelty, a revelation in those days. At the end of the eighteenth century, men for the first time, not in books but in actual fact, began to free themselves from the fatal, mysteriously oppressive world of theological tradition, and were trying to base on conscious understanding the whole political system which had grown up apart from will or consciousness. In the attempt at a rational state, as in the attempt to found a religion of reason, there was in 1793 a grand titanic poetry, which bore its fruits, but has for all that grown meagre and threadbare in the last sixty years. Our heirs of the Titans do not observe this. They are like the monks of Mount Athos, who busy themselves about their own affairs, deliver the same speeches which they delivered in the time of Chrysostom, and keep up a manner of life superseded ages ago by the Turkish power, which is now itself

THE GERMANS AND THE FRENCH

drawing to its end . . . while they go on meeting together on certain days to celebrate certain events with the same ritual, the same prayers.

Another bane of the exiles is the constant defending of themselves against each other; this is terribly destructive of intellectual effort and every sort of conscientious work. They have no objective purpose at all, the parties are obstinately conservative, any forward movement seems a weakness to them, almost a desertion; if once you have taken your stand under the banner you must go on standing under it, even if in the process of time you may have discerned that its colours are not quite what they seemed.

So the years pass—gradually everything changes about them. Where there were snowdrifts, the grass is growing; where there were bushes, there is a forest; where there was a forest are only tree-stumps—they notice nothing. Some gateways are completely fallen and are blocked up, they go on knocking at them; new outlets have opened, the light streams through them, but they look the other way.

The relations formed between the different exiles and the English might furnish wonderful illustrations of the chemical affinity of various nationalities.

English life at first dazzles the Germans, overwhelms them, then swallows them up, or rather dissolves them into inferior Englishmen. As a rule, if a German undertakes any kind of business, he at once shaves, turns his shirt collar up to his ears, says *yes* instead of *ja* and *well* where there is no need to say anything at all. In a couple of years, he writes his letters and his diary in English, and lives entirely in an English circle. Germans never treat Englishmen as equals, but behave with them as our workpeople behave with officials, and our officials behave with noblemen.

Though they enter English life, Germans do not

really become Englishmen, but affect to be English, and to some extent cease to be German. The English are as whimsical in their relations with foreigners as they are in everything else; they rush at a new arrival as they do at a comic actor or an acrobat and give him no peace, but they hardly disguise their sense of their own superiority and even a certain aversion they feel for them. If the foreigner keeps to his own dress, his own way of doing his hair, his own hat, the offended Englishman jeers at him, but by degrees grows used to recognising him as an independent person. If in his first panic the foreigner begins to adapt his manners to the Englishman's, the latter does not respect him but treats him superciliously from the height of his British haughtiness. It is sometimes hard, even with the greatest tact, to steer one's course so as not to err either on the minus or the plus side; it may well be imagined what is done by Germans who are devoid of all tact, and are familiar and cringing in their manners, too stiff and also too simple in their deportment, sentimental without reason and rude without provocation.

But if the Germans look upon the English as upon a higher species of the same race, and feel themselves to be inferior to them, it by no means follows that the attitude of the French, and especially of the French refugees, is any more intelligent. Just as the German respects everything in England indiscriminately, the Frenchman detests everything English and protests against it. This peculiarity sometimes, I need hardly say, is pushed to the most comically grotesque extreme.

The Frenchman cannot forgive the English, in the first place, for not speaking French; in the second, for not understanding him when he calls Charing Cross Sharan-Kro, or Leicester Square Lessesstair-Skooar. Then his stomach cannot digest the English dinner, consisting of two huge pieces of meat and fish, instead

THE GERMANS AND THE FRENCH

of five little portions of all sorts of ragouts, fritters, salmis and so on. Then he can never resign himself to the 'slavery' of restaurants being closed on Sundays, and the people being *bored to the glory of God*, though the whole of France is bored to the glory of Buonaparte all seven days of the week. The whole *habitus*, all that is good and bad in the Englishman, is detestable to the Frenchman.

The Englishman pays him back in the same coin, but looks with envy at the cut of his clothes and attempts like a caricature to imitate him.

All this is of great significance for the study of comparative physiology, and I am not describing it in order to amuse.

The German, as we have observed, recognises that he is, in political capacity at any rate, an inferior specimen of the race to which the Englishman belongs, and subordinates himself to him. The Frenchman, belonging to another race, not so completely different as to prevent comparison, as is the case with the Turk and the Chinaman, detests the Englishman, especially because both nations are each blindly convinced of being the foremost people in the world. The German, too, is inwardly convinced of this, particularly *auf dem theoretischen Gebiete*, but is ashamed to own it.

The Frenchman is, indeed, the opposite of the Englishman in every respect. The Englishman is a solitary creature, who likes to live apart, obstinate and impatient of control; the Frenchman is a gregarious animal, impudent but easily driven. Hence two completely parallel lines of development with the Channel lying between them. The Frenchman is for ever running ahead of things, meddling in everything, training everybody, giving instructions about everything. The Englishman waits to see, does not meddle at all in other people's business and would be readier to be taught than to teach, but has not the time—he has to get to his shop.

The two corner-stones of English life, personal independence and family tradition, hardly exist for the Frenchman. The coarseness of the English manners drives the Frenchman frantic, and it really is disgusting and poisons life in London, but behind it he fails to see the stern power with which this people has stood up for its rights, the stubbornness of character which makes it impossible to turn an Englishman into the slave who delights in his flunkey's livery and hugs his laurel-crowned chains, though by flattering his passions you may do almost anything else with him.

The world of self-government, decentralisation, developing in all directions capriciously, of its own initiative, seems to the Frenchman so savage, so incomprehensible, that, however long he lives in England, he never understands its political and civic life, its rights and its judicial forms. He is lost in the incongruous multiplicity of precedents on which English law rests, as in a dark forest, and does not observe the immense and majestic oaks that compose it, nor see the charm, the poetry and the significance of its very variety. His little Codex with its sanded paths, its lopped trees and police-gardeners in every avenue, is a very different matter.

Shakespeare and Racine again.

If a Frenchman sees drunken men fighting in a tavern and a policeman looking at them with the serenity of an outsider and the interest of a man watching a cock-fight, he is furious with the policeman for not flying into a rage and carrying off some one *au violon*. He does not reflect that personal freedom is only possible when a policeman has no parental authority, when his intervention is reduced to passive readiness to come when he is summoned. The confidence that every poor fellow feels when he shuts the door of his cold, dark, damp little den transforms a man's attitude. Of course, behind these jealously guarded, strictly watched rights, the criminal sometimes escapes—and so be it. It is far better that the clever thief should go unpunished than that every honest man should be trembling like a thief in his own room. Before I came to England, the appearance of a policeman in the house in which I lived gave me an overwhelmingly nasty feeling, and morally I stood *en garde* against an enemy. In England the policeman at your door or within your doors only adds a feeling of security.

In 1855, when the Governor of Jersey took advantage of the especial *lawlessness* of his island to persecute the journal, *L'Homme*, for Felix Pyat's letter to the Queen, and, not daring to take legal measures in the matter, ordered Victor Hugo and the other refugees who had protested against the treatment of the journal to leave the island—the common sense of the public, and all the opposition newspapers, told them that the Governor had exceeded his powers, that they ought to remain and take legal proceedings against him. The *Daily News*, together with other papers, undertook to bear the expense. But this would have been a lengthy business; besides, was it possible to win a case against the Government? The refugees published another ferocious protest, threatened the Governor with the verdict of history and proudly retreated to Guernsey.

I will describe one example of the French comprehension of English manners. One evening a refugee ran in to see me and, after a perfect volley of abuse against England and the English, told me the following 'monstrous' incident.

The French exiles had that morning been attending the funeral of one of their *confrères*. I must mention that in the dull and gloomy life of exiles the funeral of a comrade is seized upon as almost a festive occasion—an opportunity for making speeches, for waving their flag, for getting together, for walking through the streets, for noting who was there and who was not, and so the forces of exiled democracy rallied *au grand complete* An English clergyman with a prayer-book appeared at the cemetery. My friend observed to him that the dead man was not a Christian and that therefore he did not need his prayers. The clergyman, a pedant and a hypocrite, like all English clergymen, answered with affected humility and the national phlegm, 'that possibly the dead man did not need his prayers, but that it was an essential part of his duty to accompany with his prayers every dead man to his last resting-place.' A dispute arose and, as the French began to get excited and shout, the obstinate clergyman sent for the police. '*Allons donc, parlez-moi de ce chien de pays avec sa sacrée liberté!* 'added the gentleman who took the leading part in this scene, next to those of the dead man and the clergyman. 'Well,' I inquired, 'what was done by *la force brutale au service du noir fanatisme?*'

'Four policemen arrived *et le ckef de la bande* asked: "Who spoke to the clergyman?"

'I stepped forward at once,' and, as he said it, my friend who was dining with me looked as Leonidas must once have looked when he set off to sup with the gods; '"*C'est moi, Monsieur,*"[1] *car je me garde bien de dire*

[1] To illustrate the feeling which prompted my 'Red' friend to make use of the word *Monsieur* in his conversation with the police-man, to avoid abusing the word *citoyen*, I must describe the following incident. In one of the poor, dark, and dirty streets that lie between Soho and Leicester Square, where a considerable proportion of the poorer exiles are usually encamped, a 'Red '*liquoriste* opened a little chemist's shop. As I happened to be passing I went into it for a sedative drink. He was sitting behind the counter himself: tall, with coarse features, thick, overhanging brows, a big nose and a

"citoyen" à ces gueux-là. Then the *chef des sbires* said to me with the utmost impudence: "Tell the others not to make a row, bury your comrade and go to your homes. But if you make a row, I shall order you all to be turned out." I looked at him, and taking off my hat, I shouted at the top of my voice, *"Vive la République démocratique et sociale!"'*

Hardly able to restrain my laughter, I asked him: 'What did the *chef des sbires* do?'

'Nothing,' the Frenchman replied, with self-complacent pride. 'He looked at his companions, said, "Well, get on, get on with your job!" and remained quietly waiting. They knew very well that they were not dealing with English rabble . . . they have sharp noses!'

What was passing in the soul of the grave, stolid, and probably slightly tipsy constable during this performance? My friend did not dream that he might have afforded himself the satisfaction of uttering the same shout outside the Queen's window at the railings of Buckingham Palace without the slightest inconvenience. But what is still more remarkable is that neither my friend nor any of the other Frenchmen ever reflect under such circumstances that in France for a similar freak they would have been sent to Cayenne or Lambessa. If one reminds them of that fact their answer is ready:

---

mouth rather on one side—a typical provincial terrorist of 1794 with a shaven chin into the bargain. 'Sixpennyworth of Raspail water, *Monsieur,*' said I. He weighed out some sort of herb, which a little girl had come to fetch, taking no notice of my inquiry; I could observe this Collot d'Herbois at my leisure, till he had at last sealed up the corners of the paper packet and written an inscription on it. Then he turned somewhat severely to me with *'Plaît-il?'* 'Sixpennyworth of Raspail water, *Monsieur,*' I repeated. He looked at me with a ferocious expression and, scanning me from head to foot, said in a deep and dignified voice, *'Citoyen, s'il vous plaît.'*—(*Author's Note,*)

'Ah bah! C'est une halte dans la boue . . . *ce n'est pas normal!'*

And when has their freedom been normal?

The antagonism at one time expressed by a *practical* Martin Luther, and a *consistent* Thomas Münzer, lies like a germ in every embryo: the logical development, the growth of every party inevitably leads to its manifestation. We find it equally in the three *impossible* Gracchi, counting Gracchus Babœuf among them, and in the only two *possible* Sullas and Soulouques[1] of all shades. Nothing is *possible* but the middle line, the compromise, hackneyed and mediocre in class, fortune, and understanding. Lilly and the Huguenots paved the way for Henry iv., the Stuarts and Cromwell for William of Orange, the Revolution and Legitimism for Louis-Philippe. After the latter, antagonism arose between the practical republic and the consistent one; the practical one was called the Democratic, the logically-consistent the Socialist; their contests led to the Empire, but the parties remained.

The uncompromising extremists found themselves in Cayenne, Lambessa and Belle-Île, and to some extent in foreign countries, especially in England.

As soon as the exiles had recovered their breath in London, and their eyes had grown used to distinguishing objects in the fog, the old quarrel was renewed with the peculiar intolerance of exiles and the gloomy character of the London climate.

The President of the Luxemburg Committee[2] was *de jure* the leading figure among the Socialist exiles in London. The representative of the organisations of labour and the working-class *égalitaire* societies, he was

---

[1] Soulouque, a negro general and president of the republic of Haiti, in 1849 proclaimed the island an empire and took the title of Emperor Faustin 1.
[2] Louis Blanc.—(*Translator's Notes*.)

beloved by the working men; strict in his life, of irreproachable purity in his views, always at work himself, sober, a first-rate speaker, popular without familiarity, bold and at the same time cautious, he had every qualification for influencing the masses.

On the other hand, Ledru-Rollin represented the religious tradition of 1793; for him the words *Republic* and *Democracy* embraced everything: the feeding of the hungry, the right to work, the emancipation of Poland, the crushing of Nicholas, the brotherhood of nations, the downfall of the Pope. There were fewer workmen about him, his circle consisted of *capacités* —that is, of lawyers, teachers, journalists, *clubistes* and so on. The division between these parties is distinct, and so I could never understand how it was that Mazzini and Louis Blanc ascribed their final breach to personal dissensions. The split lay at the very root of their outlook, in the task they set before themselves; they could not go hand in hand, but perhaps it was not necessary to have quarrelled in public.

The difference between the cause of Socialism and the cause of Italy was rather one of order or degree. Political independence was bound to come before economic reconstruction in Italy. We saw the same thing in Poland in 1831, in Hungary in 1848. But in that there is no ground for polemics, it is rather a question of division of labour in time than of mutual annihilation. Socialist theories hindered the direct concentrated activity of Mazzini, hindered the military organisation which was essential for Italy; he was angry at this without reflecting that a similar organisation could only be mischievous to the French. Carried away by his intolerance and his Italian blood, he attacked the Socialists, and Louis Blanc in particular, in a little pamphlet which was offensive and unnecessary. Incidentally he fell foul of others too; thus, for instance, he speaks of Proudhon as 'a demon' . . . Proudhon thought of answering him, but confined himself in a later pamphlet to calling Mazzini 'the Archangel.' On two occasions I said to Mazzini in jest, '*Ne réveillez, pas le chat qui dort*,' for with such warlike combatants it was hard to get off without severe wounds.

The London Socialists answered him with equal venom, with unnecessary personalities and rudeness.

The hostility between the French of the two persuasions was of a different kind and more fundamental. Every effort to reach an understanding between formal Republicanism and Socialism was unsuccessful, and only made the insincerity of concessions and the irreconcilable difference more obvious; an agile acrobat had flung his plank over the abyss that separated them and upon it proclaimed himself emperor.

The proclamation of the Empire was a galvanic shock which horrified and disheartened the exiles.

Their faces showed the melancholy, dejected conviction of the sick man that he will never walk again without crutches. Weariness, concealed hopelessness began to master both parties. Serious argument lost its colour, was reduced to personalities, to reproaches and recriminations.

For two years longer both the French groups maintained themselves in aggressive readiness, one celebrating the 24th of February, the other the days of July. But at the outbreak of the Crimean War and Napoleon III.'s triumphal procession with Queen Victoria across London, the impotence of the exiles became evident. Even the chief of the London Metropolitan Police, Sir Robert Maine, testified to it. When the Conservatives thanked him after Napoleon's visit for the skilful measures by which he had prevented any demonstration on the part of the exiles, he replied: 'I have done nothing to deserve these thanks. Thank Ledru-Rollin and Louis Blanc.'

BARBÈS AND LOUIS BLANC

A still more ominous symptom of their approaching end was apparent about the same time in their splitting up into parties for no serious reasons, merely on personal grounds.

These parties were formed in the same way as ministries or departments are invented in Russia to find a job for some superfluous personage; or as composers sometimes invent parts for Grisi or Lablache in operas, not because those parts are needed, but because Grisi or Lablache must be employed. . . .

.   .   .   .

They stayed on till late at night recalling the year 1848; when I had seen them into the street, and gone back into my room, I was overcome by an immense sadness, I sat down at my writing-table and was ready to weep.

I felt what a son must feel on returning to the parental home after a long absence: he sees how everything has grown dingy and warped in it; his father has grown old without being aware of it, but the son is very well aware of it, and he is cramped, he feels that the grave is not far off and conceals the feeling, but the meeting depresses him instead of cheering and rejoicing him.

Barbès, Louis Blanc! Why, they were old friends, honoured friends of my effervescent youth. *L'Histoire de Dix Ans*, the trial of Barbès before the Chamber of Peers—all that had so long ago been absorbed into my brain and my heart, we were so closely akin to all these men, and here they were in person.

Their most malicious enemies have never dared suspect the incorruptible honesty of Louis Blanc, nor cast a slur on the chivalrous valour of Barbès. Every one had seen, had known both men in every position, they had no private life, they had no closed doors. We had seen one of them a member of the Government, the other half an hour from the guillotine. On the night before his execution, Barbès did not sleep, but asked for paper and began to write: those lines have been preserved, I have read them. They are full of French idealism, of religious dreams, but there is not a trace of weakness; his spirit was not troubled nor cast down; with serene consciousness he was preparing to lay his head on the block and was calmly writing when the gaoler's hand rapped violently at the door. 'It was at dawn, I was expecting the executioners' (he told me that himself), but his sister rushed in instead and flung herself on his neck. She had without his knowledge entreated from Louis-Philippe a commutation of his sentence and had been galloping with post-horses all night to reach him in time.

Louis-Philippe's prisoner rose some years later to the pinnacle of civic glory, the chains were struck off by the rejoicing populace, and he was led in triumph through Paris. But the upright heart of Barbès never wavered, he was the first to attack the Provisional Government for the murders of Rouen. The reaction grew up beside him, the republic could only be saved by reckless audacity, and, on the 15th of May, Barbès dared what neither Ledru-Rollin nor Louis Blanc did, what Caussidière was afraid to do. The *Coup d'État* failed and Barbès, this time prisoner of the Republic, was again on his trial. At Bourges, just as in the Chamber of Peers, he told the lawyers of the petty-bourgeois world, just as he had told the old sinner Paquier: 'I do not recognise you as judges, you are my enemies, I am your prisoner of war; do with me as you will, but I do not accept you as my judges.' And again the heavy doors of lifelong imprisonment were closed upon him.

By chance, against his will, he came out of prison. Napoleon III. thrust him out almost in mockery, after reading, during the Crimean War, the letter in which Barbès in an access of Gallic Chauvinism speaks of the military glory of France. Barbès retired to Spain, but the scared and dull-witted government expelled him. He went to Holland and there found a tranquil and secluded refuge.

And now this hero and martyr, together with some of the chief leaders of the February Republic, together with the foremost statesman of Socialism, had been recalling and criticising the past days of glory and misfortune!

And I was oppressed by a weight of misery, I saw with unhappy clearness that they, *too*, belonged to the history of *another decade*, which was finished to the last page, to the cover. Finished, not for them personally, but for all the exiles and for all the political parties of to-day.

Living and noisy ten, even five, years before, they had passed out of the channel and were lost in the sand, imagining that they were still flowing to the ocean. They had no longer the words which, like the word Republic, have stirred whole nations, nor the songs like the Marseillaise which have set every heart throbbing. Even their enemies were not of the same grandeur, not of the same quality: there were no more old feudal privileges of the Crown with which it was hard to do battle, there was no king's head which, rolling from the scaffold, would bear a whole system with it. You may execute Napoleon III., but that will not bring you another 21st of January, pull Mazas[1] to bits stone by stone, and that will not bring you the taking of the Bastille! In those days, amid those thunders and lightnings, a new revelation was made, the revelation of the State founded upon Reason, a new means of redemption from the gloomy slavery of mediaevalism. Since those days, the redemption by revolution has been proved unsound, the State has not

[1] Mazas, a Paris prison, built between 1845 and 1850 in the Boulevard Mazas, now the Boulevard Diderot. It was demolished in 1900. — (*Translator's Note*.)

been founded upon reason. The political reformation has degenerated like the religious one into rhetorical babble, kept up by the weakness of some and the hypocrisy of others. The Marseillaise remains a sacred hymn, but it is a hymn of the past, like *Ein' feste Burg*; the strains of the same song evoke even now a series of majestic images, like the procession of shades in *Macbeth*, all kings, but all dead.

The old is almost passed out of sight, but of the new there is still only rumour. We are in an interregnum; till the heir arrives the police have seized everything in the name of external order. There can be no question here of rights; it is lynch law in history, it is a case of temporary necessity, of executive measures, police cordons, quarantine precautions. The new régime, combining all that is oppressive in monarchy and all that is ferocious in Jacobinism, is defended, not by ideas, not by conventions, but by terrors and uncertainties. While some were afraid, others fixed bayonets and took up their positions. The first who should break through their chain might capture the chief place that had been taken by the police, but would at once become himself a policeman.

It recalls to us how on the evening of the 24th of February, Caussidière arrived at the Prefecture with a gun in his hand, sat down in the chair just vacated by the escaping Delessert, called the secretary, told him that he had been appointed Prefect, and bade him give him his papers. The secretary smiled as respectfully as to Delessert, as respectfully bowed and went to fetch the papers, and the papers went their regular course, nothing was changed, only Delessert's supper was eaten by Caussidière. Many discovered the password to the Prefecture, but never learned the watchword of history. When the time came they behaved like Alexander I. They wanted a blow to be struck at the old régime, but not a mortal blow; and there was no Benningsen nor Zubov [1] among them.

And in all this there is a vast deal of *naïveté*. Behind the declamation in the foreground there is the *mise en scène*.

The antique draperies and triumphal setting of the Convention have so impressed the French mind by their menacing poetry, that with the name of the Republic, for instance, its enthusiastic supporters call up, not an inner change, but the fête of federalisation, the beating of drums and the dismal notes of the tocsin. The country is proclaimed in danger, the people rise up in a mass to defend it while they are celebrating the triumph of Republicanism around the trees of freedom; girls in white frocks are dancing to the strains of patriotic hymns, and France in a Phrygian cap sends forth immense armies for the deliverance of the nations and the overthrow of sovereigns.

The large majority of the refugees, particularly of the French, belong to the bourgeoisie, their characters are at once defined by the fact. The mark or stamp of the petty-bourgeois is as hard to efface as the imprint of the gift of the Holy Spirit which our seminaries lay upon their pupils. Of actual merchants, shopkeepers and business men there were few among the exiles, and those few had come there as it were by accident, for the most part thrust out of France after the 2nd of December because they did not grasp the fact that upon them lay the sacred duty of changing their constitution. They were the men to be pitied, because their position was absolutely comic; they were lost in the 'Red' surroundings of which they had known nothing at home, and were simply scared; by virtue of their national weakness, they longed to display themselves as far greater radicals than they really were; but not being accustomed to

[1] The assassins of Paul 1.— (*Translator's Note.*)

the revolutionary jargon, they were always falling into 'Orleanism,' to the horror of their companions. Of course, they would all have been delighted to return home, if the *point d'honneur*, the one binding moral force of the modern Frenchman, had not forbidden their suing for permission.

The class next above them consisted of the bodyguard of the exiles' community: lawyers, journalists, literary men and a few officers.

Most of them had been aiming at nothing in the revolution but to improve their social position, but with the rapid turn of the tide they had found themselves stranded on the English beach. Others were disinterestedly absorbed by club life and agitation; their rhetoric had brought them to London, partly of their own will, but quite twice as much against it. Among them there were many single-minded and honourable men, but few of any capacity; they had dropped into the revolution through temperament, through the recklessness of a man who, hearing a shriek for help, flings himself into the river, forgetting that it is deep and that he does not know how to swim.

Behind these infants whose pointed beards, alas, were rapidly turning grey, and whose conical Gallic skulls were somewhat short of hair, stood several groups of far more serious workmen, who were held together not so much by external bonds as by spirit and general interest.

Fate itself has made them revolutionaries, poverty and enlightenment have made them practical Socialists; hence their thought is more realistic, their resolution is firmer. These men have suffered many privations, many humiliations, and, moreover, in silence, which develops greater fortitude; they have crossed the Channel not with phrases but with passions, and hatreds. Their oppressed position has saved them from the bourgeois *suffisance*, they know that they have not had time to be educated, they want instruction, while the bourgeois has learnt no more than they, but is perfectly content with his attainments.

And that is why if they come into the arena again they will be horrified by the ingratitude of men. And may they think it is only ingratitude! That is a gloomy thought, but easier to bear than many others.

But they had much better not go back at all; let them stay and tell us and our children of their great deeds. There is no need to resent this advice; what is living changes, and the unchanging becomes a monument. They have left their trace, just as those who come after them will leave theirs, and in their turn will be overtaken by the drifting snow, and then all traces, present and past, will be hidden in the universal amnesty of eternal oblivion!

Many are angry with me for saying these things openly. 'In your words,' a very worthy man said to me, 'one hears the disinterested spectator speaking.'

But I did not come to Europe a spectator. I have been turned into one. I am very long-suffering, but at last I am worn out.

For five years I have not seen one bright face, I have not heard spontaneous laughter, I have not met a glance of understanding. I have been surrounded by *feldshers*[1] and *prosectors*.[2] The *feldshers* have been continually trying their remedies, while the others have been proving to them on the corpse that they have blundered—until I too have snatched up the scalpel; perhaps through lack of practice I have cut too deeply.

I have spoken not as an outside spectator, not to find fault: I have spoken because my heart was full, because the lack of general understanding has driven me out of

[1] Male nurses or doctors' assistants.
[2] Dissecting demonstrators.—(*Translator's Notes*.)

all patience. That I was sobered earlier than the rest has been no comfort to me. Only the very lowest of *feldshers* can smile with satisfaction as they look at the dying patient and say: 'Didn't I tell you he would turn up his toes by the evening? and you see he has.' Why, then, have I endured?

In 1856 the best of all the German refugees, Carl Schurz,[1] arrived in Europe from Wisconsin. On his return from Germany, he told me how impressed he was by the moral desolation of the Continent. I had translated to him aloud my *West European Sketches*. He tried to ward off my conclusions, as though they were a ghost which a man fears, though he is unwilling to believe in it.

'Any one who understands contemporary Europe as you do,' he said to me, 'ought to abandon it.' 'That is what you have done,' I observed. 'Why is it you don't do so?' 'It is very simple. I can answer you as an honest German in a fit of proud independence has answered before me. "I have a king of my own in Swabia." I have my own people in Russia!'

Coming down from the heights to the middle levels of the refugee community, we see that most of the refugees have been drawn into exile by a generous impulse and by rhetoric. These men sacrificed themselves for words, that is, for their sound without ever giving themselves a clear definition of their meaning. They loved them ardently and believed in them, as Catholics believe in their Latin prayers, though they do not know Latin. *La fraternité universelle comme base de la république universelle*—that is final and

[1] Schurz, Carl (b.1829), fought in the revolutionary movement of 1848. In 1852 he went to the United States, where he lectured, took part in politics and fought in the Civil War, as major-general of volunteers. In 1869 he was elected to the Senate, and in 1877 appointed Secretary of the Interior. He edited a paper, and wrote lives of Henry Clay and of Lincoln.—(*Translator's Note*.)

accepted, *point de salariés, et la solidarité des peuples!* And you may blush, but that is enough to send some men to the barricades, and if a Frenchman goes to the barricade he does not run away.

'*Pour moi,* voyez-*vous, la république n'est pas une forme gouvernementale c'est une religion, et elle ne sera vraie que lorsqu'elle la sera,*' a man who had taken part in all the risings from the day of Lamarque's funeral said to me: '*Et lorsque la religion sera une république,*' I added. '*Précisément!*' he answered, much pleased at my having turned his phrase inside out.'

The lower ranks among the refugees provide something like an ever open sore of conscience before the eyes of the leaders. In them all their own defects reappear in the exaggerated and ridiculous form in which Paris fashions appear in some Russian district town.

Ill-used from childhood, they hate the social injustice by which they have been so greatly oppressed. The corrupting influence of town life and of the universal passion for gain has in many of them converted the hatred into envy. Without clearly facing the fact, they try to become bourgeois though they detest them, just as we detest a lucky rival, though passionately longing to take his place, or to punish him for his success.

But whether animated by hatred or envy, whether by the thirst for comfort or for revenge, they are all to be dreaded in the future upheaval of Western Europe. They will be in the foreground. What will the Conservatives and rhetoricians do, confronted by their workmen's muscles, their gloomy recklessness and rankling thirst for revenge? And what will all the town-dwellers do when at the workers' call the locusts of the fields and villages rise up? The Peasant Wars are forgotten; the latest fugitives among land workers date back to the days of the Edict of Nantes: the Vendée vanished in the smoke of guns. But we are indebted to the 2nd of December for the sight of refugees wearing sabots.

The country people in the South of France, from the Pyrenees to the Alps, lifted up their heads after the *Coup d'Etat*, as though asking: 'Has not our time come?' The rising was suppressed at its very outbreak by masses of soldiers, who were followed by military tribunals; a herd of tracking gendarmes and police were scattered all over the cross-roads and little villages. The peasant's hearth, his home—the things he holds sacred, were desecrated by the police; they demanded the wife's evidence against her husband, the son's against his father, and on one doubtful word from a kinsman, on the mere denunciation of a *gardechampêtre*, dragged to prison fathers of families, old men grey as badgers, lads, women; they were tried after a fashion, wholesale, and then at random some released, some sent to Lambessa, to Cayenne, while others escaped to Spain, to Savoy beyond the bridges over the Var.[1]

I do not know much about these peasants. In London I saw several men who had escaped from Cayenne in an open boat; the very recklessness, the madness of this adventure displays more of their character than whole volumes. They were almost all from the Pyrenees. Broad-shouldered, well grown, with large features, an utterly different race, not fined down like the meagre

---

[1] I was in Nice at the time of the rising in Var and Draguignan. Two peasants who had been mixed up in the rebellion made their way to the river Var, which was the boundary. There they were overtaken by a gendarme. The latter shot at one and wounded him in the leg—he fell, while the other set off running. The gendarme tried to tie the wounded man to his horse, but afraid of letting the other get off he shot the first man in the head *à bout portant*; feeling certain that he had killed him, he galloped after the other. The terribly disfigured peasant survived.—(*Author's Note*.)

Frenchman of the towns, with his thin blood and poor little beard. The destruction of their homes and their stay at Cayenne had educated them. 'We shall go back some day,' a Hercules of forty, usually silent (they were none of them very talkative), said to me,' and pay off our score!' They looked upon the other refugees, on their meetings and speeches, as somehow foreign . . . and three weeks later they came to say good-bye to me.

'We don't want an idle life, and besides it's dull here—we are going to Spain, to Santander. There they have promised to give us work as woodcutters.' I glanced once more at the rough, manly figures and muscular hands of the future woodcutters—and thought, 'It will be as well if their axes cut down nothing but chestnuts and oaks.'

Of the wild, devouring energy rankling in the breasts of the town workmen, I had a closer view later.

2

Felix Pyat—Victor Hugo and Others—Louis Blanc and the French Refugees

The French refugees, like all the other groups, carried with them into exile and jealously maintained all their dissensions, all their parties. Their nervous irritability was increased by the gloomy environment of an alien and hostile country that did not conceal that it maintained its right of asylum for the sake of its own self-respect, and not for the sake of those who seek it.

And then they are cut off from their people and from their habits, and they cannot move about freely. Misunderstandings become more spiteful, upbraidings for past mistakes more merciless, parties are so sharply divided that old friends drop all relations and cut each other in the street . . .

There were real differences, theoretical and of every other description also. Together with ideas there were personalities, together with party badges there were individual names, side by side with fanaticism there was envy, and with candid enthusiasm there was naïve vanity.

A year and a half after the *Coup d'État*, Felix Pyat arrived in London from Switzerland. A lively journalist, he had become well known through his trial, through the dull comedy *Diogenes*, which the French liked for its thin, dry apophthegms, and finally by the success of *The Rag-Picker* on the stage of Porte St. Martin. I have written a whole article[1] on this play in another place. Felix Pyat was a member of the last Legislative Assembly, sat with the Montagne, had a fight in the Assembly with Proudhon, was mixed up in the protest of the 13th of June 1848, and was in consequence obliged to leave France in secret. He got away, as I did, with a Moldavian passport, and went about in Geneva disguised as a Moor, probably in order that every one might recognise him. In Lausanne, to which he moved, a small circle of admirers from among the French exiles formed around him and lived on the manna of his witty sayings and the crumbs of his ideas. It was painful for him to pass from being the leader of a canton into being a member of a London party. There was no party that had a vacancy for a great man; his friends and admirers rescued him from this difficulty; withdrawing from the other parties, they formed themselves into the so-called *London Revolutionary Commune*.

La Commune Révolutionnaire was to represent the

[1] *Letters from the Avenue Marigny.* 'Why did you spoil your *Chiffonnier* by sticking on a happy ending which spoils the moral of the play as well as its artistic unity?' I once asked Pyat. 'Because,' he answered, 'if I had distressed the Parisians by the gloomy fate of the old man and the girl, nobody would have come to a second performance.'—(*Author's Note.*)

reddest section of Democracy and the most communistic one of Socialism. It regarded itself as for ever on the alert, in the closest relations with Marianne,'[1] and at the same time as the most faithful representative of Blanqui *in partibus infidelium*.

In the form of Felix Pyat the gloomy Blanqui, the austere pedant and doctrinaire of his cause, the ascetic emaciated in prisons, smoothed away his wrinkles, dyed his black thoughts crimson, and set the Parisian Commune shrieking with laughter in London. Felix Pyat's sallies in his letters to the Queen and to Walewski,[2] whom he called an *ex-réfugié* and *ex-polonais*, not a prince and so on, were very amusing; but where the resemblance to Blanqui came in I never could grasp; and altogether it was not easy for a plain man to see what was the characteristic difference that distinguished him from Louis Blanc, for instance.

The same thing must be said of the Jersey party of Victor Hugo.

Victor Hugo never was in the true sense of the word a politician. He was too much of a poet, too much under the influence of his imagination, to be one. Of course, I do not say this in disparagement. A Socialist and an artist, he was at the same time a worshipper of military glory, of the republican upheaval, of mediaeval romanticism, of the white *fleur-de-lys*, was a *vicomte* and a *citoyen*, a peer of Orleanist France and an agitator of the 2nd of December. He was a great, exuberant figure, but not the head of a party, in spite of the positive influence he exerted over two generations. Who

[1] Marianne, a secret society, socialistic and democratic, founded in France after the Restoration. The name was taken from Marie-Anne—the symbolic figure of the woman of the people who incited the fighting, tended the wounded, etc., in June 1848.

[2] Walewski, Count Alexandre (1810-1868), an illegitimate son of Napoleon 1., was a minister under Napoleon 111.—(*Translator's Notes.*)

has not been set thinking over the death penalty by *Les Derniers Jours d'un Condamné?* Whose conscience has not been stirred by his striking pictures of the social sores of poverty and fatal vice, full of the strange, terrible lights and shadows of a Turner?

The February revolution caught Hugo unawares; he did not understand it, was amazed, was left behind, made an infinite number of blunders, until the Reaction went too far for him. Roused to indignation by the censorship of his plays and by the proceedings at Rome, he appeared on the platform of the Assembly with speeches that resounded throughout France. Success and applause carried him on and on. At last, on the 2nd of December 1851, he rose to his full stature in face of bayonets and loaded guns, he summoned the people to revolt—under showers of bullets protested against the *Coup d'État* and withdrew from France, when it was no longer possible to act there. He retreated like an infuriated lion to Jersey; whence, hardly taking breath, he flung at the Emperor his *Napoléon le Petit* and then his *Châtiments*. Napoleon's agents tried in vain to reconcile the old poet with the new court. They could not. 'If but ten Frenchmen remain in exile, I, too, will remain with them; if three, I will be among them; if one, I will be that one—I will not return except to a free France.'

Hugo's moving from Jersey to Guernsey more than ever persuaded himself and his friends of his political significance, though it should, one would have thought, only have convinced them of the opposite. The position was as follows. When Felix Pyat wrote his letter to Queen Victoria after Napoleon's visit to her, he read it at a meeting and sent it to the editor of *L'Homme*. Swentoslawski, who published *L'Homme* at his own expense in Jersey, was at that time in London, and he came to see me, together with Felix Pyat; as he was leaving, he drew me aside and said that a lawyer of his acquaintance had told him that the journal might easily be prosecuted for this letter, as Jersey was in the position of a colony; but that Felix Pyat insisted on its appearing in *L'Homme*. Swentoslawski hesitated, and wanted to know my opinion.

'Don't publish it.'

'Yes, that is just what I think myself, only the worst of it is he will think that I am afraid.'

'Who wouldn't be afraid of losing some thousands of francs under present circumstances?'

'You are right, that I cannot do. I ought not to do it.'

Swentoslawski, after reasoning so sagaciously, went back to Jersey and published the letter.

There were rumours that the Ministry meant to do something. The English were offended at the tone in which Pyat addressed the Queen. The first result of the rumours was that Felix Pyat ceased to sleep at home —he was afraid *in England* of a *visite domiciliaire* and arrest at night for publishing an article! The Cabinet did not dream of a legal prosecution; the Ministers gave a hint to the Governor of Jersey, or whatever he is called there, and the latter, taking advantage of the illegal privileges that exist in the Colonies, ordered Swentoslawski to leave the island. Swentoslawski protested, and with him a dozen Frenchmen, among whom was Victor Hugo; then the Napoleon of the police of Jersey ordered all those who signed the protest to leave. They ought to have disobeyed the order to the last moment, let the police seize some one by the collar and fling him off the island, then it would have been possible to have brought the question of the legality of banishing them before a court. This was the course urged upon them by the English. Legal proceedings are disgracefully expensive in England; but the editors of the *Daily News* and other Liberal papers promised to collect whatever sum was needed, and to procure capable lawyers to defend them. To the French the path of legality seemed dull and long, revolting, and they proudly left Jersey, taking with them Swentoslawski and S. Téléki.[1]

The police order was delivered to Victor Hugo wirh peculiar solemnity. When the police official went in to him to red the order, Hugo summoned his sons; he sat down, motioned the official to a chair, and, when all were seated as in Russia before a journey, he rose to his feet and said: '*M. le Commissaire, nous faisons maintenant une page de l'histoire.* Read your order.' The policeman, who had expected to be kicked out of the house, was very much surprised at the ease with which he had gained the day; he bound Hugo by his signature to leave, and went away doing full justice to the courtesy of the French, who had even offered him a chair. Hugo did go, and the rest with him left Jersey. Most of them went no further than Guernsey. Others went to London; their cause was lost, and the right of expulsion remained unassailed.

There were only two real parties, *i.e.* the party of formal Republicanism and of violent Socialism: Ledru-Rollin and Louis Blanc. Of the latter I have not yet spoken, though I knew him better than almost any other of the French exiles.

It could not be said that Louis Blanc's outlook was

[1] Dumas writing in 1859 says: 'Il y a quelque chose comme seize ans que je connais Sander Téléki. Il m'a été présenté vers la fin de 1842 par Liszt. . . . Il a fait la guerre d'Hongroie sous Bem . . . échappait par miracle à la pendaison, car les Autrichiens ont cela de charmant qu'ils ne se contentent pas de tuer, ils pendent. . . . Il est accouru en Italie dès qu'il a su qu'on allait s'y battre et comme il a pensé quec'était a côté de Garibaldi que les coups pleuvraient plus rudes et plus serrés, c'est avec Garibaldi qu'il a fait la guerre.'—(*Translator's Note*.)

indefinite, it was sharply cut on all sides as with a knife. In the course of his exile, Louis Blanc gathered a great deal of information (in his own line, that is, the study of the first French Revolution) and became a little more settled and tranquil; but in reality his views never moved one step from the time when he wrote *L'Histoire de Dix Ans* and *L'Organisation de Travail*. What was settled and clarified was exactly the same as had been fermenting from youth.

In Louis Blanc's little body there lives a bold spirit firmly fitted together, '*très éveillé*,' with a strong character, with its own sharply cut quality, and at the same time absolutely French. His quick eyes and rapid movements give him an air at once mobile and highly finished, which is not without grace. He is like a man of concentration reduced to its least dimensions, while the colossal character of his opponent, Ledru-Rollin, makes him like a swollen child, like a dwarf on an immense scale, or seen through a magnifying glass. They are both splendidly fitted to take parts in *Gulliver's Travels*. Louis Blanc—and it is a great power and a very rare characteristic—has complete self-control; he has a great deal of reserve and, in the very heat of discussion, not only in public but in friendly talk, never forgets the most complex aspects of a question, never loses his temper in argument, never leaves off smiling good-humouredly and never agrees with his opponent. He is a master at telling stones, and, in spite of the fact that, like a Frenchman, he talks a great deal—yet, like a Corsican, he never says a word too much.

He is interested in nothing but France, knows nothing but France. The events of the world, the discoveries of science, earthquakes and inundations interest him only in so far as they affect France. Talking with him, listening to his subtle observations, his interesting stories, one may easily study the character of the French intellect, and the more easily as his soft and cultured manners do not provoke sarcastic irritation.[1]

Sometimes in jest I would pull him up in the generalisations which he had probably been repeating for years, never questioning them nor supposing that any one could question such respectable truths as: 'A man's life is a great social duty; a man *ought* to be continually sacrificing himself to society.'

[1] All this, except a few additions and corrections, was written ten years ago. I must confess that later events have led me to revise my opinion of Louis Blanc to some extent. He really has taken a step forward—and as might have been anticipated, away from the old Believers of Jacobinism. It has cost him something. 'What 's to be done?' Louis Blanc said to me when the Mexican War was at its height, 'the honour of our flag is compromised.' A purely French and absolutely anti-human opinion. Evidently it deeply distressed Louis Blanc. A year later at a banquet given in honour of Victor Hugo at Brussels, after the publication of *Les Misérables*, Louis Blanc said in his speech: 'Woe to the people whose conception of honour in general does not correspond with their conception of military honour.' This was a complete *volte-face*, it showed itself unmistakably at the beginning of the late war. Louis Blanc's vigorous, apt and deeply true articles published in *Le Temps* had raised a storm in *Le Siècle* and the *Opinion Nationale*: they had almost proved Louis Blanc to be an Austrian agent, and would have done so altogether, but for his well-deserved reputation for honesty.

When I came to know Louis Blanc more intimately, I was struck by his untroubled inner serenity. Everything was settled and in order in his understanding; no questions except subsidiary ones arose in it. He had settled his accounts with himself: *er war im Klaren mit sich*: he was morally free as a man is who knows that he is right. He good-naturedly recognised his personal mistakes and the blunders of his friends, but he had no theoretical qualms of conscience. He was as pleased with himself after the breakdown of the Republic in 1848 as the Mosaic God after the creation of the world. His mind, alert in details and daily affairs, was of a Japanese immobility on theoretical subjects. This unfaltering confidence in principles accepted once for all, though lightly played upon by the cold breath of reason, rested firmly on moral foundations the strength of which he never tested because he had faith in them. A religious brain and an absence of sceptical misgivings encircled him with a Chinese Wall, over which not one new idea, one doubt could be flung.— (*Author's Note*.)

'Why so?' I would ask suddenly.

'Why so? Upon my word: why, the whole aim, the whole significance of the individual is the welfare of society.'

'It will never be attained if every one is to be sacrificed and no one is to enjoy himself.'

'That is playing with words.'

'A barbarian's confusion of ideas,' I said laughing.

'I can never understand the materialistic view of the spirit,' he said once. 'Spirit and matter are after all distinct; they are closely connected, so closely that they are not manifest apart, but yet they are not the same thing'—and seeing that his exposition was not going well, he added at once: 'Now, I, for instance, shut my eyes and imagine my brother; I see his features, I hear his voice; where is the material existence of that image?'

At first I thought that he was joking; but seeing that he was speaking quite seriously, I observed that the image of his brother was at that moment in a photographic studio known as the brain, and that Charles Blanc's portrait could hardly be said to exist apart from that photographic apparatus.

'That is quite a different matter. The picture of my brother has no material existence in my brain.'

'How do you know?'

'Why, how do you?'

'From induction.'

'By the way, that reminds me of a most amusing anecdote . . . ' And then, as always, followed a story about Diderot or Mme. Tencin, very charming, but not in the least to the point. As the successor of Maximilien Robespierre, Louis Blanc worshipped Rousseau, and was somewhat cold in his attitude to Voltaire. In his history he has divided all leading men into two flocks in Biblical fashion—on the one hand, the sheep of brotherhood, on the other, the goats of envy and egoism. For the egoists such as Montaigne he had no mercy, and they caught it severely from him. Louis Blanc did not stick at anything in this classification, and meeting the speculator, Law, he boldly counted him among the sheep, which the reckless Scotsman had certainly never expected.

In 1856 Barbès arrived in London from the Hague. Louis Blanc brought him to me. I looked with emotion at the martyr who had spent almost his whole life in prison. I had seen him once before, and where? At the window of the Hotel de Ville, on the 15th of May, a few minutes before the National Guard broke in and seized him.[1]

I invited them to dine with me next day; they came, and we sat on till late at night.

Before we pass on to the savage elemental force quivering in darkness, enchained by man's violence and its own ignorance, and at times bursting like destructive fire through cracks and crevices, and arousing horror and alarm, let us linger once more over the last knights-templars and classic figures of the French Revolution, over the cultured and democratic middle classes made up of exiles, republicans, journalists, lawyers, doctors, professors of the Sorbonne, who for ten years took part in the conflict with Louis-Philippe, were carried away by the events of 1848, and remained true to them, both at home and in exile.

In their ranks there are intelligent, keen-witted men, very good-hearted, animated by ardent religion and readiness to sacrifice everything to it; but men of under-

[1] The pitch reached by the ferocity of the guardians of order on that day may be judged by the fact that the National Guard seized Louis Blanc in the boulevard, though he ought not to have been arrested at all, and the police at once ordered him to be released. On receiving this order the National Guard who held him seized him by the finger, thrusting his nails into it, and twisted the last joint backwards.—(*Author's Note*.)

standing, men who could analyse their own position, their own problems, as the man of science investigates a phenomenon or a pathologist investigates disease, are almost entirely lacking.

They prefer complete despair, contempt for men and the cause, they prefer the idleness of reproaches and recriminations, stoicism, heroism, every privation, to analysis. Or they have the same complete faith in success without weighing means, without making clear a practical object. Instead of it, they are satisfied with a flag, with a badge, with a stock phrase—the right to work, the abolition of the proletariat, the republic and order, brotherhood and the solidarity of all peoples. But how is all this to be arranged, to be realised? That is the last consideration. Only to get the power; the rest would be done by decrees, plebiscites, and if there were disobedience—*grenadiers, en avant armes! pas de charge . . . baïonnettes!*

And glimpses of the religion of terror, of the *Coup d'État*, of centralisation, of military intervention show through rents in the carmagnole and the blouse. In spite of the pedantic protest of some Attic minds of the Orleans party, the Terror was grand in its menacing suddenness, its unprepared colossal vengeance; but to dwell upon it with love, to invoke it without necessity is a terrible blunder for which we are indebted to the Reaction.

On me the Committee of Public Security always produced the same impression as Charrière's shop, Rue de l'École de Médecine; on all sides there are straight or curved sabres, scissors, saws glittering ominously, probably instruments for saving men, but certainly for hurting them. Operations are justified by success, but the Terror cannot boast of that. With all its surgery it did not save the Republic. With what object was Dantonotomy, Herbertotomy performed? They hastened the fever of Thermidor; and in it the Republic wasted away; as before and even more so, men went on raving over the Spartan virtues with Latin mottoes and classicism *à la David*; they raved on till one fine day they translated *Salus populi* into *Salvum fac Imperatorem*, and chanted it with full ecclesiastical rites in Notre Dame.

The Terrorists were not ordinary men. Their stern, austere figures stand out vividly in the fifth act, and will survive in history for ages, so long as human records last; but the French republicans of to-day do not look at it like that—they see in them patterns to be imitated, and try to be bloodthirsty in theory and in the hope of practice.

Repeating *à la Saint-Just* affected maxims from anthologies and Latin classics, moved to enthusiasm by the cold rhetorical eloquence of Robespierre, they will not allow their heroes to be judged like other mortals! Any one who should begin to speak of them without the dutiful words of eulogy which are applied to the 'illustrious dead,' would be accused of being a renegade, a traitor, a spy.

I did, however, now and then meet eccentric men who had broken away from the common path trodden by the crowd.

But even in such cases, when Frenchmen have taken the bit between their teeth and bolted with some idea that does not belong to the received currency of ideas and thoughts, they carry it to such an extreme that the man who has given them the idea defends himself with horror.

In 1854, Dr. Cœurderoi, who had sent me his pamphlet from Spain, wrote me a letter. I have rarely heard so exasperated a protest against contemporary France and its latest revolutionaries. It was the answer of France to the *Coup d'État* dealt her so lightly; he doubted the intelligence, the blood of his race; he invoked the Cossacks for the correction of the 'degenerate population,' he wrote to me because he found in my articles 'the same standpoint.' I answered that I did not go so far as advocating transfusion of blood as a remedy, and sent him *Du Développement des Idées révolutionnaires en Russie*.

Cœurderoi repaid the debt; he answered that he rested all his hopes on the troops of Nicholas, who would raze to the ground without pity or sparing the effete and corrupt civilisation which had not the strength to renew itself nor to die a natural death.

I append one of his letters which has been preserved.

M. A. HERZEN.

SANTANDER, *Mai* 27.

Monsieur,—Que je vous remercie tout d'abord de l'envoi de votre travail sur les idées révolutionnaires et leur développement en Russie. J'avais déjà lu ce livre, mais il ne m'était pas resté entre les mains, et c'était pour moi un très grand regret.

C'est vous dire combien j'en apprécie la valeur comme fond et comme forme, et combien je le crois utile pour donner conscience à chacun des forces de la Révolution universelle, aux Français surtout qui ne la croient possible que par l'initiative du faubourg St. Antoine.

Puisque vous m'avez fait l'amitié de m'envoyer votre livre, permettez-moi, Monsieur, de vous en témoigner ma gratitude en vous disant ce que j'en pense. Non que j'attache de l'importance a mon opinion, mais pour vous prouver que j'ai lu avec attention.

C'est une belle étude organique et originale, il y a là véritable vigueur, travail sérieux, vérités nues, passages profondément émouvants. C'est jeune et fort comme la race slave; on sent parfaitement que ce n'est ni un Parisien, ni un Paléologue, ni un Philiste d'Allemagne qui ont écrit des lignes aussi brûlantes; ni un républicain constitutionnel, ni un socialists théocrate et modéré —mais un Cosaque (vous ne vous effrayez pas de ce nom, n'est-ce pas?) grandement anarchiste, utopiste et poète, acceptant la négation et l'affirmation la plus hardie du xixe siècle. Ce que peu de révolutionnaires français osent faire.

. . . Sur le point particulier de la Rénovation ethnographique procnaine, j'ai trouvé dans votre livre (surtout dans l'Introduction) bien des passages qui semblent se rapprocher de mon opinion. Quoique vos conclusions ne soient pas très-nettement formulées sur ce point, je crois que vous comptez pour le succès de la Révolution sur la fédération démocratique des races slaves qui donneront a l'Europe l'impulsion générale. Il est bien entendu que nous ne difrérons pas pour le but: la resurrection du Continent sous la forme démocratique et sociale. Mais je crois que le sac de la civilisation sera fait par l'absolutisme. Là je vois toute la différence entre nous.

Oui, j'ai conçu ces convictions qu'on dit malheureuses, et j'y persiste parce que chaque jour je les trouve plus justes:

1. Que la force a quelque chose à voir dans les affaires de notre microcosme.

2. Qu'en étudiant la marche des événements révolutionnaires dans le temps et dans l'espace on se convainct que la force prepare toujours la Révolution que l'idée a démontrée nécessaire.

3. Que l'idée ne peut pas accomplir l'œuvre de sang et de destruction.

4. Que le despotisme, au point de vue de la rapidité, de la sûreté, de la possibilité d'exécutions, est plus apte que la démocratie à bouleverser un monde.

5. Que l'armée monarchique russe sera plutôt mise en mouvement que la phalange démocratique slave.

6. Qu'il n'y a que la Russie en Europe assez com-

pacte encore sous l'absolutisme, assez peu divisée par les intérêts propriétaires et les partis pour faire bloc, coin, massue, glaive, épée et exécuter l'Occident et trancher le nœud gordien.

Là. Là. Là.

Qu'on me montre une autre force capable d'accomplir une pareille tâche; qu'on me fasse voir quelque part une armée démocratique toute prête et décidée à frapper sur les peuples, les frères, et à faire couler le sang, à brûler, à abattre sans regarder derrière elle, sans hésiter. Et je changerai de manière de voir.

Avec vous je voulais seulement bien spécifier la question et la limiter sur ce seul point, le moyen d'exècution générale de la civilisation Occidentale.

Je n'ai pas besoin de vous dire que notre appréciation sur le Passé et l'Avenir est la même. Nous ne différons absolument que sur le Présent. Vous, qui avez si bien apprécié le rôle révolutionnaire de Pierre Ier, pourquoi ne pourriez-vous pas penser que tout autre, Nicolas ou l'un de ses successeurs, put avoir un formidable rôle à accomplir? Quelle autre main plus puissante, plus large, plus capable de rassembler des peuples conquérants, voyez-vous à l'Orient? Avant que la démocratic slave ait trouvé un mot d'ordre et traduit le vague secret de ses aspirations, le tsar aura bouleversé l'Europe. Le sort des nations civilisées est dans son bras, s'il le veut. Le monde ne tremble-t-il pas parce qu'il a parlé un peu plus haut que d'habitude? Je vous l'avoue, cette force me frappe tellement, que je ne puis concevoir qu'on cherche à en voir une autre. Et les révolutionnaires sentent tellement la nécessité d'une dictature pour démolir qu'ils voudraient l'instituer eux-mêmes dans le cas de réussite d'une nouvelle Révolution. A mon sens, ils ne se trompent pas sur la nécessité du moyen, seulement il n'est ni dans leur rôle, ni dans leurs principes, ni dans leurs forces de l'employer. Moi j'aime même voir le Despotisme se charger de cette odieuse tâche de fossoyeur.

Cette lettre est déjà bien assez longue. Je voulais seulement préciser avec vous le point débattu. Ce qu'il faudrait maintenant entre nous, je le sens: ce serait une conversation dans laquelle nous avancerons plus en une heure que par milliers de lettres. Je n'abandonne pas cet espoir, et ce jour sera le bienvenu pour moi. Avec un homme de révolution, de travail, de science et d'audace je crois toujours pouvoir m'entendre.

Quant aux sounds ou muets de la tradition révolutionnaire de '93, j'ai grand' peur que vous n'en fassiez jamais des socialistes universels et des hommes de liberté. Encore moins des partisans de la possession, du droit au travail, de l'échange et du contrat. C'est tellement séduisant que de rêver une place de commissaire aux armées ou a la police, ou encore une sinécure de représentant au peuple avec une belle écharpe rouge autour des reins, comme disait Rabelais, beaux floquarts, beaux rubans, gentil pour point, galantes braguettes, etc., etc. La plupart de nos révolutionnaires en sont là!

Les hommes ne sont guere plus sages que les enfants, mais beaucoup plus hypocrites. Us portent des faux cols et de décorations et se croient illustres. Les enfants jouent plus sérieusement aux soldats que les grands monarques et les énormes tribunes que les peuples admirent.

Vous voudrez bien me pardonner de vous avoir écrit sans avoir l'honneur de vous connaître personnellement.

Vous m'excuserez surtout de m'être permis de vous donner sur vos ouvrages une opinion qui n'a d'autre valeur que la sincérité. J'estime d'après mes propres impressions que c'est le moyen le plus efficace pour reconnaître un don, qui vous a fait plaisir. D'ailleurs notre commun exil et nos aspirations semblables me semblent devoir nous épargner a tous deux les vaines formules de politique banale. Je termine en vous résumant mon opinion par ces deux mots: La Force et la Destruction demain par le tzar, la Pensée et l'Ordre après-demain par les socialistes universels, les Slavs, comme les Germano-Latins.—Agréez, etc.

ERNEST CŒURDEROI.

J'espère vous publierez en volume vos lettres à Linton Esqre. que le journal *l'Homme* a données à ses lecteurs.

Pourriez-vous me dire s'il existe des traductions françaises des poésies de Pouschkine, de Lermontoff et surtout de Koltzoff? Ce que vous en dites me fait désirer infiniment de les lire. La personne qui vous remettra cette lettre est mon ami L. Charre, proscrit comme nous, à qui j'ai dédié *Mes Jours d'Exil*.

Chapter 4

I
POLISH REFUGEES

ALOYSIUS BERNACKI—STANISLAW WORCELL—THE POLISH AGITATORS BETWEEN 1854 AND 1856—THE DEATH OF WORCELL

Nuovi tormenti e nuovi tormentati!—*Inferno*.

OTHER misfortunes, other sufferers await us. We live on yesterday's battlefield: all around are the hospitals, the wounded, the prisoners, the dying. The army of Polish emigrants is the oldest of all and the most worn out by suffering, but it has remained obstinately alive. In migrating abroad the Poles, in spite of Danton's dictum, took their fatherland with them, and with heads erect they have proudly and sternly carried it about the world. Europe has stood aside with respect before the solemn procession of valiant warriors. The peoples have come forward to do them homage; the kings have turned away and averted their eyes to let them pass unnoticed. Europe was awakened for one instant by their footsteps, brought tears and sympathy for them, found money and the spirit to give it.[1] The

[1] Dr. P. Darasz told me the following incident which occurred to him. He took part in the rising of 1831, when he was a medical student. After the taking of Warsaw, the company in which he served crossed the frontier, and in small groups were making their way to France. Everywhere on their way people came out on to the road, to invite the exiles to their houses, offering them their rooms, often their beds. In one little town the woman in whose house he was sheltered noticed that his tobacco pouch, I think it was, was torn and took it to mend. Next day on the road Darasz, feeling in the pouch something unusual, found two gold pieces sewn up in it. Darasz, who had not a farthing, rushed back to restore the money. At first the woman denied it, declaring that

melancholy image of the Polish refugee, the knight-errant of national independence, has survived in the popular memory. Twenty years in exile have not weakened his faith, and at every momentous crisis, in every hour of conflict and struggle for freedom, the Poles have been the first to answer the roll-call, just as Worcell and the elder Darasz were the first to rally to the Provisional Government of 1848.

But the government of which Lamartine was one had no need of them and did not think of them at all. The most convinced republicans thought of Poland in order to make use of her by the insincere summons to war and revolt of the 15th of May 1848. They saw the deception, but the French bourgeois (with whom Poland was a fad, just as Italy was with the English) have been sulky with Poland ever since. People no longer talked in Paris with the same rhetoric of *Varsovie échevelée*, and the common people only kept, together with many Napoleonic memories, the legend of 'Poniatowski' supported by a rough woodcut in which Poniatowski is drowning on horseback in his *chapska*.

The year 1849 marks the beginning of the most depressing time for the Polish exiles. It dragged on wearily up to the Crimean War and the death of Nicholas. Not one real hope, not one drop of living water. The apocalyptic time, foretold by Krasinski, seemed to have come. Cut off from their fatherland, the refugees were cast away on other shores, and, like trees without fresh sap, were withering and fading away; they were

---

she knew nothing about it; then she began to cry and to beg Darasz to keep the money. One must remember what *two gold pieces* mean to a woman of humble means in a little German town: they probably represented the fruits of putting away in the *Sparbüchse* of various kreutzers and pfennigs, *good and bad* farthings, over many years. . . . Good-bye to all dreams of a silk dress, of a coloured mantilla, of a brilliant shawl!. I kneel in homage before such sacrifices.—(*Author's Note.*)

becoming aliens to their own people without ceasing to be aliens to the foreigners among whom they lived. The latter to some extent sympathised with them, but their misfortunes lasted too long, and there is no good feeling in man that can stand too long a strain. Moreover, the Polish question was pre-eminently a national question, and only accidentally a revolutionary one, in so far as it was a revolt against a foreign yoke.

The refugees looked backward as much as they looked forward, they were striving to re-establish—as though there were anything worth re-establishing in the past except independence—and independence alone implies nothing: it is a negative conception. Could any country be more independent than Russia? To the complex, laboriously worked-out formula of future social organisation, Poland contributed no new idea, nothing but her historical claim and her readiness to help others in the legitimate hope of reciprocity. The struggle for independence always calls forth warm sympathy, but foreigners can never make it their cause. Only those interests are common to all which by their very essence transcend nationality—such, for instance, as the interests of Catholicism and Protestantism, revolution and reaction, economics and Socialism.

.   .   .   .

In 1847 I made the acquaintance of the Polish democratic Central Committee. At that time it was held in Versailles, and the most active member was, so I fancied, Wysocki. No real intimacy was possible. The refugees did not want to hear from me what I knew; all they wanted to hear was the confirmation of their hopes and assumptions. They wanted to learn about the conspiracy that was undermining the whole political fabric of Russia, asked whether Yermolov was taking part in it . . . and I could tell them of nothing but the radical tendencies among the young people, of Granovsky's propaganda, of the immense influence of Byelinsky, of the shades of opinion in the two parties struggling at that time in literature and society—the Westerners and the Slavophils. That seemed to them of little consequence.

They had a rich past, we had a great hope; their breast was covered with scars, while we were toughening our muscles to receive them. Beside them we were like recruits beside veterans. The Poles are mystics, we are realists. They are attracted by the mysterious twilight in which outlines are blurred and phantoms hover, in which one can imagine infinite distance, infinite height, because nothing can be seen distinctly. They can live in this half-dreaming state, without analysis, without cold investigation, without gnawing doubts. In the depths of their souls there is an element of mediaevalism alien to us, and a crucifix before which they can pray at moments of grief and fatigue. In Krasinski's poetry the *Stabat Mater* drowns the national hymns, and draws us not to the triumph of life, but to the triumph of death, to the Day of Judgment. . . . We are either *more stupid* in our faith or *more intelligent* in our doubt.

This mystical tendency developed to the furthest limit after the time of Napoleon. Mickiewicz, Towianski and even the mathematician Wronski all helped to create the Messianic idea. In old days there were Catholics and Encyclopaedists, but there were no mystics. The old men who had been educated in the eighteenth century were free from theosophic fantasies. The tempering given by the classical tradition of the *grand siècle* was permanent, like that of Damascus steel. It was my luck to meet two or three specimens of such old Polish Encyclopaedists.

In Paris, and in the Rue de la Chaussée d'Antin, moreover, there lived from 1831 onwards a nuncio of the

Polish Diet, Count Aloysius Bernacki, who was minister of finance at the time of the revolution, and marshal of the nobility of some province; he presented his fellow-nobles to Alexander 1., who was playing the Liberal in Poland in 1814.

Completely ruined by the confiscations, he settled in 1831 in Paris, in a small lodging in the Chaussée d'Antin, as I have mentioned already, whence he issued every morning in a dark brown coat to take a walk and read the newspapers, and, at a later hour, came out again in a dark blue coat with gilt buttons to spend the evening with some one; in 1847 I made his acquaintance. The house he lived in was dilapidated, the lady who owned the house wanted to have it repaired. Bernacki wrote a letter to her, which so touched the Frenchwoman (not at all an easy thing to do when it is a question of money) that she entered into negotiations with him and only asked him to leave the house for a time. When she had the house done up, she let Bernacki have his rooms again at the same rent. He saw with grief the new and handsome staircase, the new wallpaper, window-frames, and furniture, but submitted to his fate.

Temperate in all things, absolutely sincere and honourable, the old man was an admirer of Washington and a friend of O'Connell. A true Encyclopaedist, he advocated egoism *bien entendu* and spent a whole life in self-sacrifice, and had sacrificed everything, from wealth and family to social position and native land, without ever showing any special regret or deigning to complain.

The French police left him in peace and even respected him, knowing that he had been a minister and a nuncio; the prefecture seriously imagined that a nuncio of the Polish Diet was something of the nature of a papal nuncio. This was known among the exiles, and so his comrades and fellow-countrymen were constantly sending him to interview the police on their behalf. Bernacki went without a murmur and wearied the officials with correctly turned complimentary speeches, until they often made concessions to get rid of him. After the complete suppression of the February revolution, the tone changed; no smiles nor tears nor compliments nor grey hairs were of any avail, and just then, as ill luck would have it, the widow of a Polish general who had fought in the Hungarian War arrived in Paris, entirely destitute. Bernacki asked the prefecture to assist her; in spite of the high-sounding title, 'Son Excellence Monsieur le Nonce,' the prefecture refused flatly. The old man appealed to Carlier; to get rid of him and at the same time to humiliate him, Carlier replied that assistance was given only to the refugees of 1831. 'If you feel such sympathy for this lady,' he added, 'send in an application for yourself for assistance on the ground of poverty; we will assign you twenty francs a month, and you can make what use you like of them.'

Carlier was caught. Bernacki received the prefect's suggestion in the most simple-hearted way and at once accepted it, thanking him effusively. From that time forward, the old man went every month to the prefecture, waited for an hour or two in the anteroom, received twenty francs and took the money to the widow.

Bernacki was a good deal over seventy, but he was wonderfully well-preserved; he liked dining with his friends, sitting up with them till two o'clock in the morning and sometimes drinking a glass or two of wine. One night we were going home with him about three o'clock in the morning; we had to pass through the Rue Lepelletier. The Opera House was glowing with lights; *pierrots* and *débardeurs*, wrapped in shawls, dragoons and police-officers were thronging in the entry. In jest, feeling confident that he would refuse, I said to Bernacki:

'*Quelle chance!* Shall we go in?'

'With the greatest pleasure,' he answered. 'I haven't seen a masked ball for fifteen years.'

'Bernacki,' I said to him jestingly, as we went into the hall, 'when are you going to begin to grow old?'

'*Un homme comme il faut*,' he answered laughing, '*acquiert des années, mais ne vieillit jamais?*'

He kept up his character to the end, and, like a well-bred man, took his leave from life quietly and on good terms with it; he felt unwell in the morning and died in the evening.

At the time of Bernacki's death I was in London. There soon after my arrival I made friends with a man whose memory is still precious to me and whose coffin I helped to carry to the Highgate Cemetery—I am speaking of Worcell. Of all the Poles I got to know then, he was the one I liked best, and the one who was least antagonistic to Russians. It was not that he was fond of Russians, but he looked at things humanely and so was incapable of wholesale condemnation and narrow-minded hatred. He was the first man with whom I discussed the founding of the Russian printing-press. After listening to me the sick man grew animated, took pencil and paper, began making calculations, reckoning how much type we should require and so on. He made out the chief orders, he introduced me to Czernecki, with whom I worked so much later on.

'My God, my God,' he said, as he held the first page of proof in his hand, 'a free Russian press in London . . . how many evil memories are effaced from my mind by that sheet of paper smeared with printer's ink!'

'We ought to go hand in hand,' he often repeated

afterwards; 'our path is one, our cause is one . . .' and he laid his wasted hand on my shoulder.

At the Polish anniversary of the 29th of November 1853, I made a speech at the Hanover Rooms with Worcell in the chair. When I had finished amidst loud applause, Worcell embraced me and kissed me with tears in his eyes.

'Worcell and you on the platform made a great impression upon me just now,' one of the Italians (Count Nani) said to me as we went out. 'It seems to me that that noble, grey-headed, frail-looking old man and your healthy, stalwart figure were the typical representatives of Poland and Russia.'

'Only add,' I said, 'that Worcell in giving me his hand and embracing me *forgave Russia in the name of Poland.*'

Indeed we might have gone hand in hand—but it was not to be.

Worcell was *not alone.* . . . But first let me speak of him alone.

When Worcell was born, his father, one of the wealthy Polish aristocrats in Lithuania, a kinsman of Eszterhazy, of Potocki, and I do not know of whom else, sent for the village-elders and young women from five of his estates, that they might be present at the christening of the little count, Stanislaw, and might remember all their lives the banquet given by their lord on the occasion. This took place in 1800. The Count gave his son the most brilliant, the most many-sided education; Worcell was a mathematician, a linguist, and familiar with the literatures of five or six countries; in his early youth he had acquired an immense amount of knowledge and at the same time he was a man of the world, belonging to the most aristocratic Polish society at one of the most brilliant periods of its decline, between 1815 and 1830; Worcell married young and was only just entering upon 'practical' life, when the rebellion of 1831 broke out. He gave up everything and threw himself heart and soul into the movement. The rebellion was suppressed, Warsaw was taken. Count Stanislaw crossed the frontier like the rest, leaving family and fortune behind.

Instead of following him, his wife cut off all relations with him. As a reward for doing so, part of the property was restored to her. They had two children, a son and a daughter; how they were brought up, we shall see later; to begin with, their mother trained them to forget their father.

Meanwhile Worcell made his way through Austria to Paris and at once found himself in perpetual exile and entirely without means. He was not in the least daunted. Like Bernacki, he adopted a life of monastic self-denial and zealously entered upon his mission, which only ceased twenty-five years afterwards, when he drew his last breath in a little damp basement room, in a wretched lodging-house in gloomy Hunter Street.

To reorganise the Polish party of progress, to extend the propaganda of its principles, to concentrate the refugees' forces, to prepare for a new rebellion and to advocate this from morning till night, to devote his whole time to it—such was the plan of Worcell's whole life, from which he never deviated and to which he subordinated everything. With this object he got into touch with all the revolutionists of France, from Godefroi Cavaignac to Ledru-Rollin; with this object he became a freemason, and kept in close relations with the followers of Mazzini, and later on with Mazzini himself. Worcell firmly upheld the banner of the revolutionary party of Poland in opposition to the party of the Czartoryzskis. He was convinced that the aristocracy had been the ruin of the revolution, he looked upon the old nobles, as the enemies of his cause, and sought support from the new, the purely democratic Poland.

Worcell was right.

The Polish aristocracy, sincerely devoted as they were to their cause, were in many ways opposed to the tendencies of our times; the image of the Poland of the past was for ever hovering before their eyes, not a new Poland, but the old Poland restored; their ideal was based as much on memories as on hopes. The fetters of Catholicism were quite enough to hold Poland back —the armour of feudal chivalry would have paralysed her completely. In joining hands with Mazzini, Worcell wished to unite the Polish cause with the general European movement for republicanism and democracy. It is clear that he was bound to seek support among the humbler gentry, among townspeople and workmen. It was only in those classes that insurrection could begin. The aristocracy would join the movement, the peasants might be drawn into it, though they never would have taken the initiative.

Worcell may be reproached with stepping into the rut in which the European revolution was already sunk and foundering, for seeing in that path the only way of salvation; but, having once taken it, he was consistent. Circumstances vindicated him completely. Where, indeed, could revolutionary forces be found in Poland, if not in the social layer to which Worcell always turned, and which was forming, growing up and gaining strength between 1831 and 1860?

However different our views may be of revolution and the methods of bringing it about, we cannot deny that everything gained by revolution has been gained by the middle classes and the workers of the towns. And the Polish question was a purely patriotic one; national independence was more precious than social revolution, even to the heart of Worcell himself.

A sort of shudder of awakening ran over slumbering Europe some eighteen months before the revolution of

February. The Cracow affair, the trial of Miroslawski, even the war of the Sonderbund and the Italian *risorgimento* were signs of it. Austria replied with an outbreak of imperial terrorism, Nicholas presented her with Cracow, which did not belong to him—but tranquillity was not restored. Louis-Philippe fell in February 1848, it was a Pole who carried his throne to be burned. Worcell at the head of the Polish democracy came forward to remind the Provisional Government of Poland. Lamartine met him with cold rhetoric. The Republic was more peaceable than the Empire.

There was a moment when it was possible to hope; that moment was missed by Poland, missed by all Western Europe, and Paskevitch announced to Nicholas that Hungary lay at his feet.

After the fall of Hungary, there was nothing more to expect, and Worcell, forced to leave Paris, moved to London.

In London at the end of 1852 I found him a member of the European Committee.[1] He knocked at every door, wrote letters, newspaper articles, worked and hoped, persuaded and entreated—and as, with all that, he had to eat, took to giving lessons in mathematics, in geometrical drawing, and even in French; coughing and breathless from asthma, he walked from one end of London to the other to earn two shillings or at the most half a crown. And then part of what he earned he gave to his comrades.

His spirit never flagged, but his body could not keep pace with it. The London atmosphere, damp, soot-laden, never warmed by the sun, was bad for his weak chest. Worcell was wasting away, but still he persevered. So he lived on to the Crimean War; he could not, I had almost said he *should* not, have survived that.

[1] Consisting of Mazzini, Kossuth, Ledru-Rollin, Arnold Ruge, Bratiano and Worcell.—(*Author's Note.*)

'If Poland does nothing now, all is lost, for many years, if not for ever, and I had better close my eyes,' Worcell said to me, as he set off with Kossuth for a tour round England.

They held meetings in all the principal towns. Worcell and Kossuth were received with loud applause, small sums of money were subscribed for the cause—and that was all. The Government and the Parliament are very good at knowing when public opinion is simply stirred, and when it is insistent. A strong Government after bringing forward a Conspiracy Bill fell in anticipation of a mass-meeting of protest in Hyde Park. There was in the meetings held by Kossuth and Worcell nothing definite, nothing forcible enough to induce the Government and Parliament to acknowledge the rights of Poland and to express sympathy with the Polish cause. The terrible reply of the Conservatives was unanswerable: 'All is quiet in Poland.' The English Government would have had, not to recognise an accomplished fact, but to bring it about, to take the initiative in revolution, to rouse Poland. Public opinion in England does not go so far as that. Moreover, *in petto*, every one was longing for the end of the war which had only just begun, was costly and, in reality, quite useless.

At intervals between the meetings Worcell returned to London. He was too intelligent not to realise their failure, he was visibly ageing, he was gloomy and irritable, and, with the feverish energy with which dying men fly to all manner of remedies, he went back to Birmingham or Liverpool, with sinister apprehensions, and obstinate hopes in his heart, to raise his lament for Poland from the platform. I looked at him with great distress. But how could he imagine that England would rouse Poland, that the France of Napoleon III. would stir up revolution? How could he build hopes on the Europe which had let Russia invade Hungary and the French invade Rome? Did not the very presence of Mazzini and Kossuth in London loudly proclaim the degradation of Europe?

. . . About the same time the long-rankling dissatisfaction of the younger refugees with the Central Committee became articulate. Worcell was petrified—he had not expected this blow, and yet it came quite naturally.

The small group of people immediately surrounding Worcell were far from being on his level. He understood this, but having grown accustomed to his chorus had fallen under its influence. He imagined that he was their leader, while the chorus that followed him directed his course as they wished. Worcell alone rose to the heights on which he could breathe freely, where it was natural for him to be—the chorus, like plebeian relations, dragged him down to the low level of personal squabbles and petty calculations. The leader, old before his time, gasped in this atmosphere from spiritual breathlessness as much as from physical.

These people did not understand the importance of the alliance which I proposed.

They looked upon it as a means of giving a different colour to the cause; their everlasting repetition of commonplaces, their patriotic phrases, their stock memories—had all grown insipid and boring. Association with the Russians would introduce a novel element. Moreover, they hoped to improve their almost bankrupt position at the expense of the Russian propaganda.

From the very beginning, there was no real understanding between the members of the Central Committee and me. Suspicious of everything Russian, they wanted me to write and publish something like a *profession de foi*. I wrote *The Poles Forgive Us*. They asked me to alter certain expressions. I did so, though I was very far from agreeing with them. In reply to my article L. Z. wrote an appeal to the Russians and sent it to me in manuscript. There was not a trace of a new idea in it; there were the same phrases, the same allusions to the past, and outbursts of Catholicism as well. Before translating it into Russian, I pointed out to Worcell the absurdities of the original. Worcell agreed and asked me to explain the matter in the evening to the members of the Central Committee. Then followed the eternal scene between Trissotin and Vadius:[1] the very passages which I criticised were, it appeared, essential to save Poland from ruin. As for the Catholic phrases, they said that whatever their personal convictions might be, they wished to keep with their people; and the people were devoted to their oppressed mother, the Latin Church.

Worcell supported me. But as soon as he began to speak, his comrades made an uproar. Worcell was coughing from the tobacco smoke and could not make himself heard. He promised me to talk to them afterwards and to insist upon the chief corrections. A week later the *Polish Democrat* came out. Not one word was altered in the appeal; I refused to translate it. Worcell told me that he too was amazed at this proceeding. 'It is not enough for you to be amazed; why did you not stop it?' I said to him.

It was evident to me that sooner or later Worcell would be faced with the question, whether to break off from the existing members of the Central Committee and remain in close relations with me, or to break off his association with me and remain on the same terms with his half-baked revolutionists . . . Worcell chose the latter course; I was grieved by this, but neither complained of it nor resented it.

At this point I must go into melancholy details. When I set up the printing-press, it was decided that all the

[1] The reference is to Molière's *Femmes Savantes.—(Translator's Note.)*

expenses of publishing (paper, type, rent, labour, etc.) should fall upon me. The Central Committee undertook the dispatch of the Russian papers and pamphlets at their own expense and through the same channels as the Polish pamphlets. All that they took to send off I gave them free of charge. It would seem that mine was the lion's share, but apparently it was not enough.

For their own purposes and principally in order to collect funds, the Central Committee arranged to send a delegate to Poland. They even wanted him to go to Kiev and, if possible, to Moscow for propaganda among the Russians, and asked me to give him letters. I refused, afraid of getting people into trouble. Three days before the delegate set off I met Z. in the street in the evening, and he asked me at once: 'How much are you giving for the expenses of the delegate?'

It struck me as a strange question, but knowing what straits they were in, I said that I would give ten pounds (250 francs), if they liked.

'What do you mean? You must be joking,' said Z. frowning. 'He will need at least sixty pounds and we need forty pounds to make that up. We cannot leave it like that, I will talk to the comrades and come to you.'

He did, in fact, come next day accompanied by Worcell and two other members of the Central Committee. On this occasion Z. simply accused me of refusing to give enough money for the expenses of the delegate, though I had agreed to give him Russian papers to take.

'Upon my soul,' I said, 'you decided to send the delegate, you think it necessary; so the cost of it falls on you. Worcell is present, let him remind you of our agreement.'

'What's the use of discussing *trifles*: as though you didn't know that we haven't a farthing!'

This tone sickened me at last.

'I think you haven't read *Dead Souls*,' I said, 'or I would have reminded you of how Nozdryov, showing the boundary of his estate to Tchitchikov, told the latter that the land on both sides of the boundary was his. That is very much like our position: we have divided our work and our burdens by arranging that both parts should fall on my back.'

The little bilious Lithuanian began to lose his temper and make an outcry about honour, and wound up his absurd and discourteous speech by the question, 'What do you want, then?'

'That you should not take me for a *bailleur de fonds* nor a democratic banker, as one German called me in a pamphlet. You think too much of my fortune and, I fancy, too little of me; you are mistaken. . . .'

'Excuse me, excuse me . . .' cried the Lithuanian, pale with fury.

'I cannot permit this conversation to go further,' Worcell, who had been sitting gloomily in the corner, observed, rising to his feet, 'or you must continue it without me. *Cher* Herzen, you are right, but think of our position: it is essential to send the delegate and we have not the means.'

I stopped him. 'In that case you might have asked me whether I could do anything, but you could not demand it; and to demand it in this coarse way is simply disgusting. I will give the money; I do so entirely for your sake, and I give you my word of honour, gentlemen, this is for the last time.'

I handed Worcell the money and they all gloomily withdrew.

The delegate went and returned, having done nothing.

The war drew near, began. The *émigrés* were dissatisfied; the younger section blamed Worcell's comrades for incapacity, laziness and seeking their own interests instead of those of Poland. Their discontent reached the point of open protests, they talked of demanding accounts from the members of the Central Committee, of making an open declaration of lack of confidence. The one thing that restrained them and made them hesitate was their love and respect for Worcell. I did all I could through Czernecki to strengthen their scruples, but blunder after blunder committed by the Central Committee was enough to drive any one out of patience.

In November 1854 there was another Polish meeting, but its spirit was different from that of the previous year. An M.P., Joshua Wolmsley, was asked to take the chair. The Poles put their cause under English patronage. To prevent the speeches from being too *red* Worcell wrote notes to some of us, on the same pattern as the one I received from him:

'You know that we have a meeting on the 20th; we cannot as on the previous occasion ask you to say a few sympathetic words for us; the war and the necessity for securing English support compel us to give a somewhat different tone to the meeting. Herzen, Ledru-Rollin and Pianciani will not speak for us. The speakers will be principally English; of our comrades, only Kossuth will make a speech in order to give an account of our position, etc'

I answered that 'I received his invitation *not* to speak at the meeting, and accepted it the more readily as it was so easy to comply with.'

Support from the English was not forthcoming; concessions were made in vain; even the subscriptions did not amount to much. Wolmsley said that he was ready to give money, but did not wish to put his name down as a subscriber, that as a Member of Parliament he could not take part officially in raising funds for an object not sanctioned by the Government.

All this, and among other things my exclusion from the platform, intensified the irritation of the younger comrades; a statement of the charges against the Central Committee was already being passed from hand to hand. As luck would have it, I was obliged to find fresh quarters for the Russian press. Z., who rented the house in which the Russian as well as the Polish press was installed, was heavily in debt; the bailiffs had been in twice already; they might be expected any day to seize our press together with the furniture. I commissioned Czernecki to move it; Z. made difficulties, was unwilling to let the type and other belongings go; I wrote him a cold letter. In answer to it Worcell, ill and agitated, came to Richmond next day to see me.

'You are giving us the *coup de grâce*; at the very moment when there is such strife raging among us you are moving the press.'

'I assure you that I am not doing so for any political reason, any quarrel, or as a protest, but simply I am afraid that everything will be distrained at Z.'s. Can you assure me that that will not happen? I will rely on *your* word of honour and not move the press.'

'He certainly is in very great straits.'

'How can you, then, wish me to risk the loss of my only weapon? Even if I should be able to recover it later on, think of the loss of time. You know how these things are done here.'

Worcell did not speak.

'I'll tell you what I can do for you: I will write a letter, saying that for business reasons I am compelled to move the press, but so far from meaning that I am breaking off from you, it will come to our having two presses instead of one. You can publish this letter if you like or show it to any one you please.'

I did in fact write this letter, addressing it to a humble

member of the Central Committee, who was in charge of the office.

'No doubt you have heard,' asked Worcell, 'that they are drawing up an act of indictment against us?'

'I have.'

'This is how I am rewarded in my old age . . . this is what I have been brought to . . .' and he shook his grey head mournfully.

'I doubt whether you are right, Worcell. They are so accustomed to love and respect you, that it was only through fear of wounding you that things have not come to a head before. You know that it is not with you they have a quarrel, let your comrades go their own way.'

'Never, never; we have done everything together, we share the responsibility.'

'You won't save them.'

'And what did you say half an hour ago about Russell's betraying his comrades?'

It was in the evening. I was standing at a little distance from the fireplace, Worcell was sitting at the window with his face towards the fire. His face, worn by illness, with the red glow of the fire quivering over it, struck me as more wasted and suffering than ever— a tear, the bitter tear of age, rolled down his hollow cheek . . . several minutes of unbearably painful silence followed . . . he got up, I went with him to his bedroom, the great trees were rustling in the garden. Worcell opened the window and said: 'I should last twice as long here with my poor chest.'

I gripped him with both hands: 'Worcell,' I said, 'stay with me; I will give you a second room, no one shall interfere with you, do as you like, breakfast alone, dine alone if you like; you will rest here for two or three months. . . . You will not be continually worried, you will be refreshed. I entreat you as a friend, as though I were your younger brother.'

'I thank you. I thank you with all my heart. I would accept your invitation at once, but under present circumstances it is simply out of the question . . . on the one hand, there is the war; on the other, our fellows will take it as meaning that I have deserted them. No, every man must bear his own cross to the end.'

'Well, sleep well to-night at least,' I said to him, trying to smile. There was no means of saving him!

In the autumn of 1856 Worcell was advised to go to Nice and to stay a little while first on the warm shores of the Lake of Geneva. When I heard of it I offered him the money necessary. He accepted it, and that brought us together again; we began seeing each other more frequently. But he was a long time preparing to go; the damp London winter with its smoky stifling fog, its everlasting humidity and terrible north-east winds, was beginning. I tried to hurry him off, but already he began to betray a sort of instinctive dread of change, of movement. He was afraid of solitude. I suggested that he should take some one with him to Geneva; there I should have handed him over to Karl Vogt.

He accepted everything, agreed to everything, but did nothing. He lived in an underground basement; it was scarcely ever light in his room, there he was fading away, ill with asthma, without air, breathing coal smoke.

Peter Taylor told Worcell's landlady to send him every week her bill for his lodging, board and washing; he paid this bill, but gave not a single pound into the old refugee's hands.

It was definitely too late for him to travel; I offered to take a good room for him in the Brompton Consumption Hospital.

'Yes, that would be very nice, but it is impossible. Only think what a dreadful distance it is from here.'

'Well, what of it?'

'Szabicki lives here and all our affairs are here; *he would have to come every morning to bring me a daily report.*'

At this point self-sacrifice bordered upon madness.

. . . The war was ending, Nicholas was dead, a new Russia was arising, we lived to see the Paris Peace, and to see the *Polar Star* and everything we published bought up to the last copy. We began publishing the *Bell* and it went well. . . . Worcell and I rarely saw each other; he rejoiced at our success with that inner suppressed but burning pain with which a mother who has lost her son watches the development of another's boy. . . . The time of the fatal alternative set by Worcell in his *oggi o mai* had come, and he was fading out of life. . . .

Three days before his end Czernecki sent for me. Worcell had asked for me—he was very ill, they were expecting the end. When I came in he was in a state of semi-consciousness not unlike a trance; he lay on the sofa, pale and waxen . . . his cheeks were terribly sunken, and these fits of unconsciousness had been frequent with him during the last few days, he was slowly growing used to death. A quarter of an hour later Worcell began to come to himself, spoke in a faint voice; he recognised me, sat up and lay half reclining.

'Have you read the papers?' he asked me.

'Yes.'

'Tell me how the Neufchâtel question is going. I can read nothing.' I told him, he listened and understood everything.

'Ah, how I want to sleep! Leave me now, I shall not sleep with you here, and I shall be easier if I sleep.'

Next day he was a little better. He wanted to say

something to me . . . twice he began and stopped . . . and only when he was left alone with me the dying man called me to his side and, feebly taking my hand, said: 'How right you were . . . you don't know how right you were! . . . it has been on my mind to tell you so.'

'Don't let us talk any more about them.'

'Go your own way . . .'—he raised his dying but bright and radiant eyes upon me. He could talk no more. I kissed him on the lips, and it was well I did, for our parting was a long one. In the evening he got up, sipped a little warm gin and water with the landlady—an excellent simple-hearted woman, who had a religious reverence for Worcell as a being of a higher order—went back to his own room, and fell asleep. Next morning Szabicki and the landlady asked whether he wanted anything more. He asked them to make a fire and let him sleep again; they did so. Worcell never woke again.

When I came he was gone. His thin, thin face and body were covered by a white sheet. I looked at him, said a last good-bye, and went to fetch a sculptor's workman to take a mask of him. His last interview, his great agony I have described in another place; I will add one terrible touch to it.

Worcell never spoke of his family. Once he was looking for some letter to give me; rummaging in the table he opened a drawer. There lay a photograph of a well-fed-looking young man with the moustache of an officer. 'A Pole and a patriot, no doubt,' I said, more in jest than by way of inquiry.

'That,' said Worcell, looking away and hurriedly taking the portrait out of my hand, 'is my son.' I learned later that he was in the Russian service in Warsaw.

His daughter had married a count and was living in wealthy style. She did not know her father.

Two days before his death he was dictating his will to Mazzini . . . his last message to Poland, his farewell to her and greetings to friends. . . . 'That is all,' said the dying man. Mazzini did not put down the pen. 'Think a little,' he said; 'is there nothing else you want at this moment? Are there no others to whom you should have something to say? 'Worcell understood, his face clouded over and he answered: 'There is nothing for me to say to them.'

I know no curse which would sound more terrible and lie more heavily upon one than those simple words.

.   .   .   .

With the death of Worcell the democratic party of the Polish emigrants in London grew pettier. It had rested upon him, upon his beautiful, his revered personality. The radical party fell apart into little cliques, almost hostile to each other. The yearly meetings split up, became poor in numbers and interest. There was still the everlasting requiem, the rehearsal of losses, new and old, and, as always in requiems, the visionary hope of the resurrection of the dead and the life everlasting, the faith in the second coming of Buonaparte and the resurrection of Poland.

Two or three worthy old men remained like grand and mournful monuments; like the grey-headed, long-bearded Israelites weeping at the walls of Jerusalem. They pointed, not like leaders, to the path ahead, but like monks, to the grave; they bring us to a standstill with their *Sta viator!*

The best of the best among them had kept a youthful heart in his decrepit body, and a gentle, childishly pure youthful light in his blue eyes. He was already on the brink of the grave, he would soon pass away, and soon, too, his opponent Czartoryzski.

Is not that really *finis Poloniae*?

Before we part for ever from the touching and sympathetic personality of Worcell in the cold Highgate cemetery, I should like to give a few more trifling details about him. So men coming from a funeral check their mourning to tell stories of the dead man.

Worcell was very absent-minded in little daily affairs; he always left behind him his spectacles, spectacle-case, handkerchief, snuff-box; on the other hand, if a handkerchief not his own lay beside him he would put it in his pocket; he came to see me sometimes with three gloves, sometimes with one.

Before he moved to Hunter Street, he lived close by in a semicircle of small houses at 43 Burton Crescent, not far from the New Road. After the English fashion all the houses in the Crescent were single dwellings. The house in which Worcell lived was the fifth from the end and, knowing his absent-mindedness, he always counted the doors. Returning one day from the opposite side of the Crescent, Worcell knocked and, when the door was opened, walked into his room. A girl, probably the daughter of the house, came out of it. Some one coughed twice behind him: a complete stranger was sitting in the armchair. 'I beg your pardon,' said Worcell, 'I am afraid you have been waiting for me.' 'Allow me,' observed the Englishman, 'before answering, to know with whom I have the honour of speaking.'

'I am Worcell, and I have not the pleasure of your acquaintance; what can I do for you?'

Here Worcell was suddenly struck by the idea that he had come to the wrong place; looking about him he saw that the furniture and everything else was not his. He told the Englishman of his plight, and apologising went off to the fifth house from the other side. Fortunately the Englishman was a very polite person, which is not a very common find in London.

Three months later the same thing happened again. This time when he knocked, the maid who opened the door, seeing a venerable old man, asked him to walk into the parlour, where the Englishman was having supper with his wife. Seeing Worcell walk in, he held out his hand good-humouredly and said: 'It's not here, you live at No. 43.'

In spite of this absent-mindedness, Worcell preserved to the end of his life an extraordinary memory; I used to refer to him as to a lexicon or encyclopaedia. He had read everything in the world and studied everything, mechanics and astronomy, the natural sciences and history. Though he had no Catholic prejudices, from the old *pit* of the Polish mind he believed in a spiritual world, unnecessary and impossible, but apart from the material world. It was not the religion of Moses, Abraham and Isaac, but the religion of Jean Jacques, of George Sand, of Pierre Leroux, of Mazzini and the rest. But Worcell had less right to it than any of them.

When his asthma was not worrying him very much and he was not very gloomy, Worcell was very charming in company. He told stories superbly, and especially reminiscences of the old life of the Polish nobility. I used to listen attentively to his tales. The world of Pan Tadewsz, the world of Murdelio . . . passed before one's eyes; a world the end of which one could not regret; on the contrary, one rejoices that it is no more, though one cannot refuse to acknowledge a sort of brilliant, unbridled poetry in it entirely lacking in the life of the Russian nobility. West European aristocracy is indeed so completely alien to us that all accounts of our grandees may be reduced to stories of savage luxury, of banquets in which a whole town takes part, of multitudes of house-serfs, of tyrannising over the peasants and poor neighbours, together with slavish cringing before the emperor and the court. The Sheremetyevs and the Golitsyns with all their palaces and great estates were in no way distinguished from their peasants, except by wearing a German coat, reading and writing French, and enjoying wealth and the Tsar's favour. They were all continually justifying Paul's dictum, that he had no one about him but servants in high positions; it was to such that he was speaking when he said it. All that is very good, but one ought to recognise it. What can be more pitiful *et moins aristocratique* than the last representative of Russian nobility and high rank whom I have seen, Prince Sergey Mihailovitch Golitsyn, and what can be more loathsome than an Izmailov?

The manners of the Polish Pans were bad, barbarous, almost unintelligible now; but they were on another plane, due to a different mould of character, and there was not a shade of churlishness in them.

'Do you know,' Worcell asked me once, 'why the Passage Radziwill in the Palais Royal is so called?'

'No.'

'You remember the celebrated Radziwill, the friend of the Regent, who drove with his own horses from Warsaw to Paris and bought a house for every night he had to sleep on the journey; the quantity of wine drunk by Radziwill was too much for his less vigorous host; the Duke became so much attached to him, that though he saw him every day, he used to send him notes in the morning. One day Radziwill wanted to tell the Regent something; he sent a lad with a letter to him. The fellow looked and looked, but could not find the place, and came back to confess his failure. "You fool," the Pan said to him, "come here, look out of window, do you see that big house?" (the Palais Royal).—"Yes, I see it"—"Well, that is where the greatest Pan here lives. Any one will show it you" The lad went off and looked and looked, but could not find the place. The fact is that the palace is screened by houses, and one has to make a *détour* by the Rue

Honoré. "Phew, what a bore!" said the Pan; "tell my steward to buy the houses between my house and the Palais Royal, and to make a street, so that this fool won't lose his way next time I send him to the Regent."'

I will give another example of how financial operations are conducted as a rule in our world.

After my arrival in London in 1852, while speaking of the low state of the Italian party funds with Mazzini, I told him that in Genoa I had proposed to his friends that they should put a tax on their incomes and pay, those with no families 10 per cent., those with a family less.

'They will all agree,' observed Mazzini, 'but very few will pay it.'

'That would be shameful; they will pay,' I said. 'I have long wished to contribute my mite to the Italian cause, it is as dear to me as my own; I will give 10 per cent, of my income at the same time. That will be about £200. Here is £140, but £60 I will keep for the present.'

In 1853 Mazzini vanished. Soon after his departure two refugees called upon me, one wearing a fur collar because he had ten years previously been in Petersburg; the other with no collar, but with a grey moustache and a little military beard. They came with a message from Ledru-Rollin; he wanted to know whether I was not intending to send a sum of money to the European Committee. I confessed that I had no such intention.

Some days later the same question was put to me by Worcell. 'Where can Ledru-Rollin have picked up that idea?'

'Why, you did give some to Mazzini.'

'That is rather a reason for not giving to any one else.'

'I believe you still have £60 to give.'

'Promised to Mazzini.'

'That is all the same.'

'I don't think so.'

A week passed; I had a letter from Mazzoletti, in which he informed me that it had come to his knowledge that I did not know to whom to send £60 still in my hands; for which reason he begged me to send the money to him as the representative of Mazzini in London.

This Mazzoletti really was Mazzini's secretary. An official and a bureaucrat by nature, he amused us by his official dignity and bureaucratic manner.

When a telegram appeared in the newspapers announcing the rising in Milan of the 3rd of February 1853, I went to Mazzoletti to find out whether he had any news. Mazzoletti asked me to wait; then came out to me with an anxious but valiant air, carrying some papers and accompanied by Bratiano, with whom he was in earnest conversation.

'I have come to you to find out if you have any news.'

'No, I only heard myself from *The Times*; I am awaiting a dispatch from hour to hour.'

Two or three others arrived. Mazzoletti was pleased, and so groaned and complained that he had no time to spare. In course of conversation he began to drop hints of news and explanations.

'How do you know that?' I asked him.

'That . . . these, of course, are my own deductions,' Mazzoletti observed, somewhat disconcerted.

'I will come to you to-morrow morning. . . .'

'If any news comes to-day I will let you know.'

'You will oblige me; from seven till nine o'clock this evening I shall be at Verrey's.'

Mazzoletti did not forget. At seven o'clock I was dining at Verrey's: an Italian whom I had seen twice walked in, he came up to me, looked about him, waited till the waiter had gone to fetch something, and saying that Mazzoletti had charged him to tell me that there was no telegram, went away.

On receiving the letter from the state secretary of revolution, I answered him jokingly, that he was wrong in picturing me as standing helpless in the midst of London, not knowing to whom to give £60; that without a letter from Mazzini I had no intention of giving the money to any one whatever.

Mazzoletti wrote me a long and somewhat wrathful note, which was intended, without lowering the dignity of the writer or exceeding the limits of parliamentary courtesy, to be sarcastic at the expense of the recipient.

Not a week had passed after these overtures when early one morning Amelia G., one of the women most devoted to Mazzini and an intimate friend of his, called upon me. She told me that the rising in Lombardy had failed, that Mazzini was still in hiding there and asking them to send him money at once, and they had no money.

'Here,' I said, 'is the famous £60; only, don't forget to tell your privy councillor Mazzoletti, and Ledru-Rollin too if occasion arises, that I did not do so badly in refusing to fling these 1500 francs into the bottomless pit of the European Committee.'

In anticipation of our Russian national inference from my story, I ought to say that no one ever profited by the money so collected.[1] In Russia some one would

[1] The Italian exiles were above all suspicion. There was one very amusing incident among the French refugees. B., who is mentioned in the account of Barthélemy's duel, collected some money on instructions from Ledru-Rollin and spent it. His desire to return to London was greatly diminished thereby, and he began to ask permission to remain at Marseilles. Billier replied that B. was so harmless in a political sense that he might have remained, but that his dishonesty in connection with his own party showed that he was an undesirable person, for which reason he refused him permission.

In this matter too the Germans carry off the palm. They gathered by collections in America and Manchester, I remember,

have stolen it: here it vanished exactly as though someone had burnt the banknotes in a candle without taking the numbers.

2

Pater V. Petcherin

'Yesterday I saw Petcherin.'

I started at the name.

'What,' I asked, '*the* Petcherin, is he here?'

'Who, the Reverend Petcherin? Yes, he is here.'

'Where is he?'

'In the Jesuit monastery, Saint Mary's Chapel, at Clapham.'

The Reverend Father Petcherin! . . . That sin too lies at the doors of Nicholas. I had not known Petcherin personally, but I had heard a very great deal about him from Ryedkin, Kryukov and Granovsky. He had returned, a young professor, from abroad, to take the Chair of Greek in the Moscow University; it was at one of the very darkest periods of the persecution by Nicholas between 1835 and 1840. We were in exile, the later young professors had not yet arrived, the *Telegraph* had been forbidden, the *European* had been forbidden, the *Telescope* had been forbiden. Tchaadayev had been declared insane.

twenty thousand francs. This sum, destined for the purposes of agitation and propaganda, legal expenses and so on, they put into one of the London banks and elected as trustees Kinkel, Ruge and Count Oscar Reichenbach, three irreconcilable enemies. They had at once grasped what a rich source of unpleasantness for one another had been put into their hands, and so hastened to make it a condition that the bank should give no payment without all three signatures. One or two of them had only to sign a cheque for the third to refuse to da so. Whatever the German refugee society might do, one signature was not sufficient. So the sum lies untouched in the bank to this, day, probably destined for the future Teutonic republic. — (*Author's Note.*)

It was not till after 1848 that the Terror in Russia went to even further extremes.

But the frenzied tyranny of the last years of Nicholas' reign was unmistakably the fifth act. By then it was already becoming apparent that something was not only breaking and ruining, but was itself being broken and dropping into ruins. There was the sound as though the floor were cracking under a collapsing roof.

In the 'thirties, on the contrary, the frenzy of power went its accustomed routine with its regular step; all around was silence and desolation, everything was dumb submission with no hope, no human dignity, and at the same time dull, stupid and petty. Any one who looked for sympathy met a flunkey's menace or panic, all turned from him or insulted him. Petcherin was gasping for air in this Neapolitan cave of slavery, he was overtaken by horror, misery, he had at all costs to escape from this accursed land. To get away he needed money. Petcherin began to give lessons, reduced his expenditure to the barest necessaries, missed the gatherings of his comrades, went out little, and after saving a small sum went away.

Soon afterwards he wrote a letter to Count Strogonov; he informed him that he should not return. Thanking him and bidding him farewell, Petcherin spoke of the unbearably suffocating atmosphere from which he was escaping, and besought him to protect the luckless young professors doomed by their culture to the same agonies, to shield them from the blows of brute force.

Strogonov showed this letter to many of the professors.

There was silence about him for some time in Moscow, then suddenly we heard with an infinitely bitter feeling that Petcherin had become a Jesuit, that he was serving his novitiate in a monastery. Poverty, friendlessness, solitude had broken his spirit. I looked through his *Triumph of Death*, and asked myself: 'Can this man possibly be a Catholic, a Jesuit? Why, he has already gone from the rule of the Tsars, where *history is made* under the stick of the policeman, and under guard of the gendarme. Why then did he so soon feel the need of other control, other authority?'

The Russian felt isolated, forlorn in the closely classified West, up to its neck in business; he was too conscious of being without kith or kin. When the cord by which he was bound was broken and his life, suddenly set free from every external guidance, was left in his own hands, he did not know what to do, could not deal with it, and thrown out of his natural orbit with no goal before him, no boundaries to restrain him, he sank into a Jesuit monastery!

At two o'clock on the day after I heard his name, I went to Saint Mary's Chapel. The heavy oak door was closed—I knocked three times with a knocker in the shape of a ring, the door opened and a thin young man of about eighteen appeared, wearing a monk's cassock; in his hand was a breviary.

'Whom do you wish to see?' the brother who acted as porter asked.

'The Reverend Father Petcherin.'

'Kindly give me your name.'

'Here is my card and a letter.' In the letter I had put an announcement of the Russian printing press.

'Come in,' said the young man, closing the door behind me. 'Will you wait here?' and he indicated two or three large chairs with antique carving on them in the spacious vestibule.

Five minutes later he returned, and told me in French, with a slight accent, that *le père Petcherin sera enchanté de me recevoir dans un instant.*

After that he led me across the refectory into a small, lofty room, dimly lighted, and again asked me to sit down. On the wall there was a crucifix carved out of stone, and, if I am not mistaken, on the other side there was also a Madonna. About the heavy, massive table there were large wooden armchairs and ordinary chairs. A door on the opposite side led by a porch into a spacious garden; its worldly greenness and the rustle of the leaves seemed somehow out of keeping.

The brother doorkeeper showed me a notice on the wall, in which was the statement that the reverend fathers saw those that had need of them between four and six. It was not yet four.

'I think you are not an Englishman and not a Frenchman?' I asked him, listening to his accent.

'No.'

'*Sind Sie ein Deutscher?*'

'*Oh, nein, mein Herr. Ich bin beinahe ihre Landsmann, ich bin ein Pole.*'

Well—the brother doorkeeper was not a bad choice, he spoke in four languages. I sat down; he went away; I felt strange at seeing myself in these surroundings. Black figures kept walking by in the garden; two men in semi-monastic dress passed close by me; they gravely but courteously bowed, looking at the ground; on each occasion I rose and as gravely bowed in return. At last a little very elderly priest came in wearing a biretta and the regular garb in which priests are dressed in monasteries. He came straight up to me, his robes rustling, and asked me with the purest French accent: 'You wish to see Petcherin?' I answered by giving my name.

'I am greatly delighted at your visit,' he said, holding out his hand; 'please sit down.'

'I beg your pardon,' I said, somewhat taken aback at not having recognised him. It had not entered my head that I should meet him in such a costume. 'Your dress . . .'

He gave a slight smile and at once went on: 'It is a long while since I have had any news of my own country, of our friends, of the university. You probably knew Ryedkin and Kryukov.'

I looked at him; his face was old, older than his years, one could see that behind those wrinkles much had passed, and passed away, *tout de bon*, that is, had died, leaving only its funereal traces on his features. The artificial clerical composure with which monks destroy as with corrosive sublimate whole sides of their heart and their mind had reached even his speech and all his movements. A Catholic priest has always something of the widow, he too is always in mourning and in solitude, he too is faithful to something which is not, and quenches his real passions by stimulating his imagination.

When I told him about our common acquaintances and about the death of Kryukov, at which I had been present, and how his students had borne him to the cemetery across the whole length of the town, and then about Granovsky's triumphs, about his public lectures, we both sank into thought. What was passing in the skull under the biretta I do not know, but Petcherin took it off as though it weighed heavily on him at that moment, and laid it on the table. Conversation did not run easily. '*Sortons un peu au jardin,*' said Petcherin, '*le temps est si beau, et c'est si rare a Londres.*'

'*Avec le plus grand plaisir,* but tell me, please, why are we talking in French?'

'Yes, indeed! Let us speak Russian. I believe I have quite forgotten it.'

We went out into the garden. The conversation again passed to our university days in Moscow.

'Oh,' said Petcherin, 'what a terrible time it was

when I left Russia! I cannot think of it without shuddering!'

'Only imagine what is being done there now; our Saul has gone completely mad since 1848,' and I told him of several atrocious incidents.

'Unhappy country, especially for the minority who have received the unlucky gift of culture. And yet what a good people! I often think of our peasants when I am in Ireland. They are very much alike; the Celtic peasant is just such a child as ours. You should go to Ireland, and you will be convinced of it yourself.'

So the conversation was prolonged for half an hour; at last when I prepared to leave him I said to him: 'I have a favour to ask of you.'

'Please tell me what it is.'

'Several of your poems came into my hands in Petersburg: among them is a trilogy—"Polikrat Samossky," "The Triumph of Death" and something else: haven't you got them, or can you not let me have them?'

'How can you recall such nonsense! They were the crude, childish productions of a certain period and a certain mood.'

'Perhaps,' I observed smiling, 'that is why I like them; but have you got them or not?'

'No, indeed!'

'And you could not dictate them?'

No, no, certainly not.'

'But if I can find them somewhere in Russia will you permit me to publish them?'

'I really look upon those trivial productions as though some one else had written them; they mean no more to me than a sick man's ravings after his recovery.'

'Since they mean nothing to you, then I can publish them—without your name, of course?'

'Do you like those verses still?'

'That's my business. You only tell me whether you will allow me to publish them or not.'

Even then he would not give me a direct answer. I did not insist further.

'Why,' observed Petcherin, as I was saying good-bye, 'you have brought me none of your publications. I remember some three years ago there was talk in the newspapers of a book published by you, I believe in German.'

'Your cloth,' I answered, 'will tell you on what grounds I could not bring it; accept my not doing so as a sign of respect and delicacy.'

'You little know our tolerance and our love; we may grieve over error, pray for its correction, earnestly desire it, and in any case love the man.'

We parted. He forgot neither the book nor my answer, and three days later wrote me the following letter in French:—

J.M. J.A., St. Mary's, Clapham,
April 11, 1853.

I cannot disguise from you the sympathy that is awakened in my heart by the word freedom—freedom for my unhappy country! Do not for one instant doubt the sincerity of my desire for the resurrection of Russia. For all that, I am far from agreeing with your programme in all respects. But that is of no importance, the love of the Catholic priest embraces all opinions and all parties. When your most precious hopes deceive you, when the powers of this world rise up against you, you will still have left an unfailing refuge in the heart of the Catholic priest: in him you will find affection without insincerity, precious tears and the peace which this world cannot give you. Come to me, dear fellow-countryman. I should be very pleased to see you once more before I go away to Guernsey. Do not forget to bring your brochure for me.

V. Petcherin.

I took him the books, and four days afterwards received the following letter:—

St. Pierre, Island of Guernsey,

J.M.J.A., Chapelle Catholique, *April* 15, 1853.

I have read both your books with great attention. One thing has particularly impressed me: it seems to me that you and your friends rest your hopes exclusively on philosophy and on *belles lettres*. Can you imagine that it is their vocation to reform society as it is? Pardon me, but the evidence of history is entirely against you. There is no instance of a society being founded or recreated by philosophy and literature. I say plainly (*tranchons le mot*), only religion has ever served as the foundation of a state; philosophy and literature, alas! are but the latest flower of the social tree. When philosophy and literature attain their apogee, when philosophers, orators and poets are the ruling power and settle all public questions, then comes the end, the downfall, then comes the death of society. That is shown by Greece and Rome, that is shown by the so-called Alexandrian period; never was philosophy more encouraged, never was literature more flourishing, yet it was a period of deep social degradation; whenever philosophy has undertaken the re-creation of the social order, it has invariably passed into a social despotism, for instance in the case of Frederick 11., Catherine 11., Joseph 11., and in all the revolutions that have failed. You have let fall a phrase felicitous or infelicitous as you like: you say that the phalanstery is nothing but the barracks in another form, and that Communism can but be the autocracy of Nicholas transformed into another aspect. In fact, I see a shadow of melancholy resting on you and your Moscow friends. Indeed, you seem yourselves conscious that you are all Onyegins, *i.e.* that you and your friends are all in negation, in doubt, in despair. Is it possible to rebuild society on such foundations?

Perhaps what I have said is a commonplace, and you know it better than I do. I write this not for the sake of argument, not to begin a controversy, but I thought myself bound to make this criticism, because sometimes the noblest minds and best hearts are mistaken in their fundamental principle, without themselves being aware of it. So I write this to you to show how attentively I have read your book, and to give you a fresh proof of the respect and love which, etc. V. PETCHERIN.

To this I answered him in Russian:

25 EUSTON SQUARE,
April 21, 1853.

HONOURED FELLOW-COUNTRAYMAN,—I thank you most sincerely for your letter, and ask your leave to say a few words *à la hâte*, on the principal points of it.

I entirely agree with you that literature like the flowers of autumn appears in all its brilliance before the downfall of states. Ancient Rome could not be saved by the witty phrases of Cicero, nor by his thin morality, nor by the Voltairianism of Lucian, nor the German philosophy of Proclus; but note that it could not be saved by the Eleusinian mysteries either, nor by Apollonius of Tyana, nor all the efforts to prolong and revive paganism.

It was not only impossible but useless. There was no need to save the ancient world, it had outlived its age, and a new world had risen up to take its place. Europe is precisely in the same position; literature and philosophy are not preserving its decrepit forms, but thrusting them into the tomb, breaking them up, setting us free from them.

The new world is approaching exactly as it was then. Do not think that I have been inconsistent in calling the phalanstery a barracks; no, all doctrines and schools of socialists that have appeared hitherto, from Saint-

Simon to Proudhon, who stands for nothing but negation, are poor, they are the first murmur, the first spelling out word by word, they are the Therapeutes and the Essenes of the ancient East. But who has not a foreboding, a glimpse of the vast issues that are dimly apparent through those one-sided efforts, and who would punish children because their teeth are cut with difficulty or come through irregularly?

The despondency of modern life is the despondency of the twilight, of transition, of forebodings. Animals are uneasy before an earthquake.

Nothing has got beyond that point. Some try to force open the door to the future, others forcibly prevent the past from going; some look to prophecies, others to memories, their work consists in hindering each other, and both alike are stuck in the bog.

Beside it is another world—Russia. Its foundation is a communistic peasantry still slumbering, with a surface scum of cultivated people reduced to the condition of Onyegin, to despair, to exile, to your fate and to mine. It is a bitter lot for us. We are victims of the fact that we are born out of our right time. For our cause that makes no difference; at any rate, it has not the same importance.

Speaking of the revolutionary movement in new Russia, I have said that from Peter the Great Russian history is the history of the nobility and of the Government. The revolutionary ferment is found in the nobility; though in Russia it has had no outlet—open, active, in the market-place—no outlet except the literary career; there too I have tracked it.

I have had the boldness to say in my letter to Michelet that cultured Russians are the most emancipated of men; we. have gone incomparably further in negation than, for instance, the French. In negation of what? Of the old world, of course.

Together with his idle despair Onyegin now is arriving at positive hopes. You have perhaps not noticed them. Abjuring Europe in its effete form, abjuring Petersburg, which is Europe again but adapted to our manners, weak and cut off from the people, we have perished. But little by little something new, grotesque in Gogol, exaggerated in the Panslavists, has been developing. This new element is the element of faith in the strength of the people, a faith full of love. With it we have begun to understand the peasantry. But we are far away from them. I am not saying that it will be our lot to re-create Russia; we must be thankful to have welcomed the common people, and to have divined that the new world belongs to them.

One word more. I am not confounding science with literary and philosophical culture. Science, if it does not re-create a state, does not really decline with it. It is a means, it is the memory of the human race, it is its conquest over Nature, its emancipation. Ignorance, ignorance alone is the cause of pauperism and slavery. The masses have been left by their educators in the condition of cattle. Science, nothing but science, can correct that now and give them bread and shelter. Not through propaganda but through chemistry, mechanics, technology, railways, it may restore the brain which has been cramped morally and physically for ages.

I shall be truly delighted, *et cetera*.

A fortnight later, I received the following letter from Father Petcherin:

J.M.J.A., ST. MARY'S, CLAPHAM,
May 3, 1853.

I answer you in French for reasons of which you are aware. I could not write to you before, I was burdened with duties in Guernsey: one has little time for philosophical theory when one lives in the midst of a reality pulsating with life; one has no leisure to settle speculative problems of the future destiny of mankind when mankind in flesh and blood comes to pour out its sorrows on one's bosom, and to beg for advice and help.

I must frankly confess that your last letter filled me with horror, and a very egoistic horror I must admit.

What will happen to us when your culture (*votre civilisation à vous*) gains the day? For your science is everything, alpha and omega. Not that broad science which embraces all the faculties of man, everything visible and invisible, science as it has been understood by the world hitherto, but a limited, narrow science which analyses and dissects matter, and knows of nothing else. Chemistry, mechanics, technology, steam, electricity—the great science of eating and drinking, the worship of the individual (*le culte de la personne*) as Michel Chevalier would have said! Woe to us if *that* science triumphs! In the days of their persecution by the Roman Emperors Christians had at least the possibility of flight into the wilderness of Egypt, the sword of the tyrants was checked at that boundary which they could not pass. But whither can one flee from the tyranny of your material civilisation? It levels mountains, excavates canals, lays down railways, sends steamers; its newspapers penetrate to the burning wastes of Africa, to the pathless forests of America. As once Christians were dragged into the amphitheatres to be exposed to the jeers of the crowd greedy for spectacles, so now they will drag us men of prayer and silence into the public market-place, and there ask: 'Why do you flee from our society? You ought to take part in our materialistic life, in our trade, in our marvellous industry. Go, make speeches in the market-place, go and preach political economy, deliberate on the fall and rise of the exchange. Go and preside at our feasts, paradise is here on earth—let us eat and drink, for to-morrow we die!' That is what moves me to horror, for where are we to find a refuge from the tyranny of matter, which is gaining more and more mastery of all?

Forgive me if I have somewhat exaggerated the gloomy colours of my picture; it seems to me that I have only carried the foundations laid by you to their legitimate conclusion. I should not have left Russia for an intellectual caprice (*caprice de spiritualite*). Russia has indeed begun with science as you understand it, and she is continuing with it. She holds in her hands the gigantic lever of material power. She calls all talents to serve her and to celebrate her material prosperity. She will become the most cultured country in the world. Providence has allotted to her the material world; she will make a paradise of it for her elect. She understands civilisation just as you understand it, the science of the material has always been her strength. But we who have faith in an immortal soul and a future life, what have we to do with this civilisation of the present minute? Russia will never have me for its subject.

I have propounded my views with simplicity, to make our position clear to each other. Forgive me if I put too much heat into my words. As I am going back to Ireland on Friday morning it will be impossible for me to come to you, but I shall be very glad if it will suit you to visit me on Wednesday or on Thursday after dinner.
—Receive, etc. V. PETCHERIN.

I answered him next day.

25 EUSTON SQUARE,
May 4, 1853.

HONOURED FELLOW-COUNTRAYMAN,—I went to see you to press the hand of a Russian whose name was familiar to me and whose position was so like my own. . . . Although life and convictions have put you among the triumphant ranks of the conquerors and me in the melancholy camps of the vanquished, I had no thought of touching upon the difference of our opinions. My wish was to see a Russian, my wish was to bring you living news of your native land. From a sense of delicacy I did not offer you my pamphlets, it was your own wish to see them. Hence your letter, my answer, and your second letter of the 3rd of May; you attack me, my opinions (exaggerated and not fully held by me), I cannot but defend myself. I only wrote to you that I reckon the sum total of our conquests over Nature and of all our culture, of course, entirely outside the domain of *belles lettres* and abstract philosophy.

But this is a lengthy subject, and I have no desire without special provocation to repeat everything that has so many times been said about it. Allow me rather to reassure you in regard to your anxiety about the future of men who love the contemplative life. Science is not a special school or doctrine, and so it can become neither a government, an arbitrary law, nor a persecution. You probably meant to speak of social ideas, of freedom. In that case, take the most 'materialistic' and 'most free' country, England. Men of the contemplative life as well as the advocates of a Utopia find in it a nook for tranquil reflection and a platform for preaching their doctrines. And yet England, a Protestant monarchy, is very far from complete tolerance.

And what is there to fear? The rumble of the wheels bringing bread to the hungry, half-clad crowd? We do not forbid men to thrash corn for fear they should disturb our poetic tranquillity.

There will always and everywhere be contemplative natures; there will be more freedom for them both as to thought and stillness; let them find themselves a quiet spot; no one will disturb and no one will summon them, no one will persecute them, no one will either oppress them or support them. I imagine it is wrong to be afraid of improving the life of the masses because the process of improving it may grate upon the ears of men who do not want to hear anything external. No one asks even for self-denial, for kindness, for sacrifice in this case. If it is noisy in the market-place you should not carry your wares there but go away from it. But the newspapers follow us everywhere—what contemplative nature is dependent for happiness on the first edition in Paris or the first edition in London?

But, you see, if instead of freedom the anti-materialistic and monarchial principles triumph, then it will be hard for us to find a place, not where we may rest undisturbed, but where we may escape the hangings, burnings, and torturings which are still to be found to some extent in Rome and Milan, in France and Russia.

Which then need feel afraid? Of course, death is of no consequence *sub specie aeternitatis*, but from that point of view, you know, everything else is of no consequence either.

Forgive me, honoured fellow-countryman, for my frank opposition to what you say, and consider that I could make no other answer.

My warmest good wishes that you may have a good journey to Ireland.

With that our correspondence ended.

Two years passed. The grey fog on the European horizon was lighted up by the glare of the Crimean War ar which made its darkness blacker than ever, and all at once, among the bloody news of campaigns and sieges, I read in the newspapers that somewhere in Ireland the Reverend Father Vladimir Petcherin had been brought up for trial for publicly burning a Protestant Bible in the market-place. The haughty British judge, taking into consideration the senselessness of the action and the fact that the prisoner was a Russian, confined himself to a paternal exhortation to a greater propriety of behaviour in the streets for the future. . . .

Can those chains weigh lightly upon him . . . or does he often take off his biretta and lay it wearily on the table?

3
THREE TRIALS

I

THE DUEL

In 1853 the celebrated communist Willich introduced me to a Parisian workman called Emanuel Barthélemy. I knew his name before from the June trial, from his sentence, and finally from his escape from Belle-Île.

He was a young man, short, but of a muscularly powerful build; his pitch-black curly hair gave him a Southern look; his face, slightly marked with smallpox, was clear-cut and handsome. Continual conflict had aroused in him an inflexible will and the power of directing it. Barthélemy was one of the most single-minded natures which it has been my lot to meet. Of bookish school education he had none except in his own line: he was an excellent mechanic. We may note in passing that it was from the ranks of the mechanics, machinists, engineers, and railway workers that the most resolute fighters on the June barricades came.

The thought of his life, the passion of his whole existence was an unflagging thirst like that of Spartacus for the revolt of the working people against the middle classes. This idea was in him inseparable from a savage desire to massacre the bourgeois.

What a commentary that man furnished me on the horrors of 1793 and 1794, on the days of September, on the hatred with which the parties nearest of kin destroyed each other! In him I saw face to face how a man can combine a thirst for blood with humanity in other relations, even with tenderness, and how a man may be at peace with his own conscience while like Saint-Just sending dozens of men to the guillotine.

'That the revolution may not be for the tenth time stolen out of our hands,' Barthélemy would say,' we must crush our worst foe at home, in our own family. At the counter, in the office, we always find him—it's in our own camp we ought to destroy him!' On his proscription lists were the names of almost all the refugees: Victor Hugo, Mazzini, Victor Schœlcher,[1] and Kossuth. He made very few exceptions; among them, I remember, was Louis Blanc. The peculiar object of his most genuine hatred was Ledru-Rollin. The keen, passionate but extremely composed face of Barthélemy would twitch convulsively when he spoke of 'the dictator of the bourgeoisie.'

He talked in a masterly fashion, a talent that is growing more and more rare. Public speakers in Paris, and still more in England, are endless in number. Priests, lawyers, members of parliament, men selling pills or cheap pencils, hired orators—secular and spiritual—in the parks, they all have a wonderful faculty for preaching, but very few can talk for the benefit of a room.

Barthélemy's one-sided logic, continually turned in one direction, acted like the flame of a blowpipe. He spoke smoothly without raising his voice or gesticulating; his choice of words, his sentences were correct, pure, and completely free from the three curses of modern French, revolutionary jargon, legal expressions and the easy familiarity of shop-boys.

[1] Schœlcher, Victor (1804-1893), was a French politician and writer, author of Histoire des Crimes de 2 décembre, etc.—(*Translator's Note.*)

Where had this workman, brought up in the stifling foundries where iron was forged and wrought for machines, in stifling Parisian alleys, between the pot-house and the forge, in prison and in penal servitude—where had he gained his true conception of beauty and proportion, of tact and grace—a conception lost by bourgeois France? How had he managed to preserve the unaffected naturalness of his language among the frigid rhetoricians, the Gascons of revolutionary babble?

It is indeed a puzzle.

It seems as though the atmosphere must be fresher about the workshops. Here is his life, however.

He was not yet twenty when he was mixed up in some *émeute* in the time of Louis-Philippe. A gendarme stopped him, and as he began to say something the gendarme gave him a punch in the face with his fist. Barthélemy, who was being held by a *municipal*, tore himself away, but could do nothing. This blow awakened the tiger in him. Barthélemy—an eager, good-humoured young working lad—got up the next day transformed.

It must be observed that though Barthélemy was arrested the police released him, finding him not guilty. As for the outrage done him, no one cared to discuss it. 'What do you want to run about the streets for when there is an *émeute* going on? Besides, how could we find the gendarme now?'

So there it was. Barthélemy bought a pistol, loaded it and took to sauntering about that part of the town; he hung about for a day or two, when all at once he saw the gendarme standing at the corner. Barthélemy turned away and cocked his pistol. 'Do you recognise me?' he asked the police officer. 'I should think I do.' 'Then you remember how you . . .?' 'Come, go along, go on your way,' said the gendarme. '*Bon voyage* to you too,' said Barthélemy, and pulled the trigger. The gendarme fell, and Barthélemy walked away. The gendarme was mortally wounded, but did not die on the spot.

Barthélemy was tried for simple murder. No one took into consideration the greatness of the insult—especially according to French ideas—the impossibility of a workman sending a challenge, the impossibility of taking legal proceedings. Barthélemy was condemned to penal servitude. This was the third school in which he was trained after the forge and the prison. When Crémieux, the Minister of Justice after the February revolution, revised sentences, Barthélemy was released.

The days of June came. Barthélemy, one of the most ardent followers of Louis Blanc, showed himself then in his full strength.

He was seized while heroically defending a barricade and carried off to the forts. Some of the victims were shot on the spot, others were crowded into the cellars of the Tuileries, while others were sent to the forts and were there sometimes shot casually, more to make room than for any other reason.

Barthélemy survived; at his trial he did not dream of defending himself, but turned the prisoner's dock into a platform from which to attack the National Guard. To him we are indebted for many details of the exploits that the guardians of order performed in secret, privately as it were. Several times the president commanded him to be silent, and at last cut short his speech with a sentence of penal servitude for fifteen or twenty years if I remember right (I have not the record of the proceedings before my eyes).

Barthélemy was sent with others to Belle-Île.

Two years later he escaped and turned up in London with a plan for going back there and arranging the escape of six of the prisoners. The small sum of money which he asked for (six or seven thousand francs) was promised, and disguised as an abbé, with a breviary in his hand, he went to Paris and to Belle-Île, arranged everything, and came back to London for the money. I am told that the plan was not carried out on account of a dispute whether Blanqui was to be released or not. The partisans of Barbès and others chose rather to leave several friends in prison than to release one enemy.

Barthélemy went away to Switzerland. He disagreed with all the parties and cut himself off from them; to the followers of Ledru-Rollin he was a sworn foe, but he was not friendly with his own side; he was too curt and angular, his extreme opinions were unpleasant to the 'leaders' and scared the weak. In Switzerland he devoted himself to the manufacture of arms. He invented a special make of gun, which was loaded as it was fired and in that way enabled a succession of bullets to be shot off at the same target one after another. With this weapon he dreamed of killing Napoleon III., but Barthélemy's wild passions on two occasions saved Buonaparte from the man whose determination was no less than Orsini's.

In Ledru-Rollin's party there was a desperate character—a duellist, rake and scapegrace called Cournet.

Cournet was one of that special class who are often met with among Polish Pans and Russian officers, particularly among retired cornets living in the country; to it belonged Denis Davydov and his boon companion Burtsov, Gagarin— 'the skull and cross bones'—and Lensky's second, Zaryetsky. In a vulgar form they are met with among the Prussian *Junkers* and in the Austrian barracks. In England they do not exist at all; in France such a man is at home, he is like a fish in water, but a fish with polished, varnished scales. These men are brave, reckless to the point of insolence and senselessness, and very dull-witted. They live all their lives on the memory of two or three incidents in which they have passed through fire and water, have sliced off somebody's ears, have stood under a shower of bullets. It sometimes happens that they have first bragged of some daring action and have then really performed it to prove their words. They are dimly conscious that their recklessness is their strength, the only point of interest of which they can boast, and they have a mortal passion for boasting. With all that, they are often good comrades, especially in good-humoured talk, and will stand up manfully for their own side till the first tiff with the latter; altogether they have more military daring than civic courage.

Idlers, reckless gamblers at cards and in life, *Lanzknechts* of every desperate enterprise, particularly if it is possible to put on a uniform with the gold lace of a general, and to get money and decorations—and afterwards to settle down again for some years in a billiard-room or a café. And whether it is in helping Napoleon in Strasbourg, or the Duchess of Berry in Blois, or the red republic in the Faubourg St. Antoine, they do not care. . . . For them and for all France bravery and success cover everything.

Cournet had begun his career in the fleet during the quarrel between France and Portugal. With a handful of comrades he crept on to a Portuguese frigate, overpowered the crew and took the frigate. This incident determined and concluded Cournet's future life. All France was talking of this young midshipman; he went no further, and ended his career with the exploit with which he began it, as completely as though he had been killed in it. Later on he was expelled from the fleet. Profound peace reigned in Europe. Cournet was bored to death and began fighting on his own account. He used to say that he had fought twenty duels; we may suppose that he had fought ten, and that is quite enough to show that he could not be considered a rational man.

How he came to be a red republican I cannot tell.

He played no particular part among the French refugees. Various anecdotes were told about him, such as that he had belaboured a police officer who had tried to arrest him in Belgium and got away, and other pranks of the same kind.

He considered himself one of the foremost swordsmen in France.

The gloomy courage of Barthélemy, who was full of an unbridled *amour-propre* of his own sort, in contact with the arrogant valour of Cournet, was bound to lead to disaster. They were jealous of each other. But belonging to different circles, to hostile parties, they might all their lives have avoided a meeting. Kind friends with brotherly zeal helped to bring it about.

Barthélemy had a grudge against Cournet on account of letters sent to him through Cournet from France which had never reached him. It is very probable that Cournet was not to blame in this matter; gossip was soon added to this grievance. Barthélemy had in Switzerland become acquainted with an actress, an Italian girl, and was living with her. 'What a pity,' Cournet said, 'that this most socialist of socialists should have let an actress keep him!' Barthélemy's friends promptly wrote to him of this saying. On getting the letter, Barthélemy threw up his work on the gun, and his actress, and galloped off to London.

I have already mentioned that he was acquainted with Willich. The latter was a pure-hearted and very good-natured man, a Prussian artillery officer; he had gone over to the side of the revolution and become a communist. He had fought at Baden for the people, being in control of the artillery during Hecker's insurrection, and when everything was crushed he went to England. He arrived in England without a halfpenny, and tried to give lessons in mathematics and German, but he had no luck. He gave up his school-books, and

THE CHALLENGE

regardless of his previous rank as an officer heroically became a workman. With some comrades he set up a workshop for making brooms and brushes. They did not meet with support. Willich did not lose hope either of the resurrection of Germany or of the improvement in his own fortunes; the latter, however, did not improve, and he carried his hopes of a Teutonic republic with him to New York, where he obtained a post as a government surveyor.

Willich perceived that the business with Cournet was taking a very unfortunate turn, and offered his services as a mediator. Barthélemy had the fullest confidence in Willich, and put his case in his hands. Willich went to see Cournet. The Prussian's firm, quiet tone had an effect on the *'premiere épée'*; he explained the matter of the letters; then in answer to Willich's question, whether he believed that Barthélemy was being kept by an actress, Cournet said that he had repeated a rumour, and that he regretted it.

'That,' said Willich, 'is quite enough. Write what you have said on paper, give it me, and I shall go home truly delighted.'

'If you like,' said Cournet, and took up the pen.

'So you are going to apologise to a fellow like Barthélemy,' observed another refugee, who had come in at the end of the conversation.

'Apologise? Why, do you take this for an apology?'

'For the act of an honest man,' said Willich, 'who having repeated a slander regrets it.'

'No,' said Cournet, flinging down the pen, 'that I cannot do.'

'Didn't you say so just now?'

'No, no, pardon me, but I cannot. Tell Barthélemy that "I said that because I chose to say it."'

'Bravissimo!' cried the other refugee.

'On you, *monsieur*, rests the responsibility for the

misfortunes that will follow,' Willich said to him, and went away.

This happened in the evening; he came to me before he had yet seen Barthélemy; he walked mournfully up and down the room, saying: 'Now a duel is inevitable. What a misfortune that that refugee was present!'

'There is no helping things now,' I thought. 'Reason is silent before the wild flare of passions, and when one adds to that French blood, the hatred of coteries and of different members of the chorus in the amphitheatre . . .!'

Two days later I was walking along Pall Mall in the morning; Willich was striding rapidly along. I stopped him; pale and agitated he turned to me.

'What is it?'

'Killed outright.'

'Who?'

'Cournet. I am running to Louis Blanc for advice what to do.'

'Where is Barthélemy?'

'He and his second and Cournet's seconds are in prison. Only one of the seconds was not arrested; by the English law Barthélemy may be hanged.'

Willich got on to an omnibus and was carried off. I was left in the street. I stood pondering, then turned and went home again.

Two days later Willich came to me. Louis Blanc had of course taken an active interest in the matter and had tried to consult some well-known lawyers. It had been thought best to put the matter so that it should not be known who fired and who was a witness. To do this it was necessary that both sides should say the same thing. All were persuaded that the English judge would not care to set police traps in the case of a duel.

This had to be conveyed to Cournet's friends, but none of Willich's acquaintances visited them nor Ledru-

Rollin. He therefore sent me to Mazzini. I found him in great irritation.

'I suppose you have come,' he said, 'about this murder.' I looked at him, paused with intention and then said, 'About the case of Barthélemy.'

'You know him, you are standing up for him; that's all very well, though I don't understand it. . . . Cournet, poor Cournet had friends too. . . .'

'Who probably did not call him a criminal for having taken part in twenty duels, in which apparently it was not he that was killed.'

'Is this the time to recall that?'

'I spoke in answer to you.'

'Well, now is *he* to be saved from the gallows?'

'I imagine that no one will feel any particular pleasure at the hanging of a man who behaved as Barthélemy did at the June barricades. Anyway, it is not a question of him alone, but also of Cournet's seconds.'

'He won't be hanged.'

'There is no telling,' a young English radical with his hair done *à la Jésus* observed coolly. He had not spoken till then, but had approved Mazzini's words with the motion of his head, the smoke of his cigar, and with indistinct polyphones in which two or three vowels flattened together made up a single sound.

'Apparently you have nothing against it?'

'We like and respect our law.'

'Is not that,' I observed, giving a good-natured air to my words, 'the reason why all other peoples respect England more than they like Englishmen?'

'*Oeua*?' inquired the radical, or perhaps it was an answer.

'What is the point?' Mazzini interrupted. I told him.

'They have already thought of that themselves and have reached the same conclusion.'

The trial of Barthélemy is extremely interesting. Rarely have the French and English characters revealed themselves in such close juxtaposition, and in such striking contrast.

Everything was absurd about the duel, beginning with the spot chosen for it: they fought near Windsor. To do so they had to go by train (which goes only to Windsor) some dozens of miles away from the coast into the heart of the country, whereas people usually fight duels near the frontier, where ships, boats, etc., are in readiness. The choice of Windsor was moreover unsuitable in itself. The Queen's palace, the favourite residence of Queen Victoria, is of course guarded by the police with double vigilance. I imagine that this place was chosen very simply because of all the suburbs of London the French only know of two: *Richemon'* and *Vinssour*.

To be ready for any emergency the seconds took rapiers with sharpened points, although they knew the duel was to be fought with pistols. When Cournet fell, all, with the exception of one second who went off by himself, and consequently managed to make his way quietly to Belgium, returned together, not forgetting to take their rapiers with them. When they reached Waterloo Station in London the police had been warned by telegraph long before. There was no need for the police to search. 'Four men with beards and moustaches, wearing caps, speaking French and carrying rapiers,' were arrested as they stepped out of the railway carriage.

How could all this happen? It is not for us, I imagine, to teach the French how to hide from the police. There is no police in the world more vicious, alert, immoral and indefatigable in its zeal than the French. In the days of Louis-Philippe both the seeker and the sought played their parts in masterly style,

ARREST

every move was calculated; now that is not necessary —the police in the Russian style say 'check' and 'mate' as they move—but Louis-Philippe's reign is not so far away. How could a man so intelligent as Barthélemy and men so experienced as Cournet's seconds have made so many blunders?

The explanation is the same in both cases, absolute ignorance of England and English law. They had heard that no one could be arrested without a '*óurrand*'; they had heard of a mysterious '*abéass korpu*' by virtue of which a man must be released on the demand of a lawyer, and imagined that they would go home, change their clothes and be in Belgium when next morning the disconcerted constable would come to fetch them, and that he would infallibly be armed with a staff (as described in French novels), and would say on seeing they were gone, '*Goddam!*' All this in spite of the fact that constables do not carry staves nor Englishmen say '*Goddam!*'

The prisoners were lodged in the Surrey prison. Then began visits to them; ladies went to see them, and friends of the deceased Cournet went to see them. The police, of course, at once perceived the state of the case and how it had happened, though indeed one cannot give them much credit for that; the friends and enemies of Barthélemy and Cournet talked at the tops of their voices in restaurants and public-houses about every detail of the duel, adding of course many which had not taken place and could not possibly have taken place. But officially the police refused to know this, so when some visitors asked permission to see Coumet's second, and others asked to see Barthélemy's second, the police officer went so far as to say to them: 'Gentlemen, we have no knowledge who are seconds and who are principals; the investigation has not yet discovered all the details of the case. Please call your friends by their names.' The first lesson!

At last the Assizes came to Surrey, and a day was fixed on which the Lord Chief Justice Campbell would try the case concerning a Frenchman, Cournet, murdered by some one unknown, and concerning the persons connected with his murder.

I was then living near Primrose Hill; at seven o'clock on a cold and foggy February morning I went out into Regent's Park to cross it on my way to the railway station.

That day has remained very vivid in my memory. From the fog that covered the park and the white swans drowsily floating on the water, shrouded in a reddish-yellow smoke, up to the minute when, long after midnight, I sat with one of the lawyers at Verrey's in Regent Street, and drank the health of England in champagne. It is as clear as though it were before my eyes.

I had never seen an English court before; the comicality of the mediaeval *mise en scène* awakens in us rather thoughts of an *opéra bouffe* than of an honourable tradition, but that could be forgotten on that day.

About ten o'clock the first masqueraders, heralds with two trumpeters, appeared before the hotel in which Lord Campbell was staying, announcing that Lord Campbell would judge such and such a case in the open court at ten o'clock. We rushed to the doors of the court, which was a few steps away; meanwhile, in a gilt carriage, Lord Campbell moved across the square, wearing a wig which was only surpassed in size and beauty by the wig of his coachman, upon which was perched a minute three-cornered hat. Behind his carriage walked some twenty attorneys and solicitors, picking up their gowns and wearing no hats, but instead woollen wigs made intentionally as little like human hair as possible. At the door I almost found myself before the bar at which the Lord was judging Cournet instead of that where Lord Chief Justice Campbell was trying Barthélemy.

In the very doorway the mass of people pressed back

THE TRIAL

by the police from the court and the superhuman crush from behind caused a stoppage: it was impossible to go forward while the crowd kept increasing behind; the police, weary of half measures, joined hands and advanced to a united attack—the front rank so squeezed me that I could hardly breathe—another assault of the besiegers, and we found ourselves pressed out, thrown out some ten paces beyond the doors into the street.

Had it not been for a lawyer of my acquaintance we should not have got in at all, the court was packed full; he took us in by a special door, and at last we were seated, mopping our faces and looking to see if our watches and our money were still on us.

It is a remarkable thing that nowhere is there a crowd so numerous, so close-packed, so terrible as in London, and it never in any case knows how to form a queue; the English always behave with their national obstinacy, they will go on pressing forward for two hours, and at last they arrive somewhere.

I have many times marvelled at the entrances to the theatres; if people would go in one behind the other, they could certainly enter in half an hour, but as they all press forward in one mass, the majority of those in front are thrust aside to the right and the left of the door, and there they are overtaken by a sort of concentrated exasperation, and begin squeezing from the sides on the slowly advancing stream in the middle with no profit whatever to themselves, but as it were avenging their ill luck on the others' ribs.

There is a knocking on the door. A gentleman, also in masquerade attire, shouts, 'Who is there?' 'The Judge,' is answered on the other side; the doors are flung open, and Campbell enters, wearing a fur coat and something like a lady's dressing-gown; he bowed to all four quarters of the compass and announced that the Assizes were opened.

The opinion of Barthélemy's case formed by the judge, that is, by Campbell, was clear from beginning to end, and he retained it in spite of all the efforts of the French to turn it aside and change it for the worse. There had been a duel. One man had been killed. Both were Frenchmen, refugees, having different ideas of honour from ours; it was difficult to make out which of them was in the right, which in the wrong. One had fought in the barricades, the other was a notorious duellist. We could not leave this crime unpunished, but we ought not to use the whole force of the English law to crush foreigners, especially as they were all straightforward people and had behaved honourably though stupidly. Therefore we shall not inquire who is the murderer; in all probability the murderer is the one who has escaped to Belgium; we charge the prisoners at the bar with being accomplices and ask the jury whether they are guilty of manslaughter or not. If found guilty by the jury, they are in our hands; we shall condemn them to one of the lightest possible punishments, and that will be the end of the case. If the jury acquit them, we have nothing more to say to them, let them go wherever they choose.

All this was a knife in the heart of the French of both parties! The partisans of Cournet wanted to seize the opportunity of ruining Barthélemy in the opinion of the court, and, without directly mentioning him, indicated him as the murderer of Cournet.

Some of Barthélemy's friends and he himself sought to cover Cournet and company with shame and ignominy through a strange fact which had been discovered during the course of the police investigation. The pistols had been procured from a gunmaker, and after the duel they were sent back to him. One pistol was found to be loaded. At the trial the gunmaker appeared with the pistol and gave evidence that a little rag had been put in under the bullet and gunpowder, so that it would not have gone off.

What had happened at the duel was this: Cournet fired at Barthélemy and did not hit him. The cap of Barthélemy's pistol snapped in the usual way, but no shot followed. He was given another cap, but the same thing happened. Then Barthélemy flung down his pistol and offered Cournet to fight with rapiers. Cournet refused. It was decided to fire again, but Barthélemy asked for another pistol, to which Cournet at once agreed. The pistol was given him, a shot rang out and Cournet fell dead.

So the pistol that was taken to the gunmaker's loaded was the very one which had been in Barthélemy's hands. How had the rag got into it? The pistols had been procured by a friend of Cournet's, Pardigan,[1]

---

[1] Pardigan was seized during the June days and flung into one of the cellars of the Tuileries; there were as many as five thousand men in them. Among them there were the wounded, the cholera-stricken and the dying. When the Government sent Cormenin to investigate their condition, he and the doctors sprang back at the stifling pestilential stench. The prisoners had been forbidden to approach the tiny windows of the soupirail. Pardigan, almost swooning for want of air, stretched up his head to breathe at one of them; a sentinel of the National Guard noticed this and told him to move away or he would shoot him. Pardigan did not do so at once, and the worthy bourgeois let fly a shot at him; the bullet tore his lower jaw and part of his cheek away, and he fell. In the evening, some of the prisoners were taken to the forts; among them they lifted up the wounded man, bound his hands and led him away.

On their way the famous panic in the Place du Carrousel occurred, in which the National Guards fired at one another in terror; the wounded Pardigan dropped, exhausted; he was flung on the floor in the police guard-house and remained with his hands bound, lying on his back, swallowing the blood from his wound. So he was found by a Polytechnic student, who swore at the cannibals and made them carry the sick man to the hospital. I have described this incident in my *Letters from France and Italy* . . . but there is no harm in repeating it, that men may not forget what the cultured Parisian bourgeoisie was like. —(*Author's Note.*)

a man who had once been on the staff of the *Voix du Peuple* and had been terribly disfigured in the June Days.

If it could have been proved that the rag had been put in intentionally, that is, that Barthélemy's enemies were taking him to be murdered, they would have been covered with ignominy and ruined for ever and ever. For this agreeable result Barthélemy would willingly have accepted ten years' penal servitude or deportation.

On investigation it appeared that the rag taken out of the pistol really had belonged to Pardigan. It had been torn off the duster with which he used to rub his patent-leather boots. Pardigan said that he had been cleaning the barrel by putting a rag on the end of a pencil, and that possibly as it was turned round on it a bit was torn off, but Barthélemy's friends asked why was the rag of a regular oval shape, why was it not crumpled up or tattered? . . .

Barthélemy's enemies for their part had prepared a perfect legion of witnesses *à déckarge* for the benefit of Baronée and his comrades; their policy was that the attorney on Baronée's side should question them about the antecedents of Cournet and the others. They would sing their praises, but would say nothing about Barthélemy and his seconds. Such unanimous silence on the part of fellow-countrymen and co-religionists must, so they thought, highly recommend the one side in the eyes of Campbell and the public, and discredit the other. Calling witnesses costs money; moreover, Barthélemy had not a whole legion of friends to whom he could give the order to say one thing or another.

Cournet's friends had succeeded in being eloquently silent already at the police investigation.

Baronée, one of the arrested witnesses, was asked whether he knew who had killed Cournet, or whom he suspected. Baronée replied that no threat, no punishment could prevail upon him to say who had deprived Cournet of life, although the dead man had been his best friend.

'If I should have to languish in chains for ten years in a noisome dungeon, even then I would not tell it.'

The solicitor cut him short with the cool observation: 'Well, you have a perfect right to refuse to answer, but you prove from your words that you know the guilty party.'

And with all that they wanted to delude—whom? —Lord Campbell? I should like to append his portrait, to show the full measure of the absurdity of the attempt. Lord Campbell, who had grown old and wrinkled, sitting in his judicial armchair, reading in an indifferent voice with a Scotch accent the most terrible *évidence*, and unravelling the most complex cases with convincing clearness—was to be deluded by a handful of Parisian *clubistes*! . . . Lord Campbell, who never raises his voice, never loses his temper, never smiles, goes no further at the most absurd or critical moments than blowing his nose. . . . Lord Campbell with the face of a peevish old woman, in which if you look intently you can clearly discern the celebrated metamorphosis that so unpleasantly surprised Little Red Riding Hood; you see that it is not grandmamma, but a wolf in a wig, a woman's dressing-gown and a fur-trimmed cape.

But his lordship paid them back with interest.

After long discussions concerning the rag and after Pardigan's evidence, Baronée's counsel began to call witnesses.

First, an old refugee who had been a comrade of Barbès and Blanqui stood up. To begin with, he took the Bible with a certain air of repugnance, then made a gesture, as though to say, well, come what may—took the oath and craned his neck forward.

'Have you long been acquainted with Cournet?' one of the lawyers asked him.

'*Citoyen*,' said the refugee in French, 'from the days of my youth, devoted to a single cause, I have given my life to the holy cause of freedom and equality . . .' and was going on in the same strain.

But the lawyer stopped him, and turning to the interpreter, observed: 'The witness has apparently not understood the question. Translate it into French.'

After him followed another. When five or six Frenchmen with beards that would go into a wineglass, bald foreheads, enormous moustaches and hair cropped *à la Nicolas* or falling on their shoulders, and wearing red neckties, had been called, one after another, to repeat variations on the following theme: 'Cournet was a man whose merits surpassed his virtues, though his virtues were equalled by his merits. He was the ornament of the refugee community, the honour of his party, his wife is inconsolable, and his friends are only consoled by the fact that the lives of such men as Baronée and his comrades have been spared.

'And do you know Barthélemy?'

'Yes. He is a French refugee. . . . I have seen him, but I know nothing about him.' With this the witness made a smacking sound with his lips *à la française*.

'Witness So-and-so . . .' said the lawyer.

'Allow me,' observed Grandmamma Campbell in a voice of soft sympathy, 'do not trouble them further. The number of witnesses testifying to the virtues of the deceased Cournet and the accused Baronée seems to us unnecessary and prejudicial, we do not regard either the one or the other as a man of such bad character that his honesty and decent behaviour need be proved with such persistence. Moreover, Cournet is dead, and we have no occasion to inquire anything about him. We are called upon to judge nothing but the manner of his murder; everything relating to that crime is of importance for us, but there is no necessity for us to hear incidents in the past life of the accused, whom we equally accept as very respectable gentlemen. For my part I have no suspicions in regard to Monsieur Baronée.'

'But why have you such sly and laughing eyes, Grandmamma?'

'Because I cannot laugh at you with my lips, dear grandchildren, on account of my rank, and so I laugh with my eyes.'

Of course, after that the witnesses with their hair on their shoulders, and those with their hair standing up in a shock, in military uniform, or with a *cache-nez* of all the seven colours of the rainbow, were dismissed unheard.

Then the case made rapid progress.

One of the lawyers for the defence, putting it to the jury that the accused, as foreigners entirely unacquainted with English law, were entitled to every indulgence, added: 'You will hardly believe, gentlemen of the jury, that Monsieur Baronée knew so little of England, that in answer to the question, Do you know who killed Cournet? he answered that if he were to be kept in chains for ten years in a prison dungeon, even then he would not tell the name. You see that Monsieur Baronée has still the most mediaeval ideas about England, since he could imagine that for refusing to answer he could be put into chains and thrown for ten years into prison. I trust,' he added, not restraining his laughter, 'that the unfortunate event through which M. Baronée has been for some months deprived of his liberty has convinced him that prisons in England have somewhat improved since the Middle Ages and are scarcely inferior to the prisons in some other countries. Let us show the accused that our courts of justice, too, are humane and just,' etc., etc.

The jury, one half of whom were foreigners, found the accused guilty.

Then Campbell turned to the prisoners in the dock, reminded them of the seventy of the English law, reminded them that a foreigner when he steps upon English soil enjoys all the rights of an Englishman and must therefore bear an equal responsibility before the law. Then he passed to the difference of national manners and said, finally, that he would not consider it just to punish them with the utmost severity of the law, and therefore condemned them to *two months'* imprisonment.

The public, the common people, the lawyers and all of us were satisfied; a sharp sentence had been expected, and no one had dared to dream of less than three or four years as the minimum.

Who were not satisfied?

The condemned men.

I went up to Barthélemy, he pressed my hand gloomily and said: 'That Pardigan has got off clear, and Baronée . . .' he shrugged his shoulders.

As I was going out of the court I met the lawyer of my acquaintance. He was standing with Baronée.

'I would rather have been sent to prison for a year than mixed up with that scoundrel Barthélemy.'

The case was over by about ten o'clock in the evening. When we reached the railway-station we found crowds of Frenchmen and Englishmen on the platform, loudly and noisily discussing the case. The majority of the French were pleased with the sentence, though they felt that it was not a victory for the other side of the Channel.

In the train the French struck up the Marseillaise.

'Gentlemen,' I said, 'justice before everything. On this occasion let us sing Rule Britannia!' And Rule Britannia we sang!

II

Barthélemy

Two years had passed. Once more Barthélemy stood before Lord Campbell, and this time the stern old man, putting on his black cap, pronounced a different sentence on him.

In 1854 Barthélemy withdrew himself more than ever from every one; for ever busy with something, he showed himself very little—he was preparing something in secret; the people who lived with him knew no more than the rest. I saw him from time to time; he always showed me great sympathy and confidence, but did not say anything special.

All of a sudden there was rumour of a double murder: Barthélemy had killed an obscure Englishman,[1] a small tradesman, and then the policeman who tried to arrest him. There was no kind of explanation, no key to the mystery. Barthélemy stood mute before his judges, remained mute in Newgate. From the very first he admitted the murder of the policeman: for this he could be sentenced to the death penalty, and so he stopped short at that admission—defending, so to speak, *his right* to be hanged for the last murder without reference to the first.

This was what we found out by degrees. Barthélemy was intending to go to Holland. Dressed for the journey with a passport *visa-ed* in one pocket and a revolver in the other, accompanied by the woman with whom he lived, Barthélemy went at ten o'clock in the evening to an Englishman, a maker of soda-water. When he knocked a maid-servant opened the door to

[1] The murdered men were called George Moore and Charles Collard, and were shot at 73 Warren Street, near Fitzroy Square, on December 8, 1854.—(*Translator's Note.*)

him; the man himself invited them into the parlour and after that went with Barthélemy into his own room.

The maid heard the conversation growing louder and passing into abuse; then her master opened the door and thrust Barthélemy out; then Barthélemy took the pistol out of his pocket and fired at him. The man fell dead. Barthélemy rushed away; the terrified Frenchwoman disappeared before he did and was luckier. A policeman who had heard the shot stopped Barthélemy in the street; the latter threatened him with his pistol, but the policeman did not let him go. Barthélemy fired. . . . This time it is more than probable that he did not mean to kill the man, but only to frighten him; but trying to pull away one arm and pressing the pistol with the other hand at such close quarters, he wounded him mortally. Barthélemy set off running, but by then the police had seen him, and he was caught.

Barthélemy's enemies, not concealing their delight, declared that this was simply an act of robbery, that Barthélemy had meant to rob the Englishman. But the tradesman was not at all rich. It is hard to suppose that any man, not utterly mad, would go to commit an act of open robbery in one of the most populous quarters of London, to a house where he was known, at ten o'clock in the evening, accompanied by a woman: and all that to steal a paltry hundred pounds. (That was about what was found in the murdered man's chest.)

Some months previously Barthélemy had opened a workshop for making stained glass with patterns and arabesques, and had printed them by a special process. He had to pay sixty pounds for the patent and wanted fifteen pounds to make up that sum; he borrowed the money from me and repaid it very punctually. It was clear that there was something more in it than simple theft. Barthélemy's ruling idea, his passion, his monomania remained. That he was going to Holland only in order to make his way to Paris was a fact known by many.

Barely three or four men stopped to ponder before this bloody affair; the others were all panic-stricken and turned against Barthélemy. To be hanged in England is not respectable; to have any connection with a man condemned for murder is 'shocking'; his nearest friends drew back in horror.

I was then living in Twickenham. When I came home one evening two refugees were awaiting me: 'We have come to you,' they said, 'to assure you that we have not had the faintest share in Barthélemy's terrible crime; —we had work in common, one has to work with all sorts of men. Now it will be said . . . it will be thought . . .'

'But have you really come all the way from London to Twickenham to tell me that?' I asked.

'Your opinion is of very great value to us.'

'Upon my word, gentlemen! Why, I was a friend of Barthélemy's myself—and worse than you, because I had no work with him; but I am not denying him now. I know nothing about the case, the verdict and the sentence I leave to Lord Campbell, while I weep to think that powers so young and so rich, that a talent that has been so trained by the bitter conflict and hard environment in which he lived—that in the flower of his age he should lose his life at the hand of a hangman.'

The English were impressed by his behaviour in prison: steady, composed, melancholy without despair, firm without *jactance*, he knew that all was over for him, and listened to his sentence with the same immovable composure with which he had once stood under a shower of bullets on the barricades.

He wrote to his father and the girl he loved. I have

read the letter to his father: not a high-flown sentence, the utmost simplicity; he tries gently to comfort the old man, as though he were not speaking of himself.

The Catholic priest who *ex officio* visited him in his prison, an intelligent and kind-hearted man, took the greatest interest in him and even petitioned Palmerston for a commutation of the sentence, but Palmerston refused. The priest's conversations with Barthélemy were gentle and full of humane feeling on both sides. Barthélemy wrote to him, 'I am very grateful to you for your kind words, for your consolations. If I could have been turned into a believer, you only could have converted me; but what is to be done? I have no faith!' After his death the priest wrote to a lady of my acquaintance: 'What a man that unhappy Barthélemy was! Had he lived longer, his heart might have been opened to grace. I pray for his soul!'

I dwell on this story partly because *The Times* related with malicious spite Barthélemy's mockery at the sheriff.

A few hours before he was hanged, one of the sheriffs, learning that Barthélemy had refused spiritual ministrations, thought it his duty to turn him into the path of salvation, and began plying him with the pietistic twaddle printed in English halfpenny tracts and given away freely at the street corners. Barthélemy was bored by the exhortations of the sheriff; the apostle in the gold chain observed this and, assuming a solemn air, said to him: 'Only think, young man, that in a few hours you will be answering not me but God.'

'And what do you think?' Barthélemy asked. 'Does God speak French? If He doesn't I shan't be able to answer Him.'

The sheriff turned pale with indignation, and his pallor and indignation passed through the sighs and smiles of all the sheriffs, mayors and aldermen seated in the court, until it reached the immense sheets of *The Times*.

But no proselytising sheriff prevented Barthélemy from dying in that grave and nervously exalted spirit which he sought and which it is so natural to seek in the last hours of life. The sentence was read. Barthélemy observed to one of his friends that if he was to die he would have preferred to go out quietly, without witnesses, in prison, rather than to be strangled by the hangman in a public place before crowds of people.—'Nothing is easier; to-morrow, next day, I will bring you strychnine.' As though one was not enough, two undertook to do it. By that time he was guarded as a condemned criminal, that is, very strictly; nevertheless, a few days later his friends obtained strychnine and passed it in to him concealed in his linen. They waited to make sure that he had found it. They were satisfied of this, too. . . .

Afraid of being held responsible, one of them, upon whom suspicion might have fallen, wanted to leave England for a time. He asked me for the loan of a few pounds for the journey; I agreed to give it him. Could anything be simpler? But I mention this insignificant incident to show how every secret plot of the French is discovered, how through their love of a fine *mise en scène* numbers of outsiders are compromised in every affair in which they have a hand.

On Sunday evening there were several people, Italian and other refugees, at my house as usual. There were ladies of the party on that day. We sat down to dinner very late, at eight o'clock. At nine o'clock a man I knew pretty well came in. He used often to come and see me, and so there was nothing striking about his dropping in; but he so distinctly expressed all over his face, 'I am saying nothing,' that my visitors looked at each other.

'Won't you have something to eat or a glass of wine?' I asked.

'No,' said the visitor, sinking into a chair as though weighed down by the burden of his secret.

After dinner, before every one, he called me away into another room and, after telling me that Barthélemy had received the poison (a fact which I knew already), asked me for the money for the man who was leaving England.

'With the greatest pleasure; I will bring it you at once,' I said.

'No. I am staying the night in Twickenham. I shall see you to-morrow morning. I need not tell you —beg you—that no human being . . .'

I smiled.

When I went back into the dining-room a young girl said inquiringly: 'I suppose he had something to tell you about Barthélemy . . .?'

At eight o'clock next morning Francois came in and said that a Frenchman whom he had never seen before insisted upon seeing me.

This was the very friend of Barthélemy who wanted to get away 'unnoticed.' I flung on my overcoat and went out into the garden, where he was waiting for me. There I met a sickly-looking, fearfully thin, black-haired Frenchman (I afterwards learned that he had spent years in Belle-Île, and afterwards had been literally dying of hunger in London). He was wearing a shabby overcoat, which nobody would have noticed; but the travelling cap, the immense scarf wrapped round his neck would have attracted attention in Moscow, in Paris or in Naples.

'What has happened?'

'Has So-and-so been to you?'

'He is here now.'

'Did he speak of the money?'

'That is all settled, the money is ready.'

'I am really very grateful.'

'When are you going?'

'To-day or to-morrow.'

Towards the end of our conversation our common acquaintance joined us. When the would-be traveller had gone: 'Tell me, please, why did he come?' I asked, left alone with my friend.

'For the money.'

'But you could have given it him.'

'That is true, but he wanted to make your acquaintance; he asked me whether you would like it. What could I say?'

'Very much, of course; only I don't know whether he has chosen a good moment.'

'Why, has he hindered you?'

'No; but I hope the police won't hinder his getting away.'

Fortunately this did not occur. While he was on his way his comrade began to have doubts of the poison they had procured; after pondering a little, he gave the remains to his dog. The day passed, the dog was still alive; another passed, still alive Panic-stricken, he rushed off to Newgate, obtained an interview with Barthélemy through a grating and, seizing a favourable moment, whispered to him, 'Have you got it?'

'Yes, yes.'

'Well, you see, I have great doubts. You had better not take it. I have tried it on my dog, it had no effect!'

Barthélemy's head sank—then, raising it with his eyes full of tears, he said: 'What are you doing to me!'

'We will get something else.'

'No need,' answered Barthélemy. 'If it is inevitable, so be it.'

And from that moment he began to prepare for death, thought no more of poison and wrote some memoir, which was not given after his death to the friend to whom he had bequeathed it (the one who was hurrying away).

On Saturday, the 19th of January, we learnt that the priest had visited Palmerston, and his petition had been refused.

A painful Sunday followed that day. A small group of visitors dispersed gloomily in the evening. I was left alone. I went to bed, fell asleep and at once woke up. And so in seven, then six, then five hours he, full of strength, youth and passion, in perfect health, would be led out and killed—killed without pity, without anger or satisfaction, and, what is more, with a sort of pharisaical compassion. . . . Seven o'clock began striking in the church tower. *Now* the procession was moving and Calcraft was on the spot: would his iron nerves serve poor Barthélemy now? My teeth were chattering.

At eleven o'clock in the morning D. came in.

'Is it over?' I asked.

'It is over.'

'Were you there?'

'Yes.'

The Times told me the rest.

Opposite the article in *The Times* Abbé Roux had printed: 'The Murderer Barthélemy.'

When all was in readiness—so *The Times* tells the story—he asked for the letter of the girl to whom he used to write, and I believe a lock of her hair, or some such souvenir; he held them tight in his hand when the hangman went up to him . . . and there crushed in his stiffened fingers they were found by the men who went to take his body from the gibbet. 'Human justice,' so says *The Times*, 'was satisfied.' I suppose so —but it would not have seemed too little for the devil's!

At this point I should stop. But in my story, just as in life itself, beside the giant's footprints let the hoofprints of asses and swine remain too.

When Barthélemy was arrested he had not enough money to pay a solicitor: besides, he did not want to employ one. An unknown lawyer, called Hering, offered to defend him, obviously as a means of advertising himself. His defence was feeble; but it must not be forgotten that his task was exceptionally difficult; Barthélemy kept silent and did not want Hering to speak about the principal charge. Anyway, Hering did a great deal, wasted time, bustled about. When the day of execution was fixed, Hering came to the prison to say good-bye; Barthélemy was touched, he thanked him and among other things said to him: 'I have nothing, I cannot repay your trouble with anything but my gratitude. I should have liked to leave you something, at least for a keepsake, but I have nothing I could offer you. Perhaps my overcoat?'

'I shall be very grateful to you, I meant to ask you for it.'

'With the greatest pleasure,' said Barthélemy, 'but it is a wretched thing.'

'Oh, I am not going to wear it; I will tell you frankly, I have already disposed of it, and very well too.'

'Disposed of it?' repeated Barthélemy in astonishment.

'Yes, to Madame Tussaud for her special gallery.'

Barthélemy shuddered.

When he was being taken to be hanged, he suddenly thought of this and said to the sheriff: 'Oh, I was quite forgetting to ask you, on no account let my overcoat be given to Hering.'[1]

---

[1] Barthélemy's last words are said to have been: 'Now I shall know the secret,' alluding to a future life in which, of course, he did not believe. His case has become famous, because it is often quoted as an argument in favour of capital punishment. Obviously, had he suffered the death penalty for the murder of the gendarme in Paris, three other men would have escaped being killed by him,—· (*Translator's Note*.)

III

Not Guilty

'Dr. Simon Bernard was arrested yesterday at his own lodging, in connection with the Orsini affair. . . .'

One has to have lived some years in England to understand how surprising such news is . . . how at first one cannot believe it . . . what *Continental* emotions it stirs in one's heart!

The public suffers in England, and fairly frequently, from periodical panics, and in such times of fluster woe to anything that comes in its way. Panic is, as a rule, unsparing and merciless, but it has the advantage of being quickly over. Panic is not vindictive, it seeks to be forgotten as quickly as possible.

It must not be assumed that the cowardly feeling of cautious and uneasy self-preservation is innate in the English character. It is the effect of growing fat and rich and of all thoughts and passions being set on acquiring wealth. Timidity has been instilled into the English by the capitalists and petty-bourgeois; they give a nervous instability to their official world, which in a country of representative institutions is continually adapting itself to the character, the votes and the money of the possessing classes. They are the dominant element, and they lose their heads at every unexpected incident and, having no need to stand on ceremony, they show themselves in all their helpless, clumsy cowardice, undisguised by the tawdry and faded *foulard* of French rhetoric. One must know how to wait for Capital to recover itself and to be reassured on the score of profits, then all will go on its accustomed way again.

By the arrest of Bernard, they thought to escape from the wrath of Caesar for Orsini's having prepared his bombs on English soil. Pusillanimous concessions commonly cause irritation, and, instead of saying thank you, the menacing notes grew still more menacing, the warlike articles in the French newspapers smelt more strongly than ever of gunpowder. The capitalists turned pale and dizzy, they already saw in their mind's eye screw-steamers, red trousers, red bullets, a red glow in the sky, the Bank turned into *Mabille,* with the historical inscription: *Ici l'on danse.* What were they to do? They were ready not only to give up and demolish Dr. Simon Bernard, but possibly to undermine and demolish Mount St. Bernard, if only the damnable vision of red trousers and black beards could be dissipated, if only the wrath of their ally could be changed to mercy.

The finest meteorological instrument in England, Palmerston, who indicated with the greatest fidelity the temperature of the middle classes, translated 'Very alarming' into the Conspiracy Bill. By this Bill, if it had become law, every embassy with a little vigilance and zeal might have thrown any enemy of their respective governments into prison, and in certain cases have shipped them off home.

But fortunately the temperature of the island is not alike in all classes, and we shall soon see the great wisdom of the English distribution of wealth, which releases a considerable proportion of the people from all anxiety about capital. If every man in England were a capitalist, the Conspiracy Bill would have been passed, and Simon Bernard would have been hanged or sent to Cayenne. On hearing of the Conspiracy Bill and the overwhelming probability of its passing, the old Anglo-Saxon feeling of independence was stirred; men felt sorry to lose their ancient right of asylum, of which all sorts of people had taken advantage, from the Huguenots to the Catholics of 1793, from Voltaire and Paoli[1] to

[1] Paoli, Pasquale de (1726-1807), the Corsican patriot, was in 1755 elected chief of the island, which he governed with wisdom

Charles x. and Louis-Philippe. The Englishman has no special love for foreigners, still less for refugees, whom he regards as guilty of poverty, a vice he never forgives —but he clings to his right of asylum; he will not permit it to be touched with impunity, any more than his right of public meeting and of the freedom of the press.

When he proposed the Conspiracy Bill, Palmerston reckoned, and very confidently, on the depression of the British spirits; he was thinking of one class which is very powerful, but forgot the other, which is very numerous.

A few days before the Bill came before the House, London was covered with placards; a committee formed for the purpose of opposing the new law was calling a meeting for the following Sunday in Hyde Park, at which it would propose an address to the Queen. This address demanded that Palmerston and his associates should be declared traitors to their country and should be brought up for trial, and petitioned the Queen, should the Bill be passed, to exercise her prerogative and refuse to ratify it. The number of people expected in the Park was so great that the committee announced that it was impossible to make speeches, and arranged to present the parts of the address to the people by telegraphic signs. There were rumours that young working men from all parts of England were arriving for Saturday, that the railways would bring tens of thousands of men violently opposed to the Bill. A

and prudence, and almost delivered from the rule of the Genoese. But in 1768 the Genoese sold Corsica to the French, and a year later Paoli was overpowered by a French army and forced to escape to England. Here he became an intimate friend of Dr. Johnson, who described him as having 'the loftiest port of any man he had ever seen.'

At the French Revolution Paoli returned to Corsica, but after an unsuccessful attempt to restore its independence, came back in 1796 to England.—(*Translator's Note.*)

meeting of two hundred thousand men might be reckoned on. What could the police do with them? To use troops against a lawful and unarmed meeting assembled in order to send a petition to the Queen was impossible; moreover, in order to do so, the Mutiny Bill was essential. And the meeting would have had to be prevented. On Friday, Milner Gibson made his speech against Palmerston's Bill. Palmerston was so convinced of his triumph, that he waited smiling for the division. Influenced by the prospect of the meeting, a proportion of his own followers voted against him, and when a majority of more than thirty votes in support of Milner Gibson was announced, Palmerston thought that the teller had made a mistake, questioned him, stood up to speak, said nothing, but in a dazed way uttered a few incoherent words, accompanying them with a forced smile, and then sank into his chair to the din of hostile applause.

The meeting was made impossible, there was no longer any reason to travel from Manchester, Bristol, Newcastle-on-Tyne. . . . The Conspiracy Bill had fallen, and with it Palmerston and his colleagues.

The classically bombastic and frigidly conservative Ministry of Derby, with the Jewish melodies of Disraeli and the diplomatic subtleties of the days of Castlereagh, replaced them.

On Sunday between three and four o'clock I went to call on Mrs. Milner Gibson. I wanted to congratulate her. She lived near Hyde Park. The placards had been removed, and men were walking with printed proclamations hanging before and behind them, announcing that there would be no meeting on account of the defeat of the Bill and the fall of the Ministry. Nevertheless, since two hundred thousand visitors had been invited, it could hardly be expected that the Park would be empty. Everywhere there were dense throngs of people, orators mounted on chairs or tables were delivering speeches, and the crowds were more excited than usual. A few policemen sauntered about with maidenly bashfulness, noisy groups of street boys sang at the top of their voices, 'Pop goes the weasel!' Suddenly some one pointing to the meagre figure of a Frenchman with moustaches, in a shabby hat, shouted: 'A French spy! 'Instantly the boys rushed after him. The frightened' spy 'tried in vain to make off and, thrown down on the ground, progressed no longer on his feet, but was dragged triumphantly by the hair to the shout of 'French spy! Into the Serpentine with him!' The boys dragged him to the water, dipped him in (it was February), pulled him out and laid him on the bank, laughing and whistling. The drenched and shivering Frenchman floundered on the sand, shouting *in the Park*: 'Cabman! Cabman!'

So was repeated, fifty years afterwards in Hyde Park, the famous scene of Turgenev's 'We are drowning a Frenchman!'[1]

This prologue *à la Priestnitz*[2] to Bernardyears's trial showed how widely spread was the general indignation. The English people really were angry, and saved their country from the slur with which the 'conglomerated mediocrity,' to use J.S. Mill's expression, would certainly have disgraced it.

England is great and endurable *only* with the fullest preservation of its rights and liberties, which are not harmonised into one, nor freed from the trappings of mediaevalism and the broadcloth of puritanism, but yet give free play to the Englishman's proud independence and unwavering confidence in the basis of law.

[1] A quotation from one of Turgenev's *Sportsman's Sketches*, 'The Peasant-Proprietor Ovsyanikov.years'
[2] Priestnitz, Vincenz (1790-1851), was a famous doctor, who first introduced the water cure.— (*Translator's Notes.*)

What the English people instinctively understood was as little grasped by Derby as by Palmerston. Derby's anxiety was to reassure the capitalists and to make every possible concession to the irate ally; he wanted to show the French that even without the Conspiracy Bill he could do wonders. In his excessive zeal he made two mistakes.

Palmerston's Ministry had demanded the conviction of Bernard on a charge of *misdemeanour*, namely for bad behaviour, for rascally conduct, in short for a misdeed which did not involve a greater punishment than three years' imprisonment. And so neither the jury nor the lawyers nor the public would have taken any particular interest in the case, and it would probably have gone against Bernard. Derby insisted on trying Bernard for *felony*, that is, for serious crime, which entitles the judge in case the prisoner is found guilty to sentence him to be hanged.[1] This could not be allowed to pass; moreover, to increase the gravity of the charge while the accused is on his trial is utterly opposed to the sense of justice of the English.

Palmerston, in one of his acutest panics after Orsini's attempt, had pitched on a harmless little book by a man called Adams, discussing the question when tyrannicide is permissible and when it is not, and brought the publisher of it, Truelove, to trial.

All the independent press looked with indignation at this Continental proceeding. The prosecution of the pamphlet was utterly senseless. There are no tyrants in England, and no one in France would hear about a pamphlet written in English; besides, worse things are published in England every day!

---

[1] Dr. Simon Bernard was tried on the charge of being an accessory before the fact to the murder of two persons who were among the victims of Orsini's attempt to assassinate Napoleon III. He was tried in April 1858 at the Central Criminal Court, before the Lord Chief Justice and other judges, and the trial lasted six days. Bernard's solicitor was William Shaen.—(*Translator's Note.*)

Derby, accustomed to the turf and horse-racing, wanted to overtake and if possible outstrip Palmerston. Felix Pyat had, in the name of the revolutionary commune, written a manifesto justifying Orsini; no one was willing to publish it; the Polish refugee, Tchorszewski, put the name of his bookshop on Pyat's pamphlet. Derby ordered the copies to be seized, Tchorszewski to be brought up for trial.

Every drop of Anglo-Saxon blood that was still full of iron and untainted by gold was fired by this new insult; all the organs of Scotland, Ireland, and of course England (except two or three *kept* journals), looked upon these efforts as a criminal attempt upon the freedom of the press, and asked whether the Government was in its senses, or had gone out of its mind.

It was in this atmosphere so favourable to the Government prosecution that the trial of Bernard, this judicial Waterloo of England, as we said at the time in the *Bell*, began in the Old Bailey.

I watched Bernard's trial from beginning to end. I was at all the sittings in the Old Bailey (only, once I was two hours late) and I do not regret it. The first trial of Barthélemy and the trial of Bernard showed me clearly how far more mature in the sphere of law England is than France.

The French Government and the English Ministry took immense pains to secure Bernard's conviction; the trial cost the two Governments as much as thirty thousand pounds sterling, *i.e.* 750,000 francs. A regular mob of French spies stayed in London, travelled to Paris and back again to say one word; to be in readiness in case of need, families were sent for, doctors of medicine, jockeys, governors of prisons, women, children . . . and all this crew stayed in expensive hotels, receiving £1 (25 francs) a day for their keep. Caesar was terrified, the Carthaginians were terrified. And the scowling, slow-moving Englishmen saw it all, and, while the case was being got up, the French spies in the Haymarket and Coventry Street were pursued by boys, hissed and pelted with mud; more than once the English police had to protect them.

Edwin James based his defence on this hatred for political spies and for their unceremonious invasion of London. His treatment of the English spies surpassed all imagination. I do not know how Scotland Yard or the French Government could have compensated them for the torture that Edwin James made them endure.

An individual called Rogers bore witness that at a club in Leicester Square Bernard had said this and that about the coming end of Napoleon.

'Were you there?' asked E. James.

'Yes.'

'So you are interested in politics?'

'No.'

'What leads you to go to political clubs, then?'

'The duties of the service.'

'I don't understand; what sort of service?'

'I serve under Sir Richard Maine.'[1]

'Oh . . . well, are you given instructions?'

'Yes.'

'What are they?'

'I am told to listen to what is said, and to report it to my superiors.'

'And you get a salary for that?'

'Yes.'

'In that case you are a spy. You might have told me that before.'

The Queen's Counsel, Fitzroy Kelly, turning to Lord Campbell, one of the four judges summoned to judge Bernard, asked him to protect the witness from the lawyer's impertinent hints. Campbell with his in-

[1] The head of the Metropolitan Police.

variable dispassionateness advised James not to insult the witness. James protested that he had no intention of insulting him; 'The word spy,' he said, 'is a plain English word, and is the word that describes his duty.' Campbell assured him that it would be better to use another word. The lawyer looked up some dictionary and read the definition of the word spy: 'Spy—a person employed by the police for the purpose of listening,' etc.—'and Rogers has just told us that he is employed for pay by Sir Richard Maine (here by a motion of the head he indicated Sir Richard Maine himself) to listen at clubs and report what takes place there.' And so he begged his Lordship to excuse him, but he could find no other name, and then, turning to the wretched creature upon whom all eyes were fixed, and who was mopping his perspiring brow for the second time, he asked: 'Spy Rogers, possibly you have received pay from the French Government, too?'

The tortured Rogers was roused to fury and replied that he had never served any despotic government. Edwin James, addressing the public, said, amid Homeric laughter, 'Our spy Rogers is for representative government.'

Cross-examining the police agent who had seized Bernard's papers, he asked him by whom he had been accompanied? (The maid had testified that he had not been alone.)

'My uncle.'

'And what is your uncle's calling in life?'

'He is an omnibus conductor.'

'What did he go with you for?'

'He asked me to take him with me, as he had never seen a man arrested or papers seized before.'

'Your uncle is of an inquiring turn of mind. And by the way, you found a letter from Orsini at Dr. Bernard's; that letter was in Italian, but you had it translated; it was not your uncle, I suppose, translated it?'

'No, the letter was translated by Ubicini.'[1]

'An Englishman?'

'Yes, an Englishman.'

'I have never happened to hear that English surname. Is Mr. Ubicini a literary man, then?'

'He translates as part of his duties.'

'So your friend, perhaps, like the spy Rogers, serves under Sir Richard Maine' (again a nod in the direction of Sir Richard).

'Just so.'

'You should have told me that before.'

He did not go so far with the French spies, though they caught it from him, too.

What I liked more than anything was that, having called into the witness-box some French or Belgian tavern-keeper to put a very unimportant question to him, he suddenly stopped, and turning to Lord Campbell said: 'The question I wish to put to the witness is of such a nature that it may embarrass him to answer it in the presence of the French agents. I ask you to send them out of the court for the time.'

'Usher, show the French agents out of the court,' said Campbell, and the usher, wearing a silk mantle and carrying a staff in his hand, led a dozen spies with little beards and wonderful moustaches, wearing little gold chains and signet rings, across the crowded court. Such a procession, accompanied by scarcely suppressed laughter, must have been an ordeal in itself.

The details of the case are well known. I will not describe it.

When the witnesses had been cross-examined and the prosecutor and the defending counsel had delivered their speeches, Campbell coldly summed up the case, reading through the whole of the evidence.

Campbell was summing up for two hours.

[1] I believe that was the name.— (*Author's Notes*.)

'How can his chest and lungs stand it?' I said to a policeman.

The policeman looked at me with a feeling of pride and, offering me his snuff-box, observed: 'That is nothing for him! When Palmer was tried, he was summing up for six hours and a half and was none the worse—he is a man!'

Englishmen have marvellously powerful constitutions. How they store up such a reserve of strength and how it lasts so long a period is a problem. We in Russia have no conception of such activity and such work, especially in our three upper 'grades.' Campbell, for instance, had reached the Old Bailey precisely at ten o'clock; he was presiding over the case without a break till two. At two the judges went out for a quarter of an hour or twenty minutes and then remained in court till five or half-past. Campbell wrote down the whole of the evidence with his own hand. In the evening of the same day he appeared in the House of Lords and delivered long speeches in the correct style with unnecessary Latin quotations, pronounced in such a way that Horace himself would not have understood his own lines.

Gladstone, having a year and a half to spare between his first appointment as Chancellor of the Exchequer and his second, wrote commentaries on Homer. And the ever-youthful Palmerston gallops about on horseback, turns up at soirées and dinner-parties, everywhere polite, everywhere talkative and inexhaustible, displays his learning at examinations and prize-givings, and his liberalism, patriotic pride and generous sympathies in after-dinner speeches, looks after his own ministry, and to some extent all the others, as well as controlling Parliament!

This toughness and habit of intense work is the secret of the English constitution, education and climate. The

Englishman studies little, slowly and late; from his earliest years he drinks port and sherry, overeats himself and builds up a constitution of iron; though he practises no school gymnastics of the German Turner-Uebungen style, he gallops over hedges and ditches, drives every sort of horse, rows in every kind of boat and can make any one see rainbow-stars with his fists. At the same time, life is set in a definite rut and passes regularly from a certain sort of birth by certain avenues to a certain sort of funeral; passions trouble it little. An Englishman loses his fortune with less fuss than a Frenchman gains his; he shoots himself more simply than a Frenchman travels to Geneva or Brussels.

'*Vous voyez, vous mangez votre veau froid chaudement,*' an old Englishman said, wishing to explain to a Frenchman the difference between the English character and the French. '*Et nous mangeons notre bœuf chaud froidement.*' That is why they last out till they are eighty....

Before I go back to the trial I must explain why the policeman offered me his snuff-box. On the first day of the trial I was sitting on the reporters' bench; when Bernard was led into the dock he looked round the court, which was packed to overflowing—not one face he knew; he dropped his eyes, glanced near at hand and, meeting mine, gave me a slight nod, as though asking whether I cared to recognise our acquaintance or not; I got up and greeted him like a friend. This was at the very beginning, that is, in one of those moments of absolute stillness, in which every rustle is heard, every movement noticed. Saunders, one of the heads of the detective police, whispered to one of his men and bade him keep an eye on me, that is, he very simply pointed to me with his finger, and from that minute the detective was continually beside me. I cannot express my gratitude for this official care. If I went away for a quarter of an hour, while the judges were having lunch, to get a glass of ale at a tavern, and could not find a seat on my return, the detective nodded to me and indicated where to sit. If another policeman stopped me in the doorway, my man made a sign to him, and the policeman let me in. On one occasion, I put my hat down in the window, forgot about it, and by the crush of the crowd was completely cut off from it. When I grasped the situation, there was no possibility of getting to it; I stood up to see if I could creep through anywhere, but my detective reassured me: 'I expect you are looking for your hat; I have taken care of it.'

After that, it is easy to understand why his comrade regaled me with some reddish Scotch Cavendish.

My agreeable acquaintance with the detective served me well later on also. One day, after buying some books at Trübner's, I got into an omnibus and forgot them there; as I was walking off, I recollected them, but the omnibus had driven away. I set off to the City to inquire at the omnibus station; my detective turned up and greeted me. 'Delighted to see you,' I said; 'perhaps you can tell me how I can get back my books.'

'What was the name of the omnibus?'

'So-and-so.'

'At what time was it?'

'Just now.'

'That is easy, then; come along,' and a quarter of an hour later the books were in my hands.

Fitzroy Kelly delivered his speech for the prosecution, dry, *cassant,* with a mixture of venom in it. Campbell summed up the evidence, and the jury retired.

I went up to the lawyer's bench and asked a solicitor of my acquaintance how he thought things were going.

'Not well,' he said; 'I am almost certain the jury will give a verdict against him.'

'That is bad. And is it possible he will be . . .?'

'No, I don't think so,' the solicitor interrupted me, 'but he will be deported. It will all depend on the judges.'

There was a terrible noise, laughter, conversation, coughing in the court. An alderman took off his gold chain and showed it to some ladies; the solid chain passed from hand to hand. 'Surely somebody will steal it,' I thought. Two hours later a bell rang, Campbell came in again and then Pollock, a thin, decrepit old man, who had once been Queen Charlotte's lawyer, and two other judges. The usher announced to them that the jury were agreed. 'Bring in the jury,' said Campbell.

A deathly stillness reigned. I looked round; people's faces changed, looked paler, graver, eyes glowed, ladies shuddered. In this stillness, in the presence of this crowd, the accustomed ritual of questions, of taking the oath, was extraordinarily impressive. With his arms folded, Bernard stood calmly, a little paler than usual (his deportment throughout the trial had been excellent).

In a quiet but distinct voice Campbell asked: 'Are the jury agreed, have they chosen one of their number as foreman, and who is he?'

They had chosen as foreman a city tailor of no great wealth.

When he had taken the oath and Campbell, rising to his feet, told him that the court was awaiting the verdict of the jury, I held my breath, my heart stood still.

'. . . Before God and the prisoner in the dock, we declare that Dr. Simon Bernard, accused of being an accomplice in the attempt of the 12th of January to assassinate Napoleon, and of murder'—he raised his voice and added loudly—'Not guilty!'

A few seconds of silence, then a sigh of relief seemed to run through the crowd and was followed by frantic shouts, a thunder of applause, an outburst of joy . . .

ladies waved their handkerchiefs, lawyers jumped on to their benches, men with flushed faces and tears streaming down their cheeks shouted frantically 'Hurray, hurray!' Two minutes passed, the judges, displeased at this lack of respect, told the ushers to restore silence; two or three pitiful figures waved their staves and moved their lips, but the noise did not cease nor grow less. Campbell went out, and his colleagues went out, no one paid attention to that, the shouting and hubbub continued. The jury were triumphant.

I went up to the dock, congratulated Bernard and would have pressed his hand, but, though he stretched down and I stretched up, I could not reach his hand. All at once two lawyers, strangers to me, wearing their gowns and wigs, said to me, 'Stay—wait a minute,' and before I could answer, they seized me and shoved me up so that I could reach his hand.

As soon as the shouts began to subside, it was as though a sea were beating upon the walls and bursting with a hollow splash in at all the doors and windows of the building; this was the shouting on the stairs and in the outer hall. It retreated and approached again, spread wider and wider and melted at last into a roar: it was the voice of the people.

Campbell came in and announced that Bernard was acquitted by the court on this charge, then he went out again with his 'brother judges'; I, too, went out. It was one of those rare moments when a man looks at the crowd with love, when he feels at ease with his fellows. . . . Many of England's sins will be forgiven her for that verdict and the delight with which it was received.

I went out, the street was crowded with people.

A coal-heaver came out of a side-street, looked at the crowd and asked: 'Is it all over?'

'Yes.'

'What's the verdict?'

'Not guilty.'

The coalman laid down the reins, took off his leather cap with its huge flap at the back, threw it up in the air and began shouting in a terrific voice, 'Hurray, hurray!' and the crowd began shouting 'Hurray!' again.

At that moment, the jurymen came out of the doors of the Old Bailey, escorted by the police. The crowd greeted them by taking off their hats and uttering endless shouts of approval. The police had no need to clear a way for them. The people parted of their own accord —the jurymen went to a tavern in Fleet Street, the crowd following them; as fresh crowds came up, they shouted 'Hurray!' to them and flung their hats in the air.

This was between five and six. At seven o'clock, in Manchester, Newcastle, Liverpool and other towns, the workmen rushed about the streets with torches announcing Bernard's acquittal. The news was telegraphed to them by their friends; crowds had been waiting at the telegraph offices since four o'clock.

So England celebrated a fresh triumph of her freedom!

After Palmerston's defeat over the Conspiracy Bill and the failure of Derby's followers in the Bernard case, the proceedings taken by the Government against the two pamphlets became impossible. If Bernard had been found guilty, hanged or sent to twenty years' penal servitude, and public opinion had remained unmoved, then it would have been easy to complete the sacrifice with two or three Isaacs in the publishing trade. The French agents had already pounced upon other pamphlets, including Mazzini's letter.

But Bernard had been acquitted, and that was not all. The ovation received by the jury, the enthusiastic uproar in the Old Bailey, the delight all over England, did not promise success. The case of the pamphlets was transferred to the Queen's Bench.

This was their last effort to secure the conviction of the accused. The jury at the Old Barley could not, it seemed, be relied upon; city men, who firmly maintained their rights and were from tradition somewhat in opposition, did not inspire confidence; while the jury of the Queen's Bench came from the West End and were mostly wealthy tradesmen, who firmly upheld the religion of order and the tradition of profit, but even this jury could hardly be reckoned on after the tailor's verdict.

Moreover, every newspaper in London and throughout the kingdom, with the exception of a few sheets, obviously in the pay of the Government, rose without distinction of party against the assault on the freedom of the press. Meetings were called, committees were formed, subscriptions were got up to pay fines and legal expenses, in case the Government should succeed in and peti the conviction of the publishers; addresses securingtions were signed.

The position was growing more difficult and more absurd every day. France in full trousers, *couleur garance*, with a *képi* a little on one side, was gazing across the Channel with a sinister air, waiting for the end of the proceedings taken in defence of her master. Bernard's release had deeply offended her, and she had drawn her sabre from its sheath, swearing like a corporal.

> 'The heavy heart grew heavier
> Beneath its weight care. . . . of care. . . .'[1]

The capitalists, pale as their own silver, looked to the Government; the Government like a mirror reflected their panic. But all this was nothing to Campbell and the judicial powers not of this world. They recognised one thing, that proceedings against the freedom of the press were opposed to the spirit of the whole nation,

[1] From a poem of Ogaryov's.—(*Translator's Note*.)

and that a severe sentence would deprive them of all popularity and provoke a fierce protest. The only course left them would be to pass a trivial sentence, a farthing damages or one day's imprisonment. . . . While France with her *képi* on one side would take such a sentence as a personal insult.

It would be worse still if the jury acquitted Truelove and Tchorszewski, then the whole blame would fall on the Government for not having ordered the *Préfet de Londres*, or the Lord Mayor, to select the jury from the *Service de sûreté* or at least from the *friends of order* . . . and after that '*Tambourgi, tambourgi, they 'larum afar!*'

The Ministers of the Queen and her lawyers thoroughly grasped this awkward position and, perhaps, they would have done something, if it were possible in England to perform what the English call a 'coop detty' and the French a '*coup d'état*,' while, moreover, the example of the resourceful, indefatigable, elusive, youthful old Palmerston was so fresh. . . .

'Oh Lord, what a task it is
To be the ruler of a grown-up nation!'[1]

The day of the trial arrived. The evening before, our B. went off to the Queen's Bench and gave a policeman five shillings to let him in next day. B. laughed and rubbed his hands; he was persuaded that we should be unable to get seats, or should be stopped at the door. He forgot that there is as a fact no door to the Queen's Bench Court, but only a big archway. I arrived an hour before Campbell; there were not very many people

[1] The lines:

'Oh Lord, what a task it is
To be the father of a grown-up daughter!'

occur in Griboyedov's famous comedy, *Woe from Wit.*—(*Translator's Note.*)

and I got an excellent seat. Twenty minutes later I saw B. enter, looking in all directions, hunting about and apparently uneasy. 'What do you want?'

'I am looking for my policeman.'

'What do you want him for?'

'Why, he promised to keep a seat for me.'

'Upon my soul, why, there are a hundred seats at your service.'

'The policeman has cheated me,' said B. laughing.

'How has he cheated you? Why, you have got a place.'

The policeman of course did not show himself.

An eager conversation was going on between Tchorszewski and Truelove. Their solicitors were taking part in it too; at last, Tchorszewski turned to me and said, handing me a letter: 'What do you think of this letter?' The letter was from Truelove to his lawyer; in it he complained of having been arrested and said that, though he had printed the pamphlet, he had no intention of publishing such books; the letter was signed. Truelove was standing close by.

It was not for me to advise Truelove. I got out of it with some meaningless phrase, but Tchorszewski said: 'They want me to sign a letter like that; I won't do that. I'd rather go to prison than sign a letter like that.'

'Silence,' cried the usher. Lord Campbell appeared. When all the formalities were completed and the jury had taken the oath, Fitzroy Kelly got up and informed Campbell that he had a communication from the Government. 'The Government,' he said, 'in view of Truelove's letter, in which he undertakes this and that, and, taking into consideration this and that, abandons the prosecution.'

Campbell turning to the jury said to this: 'That the guilt of the publisher of the pamphlet on tyrannicide is unquestioned, that the English law, while allowing every possible freedom of the press, nevertheless provides measures for punishing a provocation to so terrible a crime, and so on. But since the Government, owing to certain considerations, abandons the prosecution, he is ready, if the jury consent, to cut short the proceedings; if, however, they do not choose that this should be done, he will continue the trial.'

The jurymen wanted their lunch and wanted to go about their business, and so, without leaving the box, they turned their backs and, after consulting together, answered, as might have been expected, that they agreed that the proceedings should be stopped.

Campbell informed Truelove that he was at liberty to leave the court. There was no applause at this, nothing but laughter.

An *entr'acte* followed at this moment. B. remembered that he had not had his morning tea, and went off to a neighbouring tavern. I note this trait especially because it is typically Russian. The Englishman eats a great deal of rich food, the German eats a great deal of inferior food, the Frenchman eats little but with enthusiasm; the Englishman drinks beer and everything else heavily, the German drinks beer, too, and beer instead of anything else; but neither Englishman, Frenchman nor German is so completely dependent on the habits of his stomach as the Russian. He is bound hand and foot by them. To miss his dinner . . . impossible . . . better arrive a day late, better not see some one at all. B. paid for his tea, 'Stanislasbesides his two shillings, with the following superb scene.

When Tchorszewski's turn came Fitzroy Kelly rose, and again announced that he had a communication from the Government. I strained my ears; what cause could he have invented? Tchorszewski had written no letter.

'Though the accused,' began Fitzroy Kelly, 'Stanislas Trou . . . Torf . . . Tush . . .' and he stopped, adding: 'This is impossible! The foreign gentleman at the bar is certainly guilty of the publication and sale of Felix Pyat's pamphlet, yet the Government, taking into consideration that he is a foreigner and ignorant of the English law, and that this is his first offence, abandons the prosecution.'

And the same farce was repeated. Campbell asked the jurymen. The jury instantly acquitted Tchorszewski.

On this occasion, too, the French were displeased. They wanted a grand *mise en scène*, they wanted to thunder against tyrants and champion *la cause des peuples* . . . possibly Truelove and Tchorszewski would incidentally have been fined or condemned to prison; but what does prison, ten years of prison, signify . . . beside the opportunity of repeating in the face of all people the great principles that outlaw tyrants and their Zaids[1] . . . the everlasting principles of 1789 on which the freedom of France stands so firmly . . . in exile I

The Government, frightened by its neighbour, had for the second time struck upon the granite rock of English freedom, and had meekly given way; could there have been a greater triumph for the freedom of the press?

[1] Zaid was the favourite slave and one of the first disciples of Mahomed. —(*Translator's Note.*)

Chapter 5

Golovin

IT was a few days after I had been visited by the police and my papers had been seized during the June struggle, that I was visited for the first time by I. Golovin, until then only known to me from his dull writings and from the exceedingly bad reputation he had made for himself as an insolent and quarrelsome man. He had been at Lamoricière's, had without the slightest suggestion on my part fussed about my papers, succeeded in doing nothing and came to me to reap the modest laurels of gratitude and to take advantage of the opportunity to force his acquaintance upon me.

'I said to Lamoricière,' he told me, '"General, it is a shame to worry Russian republicans and to leave the agents of the Russian Government in peace."

'"You know them, then?" Lamoricière asked me.

'"Who does not know them!"

'"*Nommez-les, nommez-les.*"

'"Well, Yakov Tolstoy and General Zhomini."

'"To-morrow I will order the police to visit them."

'"But is Zhomini a Russian agent?" I asked.

'"Ha, ha, ha—that we shall see now."'

There you have the man.

The Rubicon was crossed, and, do what I would to restrain Golovin's affection and above all his visits, everything was in vain. Twice a week he would come to us, and the moral level of our home was at once lowered —slander, quarrels, personalities arose. Five years later when Golovin tried to provoke me to fight, he said that I was afraid of him; when he said it, he did not suspect, of course, how many years I had been afraid of him before the London quarrel.

Even in Russia I had heard of his indelicacy, his lack of ceremony in money matters.

Shevyryov, returning from Paris, described to us the legal proceedings in which Golovin figured with a footman, with whom he had fought, and put this down to the discredit of us Westerners, among whom he reckoned Golovin. I observed to Shevyryov that the West ought only to be blamed for the fact that they fought, for in the East Golovin would simply have given the footman a beating and no one would have said anything about it.

His now forgotten writings about Russia disposed me even less to make his acquaintance. They were a hotchpotch of French rhetoric, the liberalism of the Roteck School, anecdotes flung in pell-mell, platitudes and continual personalities with no logic, no definite view, no coherence. Pogodin wrote minced prose, but Golovin thought in minced ideas.

I avoided his acquaintance so far as it was possible. His quarrel with Bakunin assisted me. Golovin sent an aristocratically liberal little article to some paper in which he referred to him. Bakunin announced that he had nothing in common either with the Russian aristocracy or with Golovin.

We have seen that after the June days I failed to steer clear of his undesirable acquaintance.

Every day showed me how right I had been to try to do so. In Golovin was combined all that is hateful to us in a Russian officer and in a Russian landowner, together with a mass of petty European defects, and that without any eccentricity, any talent or humour. His exterior—vulgar, aggressive and offensive—is like the characteristic label of a whole class of people, who hang about with cards or without cards at Spas and in great cities, invariably dining well, whom everybody knows, and about whom everything is known, except two things—what they live on and what they live for. Golovin was a Russian officer, a French *brouilleur*.

hâbleur, an English swindler, a German *Junker*, as well as our native Nozdryov and Hlestakov *in partibus infidelium*.

Why had he left Russia? What was he doing in Europe, he so well placed in the officers' circle of his brothers described by himself? Uprooted from his native soil, he could not recover his centre of gravity. After completing his studies at Dorpat University Golovin got a job in Nesselrode's department. Nesselrode mentioned to him that his handwriting was bad, Golovin took offence and went off to Paris.

When he was summoned to return, he answered that he could not do so yet, as he had not finished his calligraphic studies. Then he published his compilation, *La Russie sous Nicolas*, in which he offended Nicholas most of all by saying that he made mistakes in spelling. He was commanded to return to Russia. He did not go. His brothers[1] took advantage of the fact to put him on short commons—they sent him much less money than was his due. That is the whole story.

The man had not a particle of artistic feeling, of aesthetic taste, he had no desire to learn, no serious occupation. His imagination was turned on himself, he liked to pose, to preserve an *appearance*; he retained the habits of an ill-bred landowner of the middling sort all his life; they seemed easily compatible with the foraging nomadic life of the semi-refugee and semi-Bohemian.

Once I found him in Turin at the gates of the Hotel

---

[1] *A propos* of his brothers, one of them, a general in the cavalry, who was particularly in favour with Nicholas, because he had distinguished himself on the 14th of December, went to Dubbelt with the following question:

'My dying mother,' he said,' has written a few words of farewell to her son Ivan . . . that unfortunate fellow; here is a letter . . . I really don't know what I ought to do with it.' 'Take it to the post . . .' said Dubbelt, smiling amiably.—(*Author's Note*.)

Feder with a whip in his hand . .. before him stood a Savoyard, a half-naked barefoot boy of twelve. Golovin was flinging him *sous* and for every *sou* lashed him on the legs; the Savoyard hopped about, showing that it hurt a good deal, and asked for more. Golovin went on laughing and throwing halfpence. I do not suppose that he was whipping him very hard; still, he was whipping him, and how could it amuse him?

After Paris we met first again in Geneva and afterwards in Nice. He, too, had been turned out of France and found himself in a very unenviable position.[1] He had absolutely nothing to live upon in spite of the fabulous cheapness of everything in Nice at that time. How often and ardently I desired that Golovin would come in for a legacy or marry an heiress . . . that would have freed my hands.

From Nice he went away to Belgium, whence he was turned out; he went off to London, and there was naturalised, boldly adding to his surname the title Prince Hovra, to which he had no right. He returned to Turin, an English subject, and began publishing a paper. In it he annoyed the Ministers to such a point that they turned him out of the country. Golovin tried to obtain the protection of the English Embassy. The ambassador refused it him and again he drifted away to London. Here in the character of a knight of industry,

1 The French police could not forgive him one prank. At the beginning of 1849 there was a small demonstration. The president, i.e. Napoleon III., made the rounds of the boulevards on horseback. All at once Golovin made his way up to him and shouted '*Vive la République!*' and '*A bas les Ministres!*' 'Vive la République!' muttered Napoleon. '*Et les Ministres?*''*Onleschangera!* 'Golovin held out his hand to him. Five days passed, the ministers remained and Golovin published an account of his interview in La Réforme, adding that since the president had not carried out his promise, '*il retire sa poignée de main.*' The police said nothing, and only turned him out some months later on the pretext of the 13th of July. — (*Author's Note.*)

in the department of revolution, he unsuccessfully attempted to get into various political circles, made the acquaintance of every one in the world and published inconceivable trash.

Towards the end of November 1853, Worcell came to see me to invite me to say something at the Polish anniversary. Golovin dropped in on us and, catching the subject of discussion, at once attacked Worcell with the question: 'Might he make a speech?'

Worcell was annoyed. I was doubly so. Nevertheless he replied, 'We are inviting every one, and shall be very glad; but that the meeting may have unity, we must know *à peu près* what each person is going to say. We are meeting on such a day, come to our discussion.'

Golovin, of course, accepted the invitation. Worcell, as he went away, said to me, shaking his head, in the hall: 'What ill wind brought him?'

With a heavy heart I went to the preliminary meeting. I foresaw that it would not pass off without a scandal. We had not been there five minutes before my presentiment was justified. After two or three jerky generalisations, Golovin suddenly turned to Ledru-Rollin, first reminded him that they had met somewhere, of which Ledru-Rollin had no recollection, then, *à propos* of nothing at all, fell to proving to him that it was a blunder to be continually irritating Napoleon, that it would be better policy to spare him for the sake of the Polish cause. Ledru-Rollin changed countenance, but Golovin went on that Napoleon alone could save Poland, and 'that,' he added, 'is not only my personal opinion, Mazzini and Kossuth see that now, and are doing their utmost to approach Napoleon.'

'How can you believe anything so absurd?' said Ledru-Rollin, beside himself with emotion.

'I have heard it.'

'From whom? From spies; an honest man could not have told you that. Gentlemen—I do not know Kossuth personally—still, I am convinced that this is not true; as for my friend Mazzini, I boldly take it upon myself to answer for him that he has never dreamed of such a compromise, which would be a terrible calamity, and at the same time false to his own religion.'

'Yes, yes, of course,' people said on all sides. It was clear that Golovin's words had incensed every one. Ledru-Rollin turned to Worcell and said:

'You see my apprehensions were well founded; the composition of your meeting is too varied to avoid the expression of opinions which I cannot accept nor even listen to. Allow me to withdraw and decline the honour of delivering a speech on the 29th.'

He got up, but Worcell, stopping him, observed that the committee for arranging the meeting had elected himself as their president, and in that capacity he must beg Ledru-Rollin to remain, while he put the question to their comrades whether after what had just been said they preferred to let Golovin make a speech and lose the co-operation of Ledru-Rollin, or the reverse.

Then Worcell turned to the members of the Central Committee. There could be no doubt about the result. Golovin foresaw it very well and so, without waiting for an answer, rose and disdainfully flung Ledru-Rollin the words: 'I yield place and honour to you, and refuse to speak on the 29th of November as I had intended.' After which with a heavy and valiant tread he walked out.

To put an end to the business at once, Worcell asked me to read them my speech or tell them the gist of it.

Next day the meeting, one of the last of the brilliant Polish meetings, took place. It was successful, there were masses of people. I arrived at eight o'clock—every place was taken and I had difficulty in making my way to the platform prepared for the speakers.

'I have been looking for you everywhere,' Dr. Darasz said to me; 'Ledru-Rollin is waiting for you in our anteroom here and insists that he must speak to you before the meeting.'

'What has happened?'

'Oh, it's all that cad Golovin.'

I went in to Ledru-Rollin—he was violently angry and with good reason.

'Look here,' he said to me, 'what a letter that wretch sent me a quarter of an hour before I came here.'

'I am not responsible for him,' I said, opening the letter.

'Of course not, but I want you to know the sort of man he is.'

The letter was rude and stupid. It was pure swagger on his part; he wanted to cover his fiasco. He wrote to Ledru-Rollin that, if the latter had none of the French courtesy, he must show at least that he was not devoid of French courage.

'I always knew he was a troublesome and impudent man,' I said, giving back the note, 'but I certainly did not expect this. What do you intend to do?'

'Give him such a lesson as he will not forget for some time. Here before the meeting I will tear the mask from this *aventurier*, I will describe our conversation—I will call upon you as a witness and a *Russian* too—and will read his letter—and then we shall see—I am not accustomed to swallow such sugar-plums.'

'It is a pleasant prospect,' I thought; 'Golovin with his suspicious reputation will be faced with complete ruin. His one way of escape will be a duel. Such a duel must not be permitted, because Ledru-Rollin is perfectly right and has done nothing offensive. In his position he cannot fight with every stray person he meets. And what a disgrace—at a Polish meeting for one Russian exile to be plunged in the mud while another assists.'

'But can't you put it off?' I asked.

'To lose this opportunity!'

I still tried to stop it, putting in a suggestion of a court, a jury *d'konneur*—nothing had much effect. . . .

Then we came out on to the platform—and were greeted with frantic applause. Applause and the noise of the crowd are an intoxicating influence, as we all know—I forgot about Golovin and thought about my own speech. Of that speech I have spoken in another place. My very appearance on the platform was greeted with the utmost warmth by Poles, Italians and French. When I had finished, Worcell, president of the meeting, came up to me and, as he embraced me, repeated, deeply moved: 'Oh I thank you, I thank you!' The applause and hubbub was redoubled, and it was to the sound of this uproar that I returned to my place. . . . At that moment Golovin came into my head, and I was panic-stricken at the approach of the moment when the tribune of 1848 would make mincemeat of that buffoon. I took out a pencil and wrote on a scrap of paper: 'For God's sake, manage so that the nasty Golovin affair should not spoil your meeting.' The platform was in the shape of an amphitheatre; I handed the note to Pianciani, who was sitting in front of me, that he might pass it to Worcell. Worcell read it, scribbled something in pencil and passed it in the other direction, that is, towards Ledru-Rollin, who was sitting higher up. Ledru-Rollin reached over and put a hand on my shoulder and, nodding good-humouredly, said: 'For your speech and for your sake I will put it off until to-morrow,' and, more pleased than I can say, I went off to supper with Ruge and Coppingham at the American Stores.

GOLOVIN AND LEDRU-ROLLIN

Before I had time to get up next day my rooms were filled with Poles. They came to thank me, but probably they could have deferred their gratitude to a later hour. A more important matter was their impatience to settle the dispute, the Golovin business. Their fury found full vent. They had drawn up a document, in which Golovin was reviled, and an address to Ledru-Rollin, in which they declared that they absolutely refused to allow him to fight the duel. A dozen men were ready to fight Golovin. They had come to insist on my signing both the document and the address.

I saw that one scandal would give rise to half a dozen and, taking advantage of my success of the previous day, *i.e.* of the prestige it had given me, said to them: 'What is your object? Is it to settle the business, so that Ledru-Rollin should be satisfied and the unfortunate incident which all but ruined your meeting should be obliterated; or to punish Golovin at all costs? In the latter case, gentlemen, I will have no hand in it, and you may do what you think best.'

'Of course, our chief object is to settle the matter.'

'Good; have you confidence in me?'

'Yes, yes, of course.'

'I am going alone to Golovin . . . and if I arrange things so that Ledru-Rollin is satisfied, that shall be the end of it.'

'Good; but if you don't succeed in doing so?'

'Then I will sign your protest and address.'

'Right.'

I found Golovin gloomy and embarrassed, he was evidently expecting a storm, and I doubt whether he was pleased that he had provoked it.

Our interview was brief. I told him that I had saved him from two unpleasant experiences, and proffered my services to relieve him from the third, that is, to reconcile him with Ledru-Rollin. He was longing to end the trouble, but his conceit would not allow him to recognise that he was in fault, still less to admit it.

'It is only for your sake that I consent,' he muttered at last.

Whether for my sake or any one else's, the affair reached a settlement. I went to Ledru-Rollin, waited a couple of hours in a cold room and caught a chill; at last he arrived, courteous and good-humoured.

I told him the whole story from the arrival of the chivalrous sons of Poland to the wrigglings of our matador, and Ledru-Rollin agreed, laughing, to consign the matter to oblivion and receive the penitent sinner. I went to fetch him.

Golovin was waiting in great agitation; learning that all had gone off well, he flushed, and stuffing all the pockets of his greatcoat with papers of some sort, drove off with me.

Ledru-Rollin received him like a true *gentleman* and at once began talking of other things.

'I have come to you,' said Golovin, 'to say that I am very sorry . . .'

Ledru-Rollin interrupted him with the words, *'N'en parlons plus* . . . here is your note, throw it in the fire,' and without a pause went on with the story he was telling. . . . When we rose to take leave, Golovin drew a heap of pamphlets from his pockets and, handing them to Ledru-Rollin, said that these were his latest brochures, and he begged him to accept them as a sign of his particular respect. Ledru-Rollin, overflowing with gratitude, put the heap down with careful respect, and most likely never touched them again.

'Here you have our literary age,' I said to Golovin as we got into the cab. 'I have heard of clever people taking a corkscrew with them to a duel, but to arm oneself with pamphlets is something new!'

Why did I save the man from public disgrace? Really, I don't know and I simply regret it. Every time we show forbearance, spare, whitewash or rescue a man, we have to pay for it, in accordance with the great principle laid down by Byelinsky, that 'The strength of scoundrels lies in the fact that they treat honest men as though they were scoundrels, while honest men treat them as though they were honest.' The bandits of the journalistic and political world are dangerous and unpleasant, owing to their senseless and difficult position. They have nothing to lose and everything to gain. When you save such men you only restore them to their former[1] . . .

There is not one word of exaggeration in my story. Imagine then what was my astonishment when ten years later Golovin published in Germany a statement that Ledru-Rollin had *apologised to him* . . . though he knew that both Ledru-Rollin and I, thank God, were alive and well. . . . Was not that a stroke of genius?

The meeting had taken place on the 29th of November, 1853. In March 1854 I published a brief appeal to the Russian soldiers in Poland, in the name of the 'Russian Free Commune' in London. Golovin was offended at this and brought me the following protest to be printed:—

'I have read your "announcement" on Annunciation Day. It is headed "The Free Russian Commune in London," and yet the words occur: "*I* do not remember in which province."

'Consequently it is a mystery to me whether this Commune consists of you and Engelson or you alone.

'This is not the place to discuss the contents of the appeal, which was not shown me in manuscript. To refer to one thing only, I should not have signed a promise not to refrain from advising people who do not ask my

---

[1] The following word is undecipherable in the MS.— (*Note to the Russian edition.*)

advice. Neither modesty nor conscience would allow me to say that I have reconciled the name of the Russian people to the peoples of the West.

'Therefore I feel bound to ask you to announce at the earliest opportunity that I have hitherto had nothing to do with any appeals printed by your press in Russian.

'Hoping that you will not compel me to resort to any other form of publicity,—I remain your servant,

'IVAN GOLOVIN.

'LONDON, *March* 25, 1854.

'*To* M. HERZEN (Iskander).

'*P.S.*—I leave it to your discretion to publish my letter in its present form or a summary of its contents.'

I was unspeakably delighted at this protest. I saw in it the beginning of a breach with this insufferably tiresome man, and a public announcement of the difference of our views. Europe and the Poles themselves have such a superficial view of Russia—especially in the intervals when she is not beating her neighbours or annexing whole kingdoms in Asia—that I had had to work for ten years to escape being mixed up with the famous Ivan Golovin.

Golovin followed up his protest by sending me a long incoherent letter, which wound up with the words: 'It is possible that apart we may be yet more useful to the common cause if we do not waste our strength on conflict with each other.'

To this I answered:—

'*March* 30, *Thursday*.

'It is my duty to thank you for your letter received yesterday, of which the good intention—that of softening your published announcement—I fully appreciated.

'I entirely agree with you that we shall be of more use apart. As for the conflict of which you write, it has never entered my head. I shall take no initiative in it, having nothing against you, especially if each of us goes his own way. Remember how long ago and how often I have told you in private what you now say in public. Our manners, opinions, likes and dislikes are all different. Permit me to remain on terms of civility with you, but accept our separation for a *fait accompli*, and both you and I will feel more free.

'My letter is an answer. There are no questions in it. I beg you not to prolong this correspondence, and I rely upon your delicacy that our final parting shall not be accompanied either by rude language or by hostile action. With all good wishes.'

That Golovin did not in the least wish to break off relations with me was obvious; what he wanted was to vent his anger over our publishing an appeal without him and then to be reconciled, but I did not want to let slip this ardently desired opportunity.

Two or three weeks after my letter, I received a parcel from him; I opened it, a sheet of black-edged paper. . . . I looked, it was half of the invitation to the funeral sent out on the 18th of May, 1852. In answer to his letter from Turin I had sent it him, adding: 'Your letter touched me, I have never doubted the kindness of your heart. . . .' Upon this letter, he wrote that he begged me to see him, gave me a new address, and added: '*il ne s'agit pas d'argent.*' I answered that I could not go and see him, because it was not I who had business with him but he with me, because he and not I had begun the breach between us, and, finally, because he had brought that to the knowledge of outsiders. But that I was prepared to receive him when he liked to call.

He appeared next morning, meek and soft as silk. I answered him again and again that no hostile step would be taken on my side, but that our opinions and manners were so utterly dissimilar that it was useless for us to meet.

'But how is it you did not notice that before . . .?'

I did not answer.

We parted coldly but civilly.

One would have thought it was all over. No! Next day Golovin treated me to the following letter:[1] —

'*Ad Usum Proprium.*

'After to-day's conversation I cannot refuse you the satisfaction of having a Commune—have it! I have no intention of beginning an attack upon you, so consequently be sure to avoid anything that could give grounds for it.

'When your new friends fail you, you will find in me one always devoted to you.

'My advice is to write to the *Morning Advertiser* that you are not taking proceedings against them only because you despise the ignorance which cannot distinguish a patriot and a friend of freedom from a spy, which commends Brunov and slanders Bakunin.

'I will not come and see you, as I shall be occupied with more important affairs than seeking sympathy.

'When you care to visit me I shall always be glad to see you, especially as, having something in common, we shall always have something to talk over.

'GOLOVIN.

'*April 26, 1854.*'

At the approach of summer I moved to Richmond, and for some time heard nothing of Golovin. All at

[1] The *Morning Advertiser*, at that time in the hands of Karl Blind and German democrats of the Marx persuasion, published a very stupid article seeking to prove that my views were identical with those of the Russian Government. Golovin who gave such good advice resorted himself to the same means of attack, and in the same *Morning Advertiser*.

once I had a letter from him. Mentioning no names, he wrote that it had reached his ears that 'I had jeered at him' in my own house, and asked (as though I had been his mistress) that I should send back his portrait which he had presented to me in Nice. In vain I rummaged about and hunted among my papers, I could not find the portrait.

It was annoying . . . but I had to tell him that I had lost the portrait. I asked Savitch, a common acquaintance, to tell him that I had looked for it in vain, and to repeat that I wished him no harm whatever, and begged him to leave me alone.

In answer to this came the following letter:—

'HONOURED ALEXANDR IVANOVITCH,—You told Savitch that if I wrote you a letter you would send back ten pounds. My intention was to send you twenty pounds —all that I had—and you wrote yourself that of the hundred pounds you would take only twenty. I had hoped to be out of my difficulties soon, but it has turned out otherwise. However, in a week or at most a fortnight, I could return you the ten pounds. You say that you are not my enemy, and I ask you to do this, not as a favour to a friend but as an act of justice. If you think otherwise, refuse, without buzzing it about among your admirers. I. GOLOVIN.

'*August* 16.'

To this letter I made no answer. I need hardly say that I had given Savitch no message whatever about money. Golovin had purposely muddled things up, in order to give an appearance of a transaction to what was simply asking a favour. Of Savitch himself—one of the most amusing wild flowers of our native soil flung into a foreign land—we will speak some other time.

Following upon this came a second letter. He grasped that the absence of reply meant a refusal and, of course, appreciated the imprudence of the line he had taken.

Scared, he determined to attack the position by storm—he wrote to me that I was a German or a Jew,[1] and sent me back my letter B, writing upon it 'You are a coward.' Then came two letters in a disguised handwriting filled with abuse after the style of C.[2] I regret

---

[1] Here between the sheets of Herzen's MS. are gummed copies of two of his letters to Golovin:—

'*Aug.* 22, 1854, RICHMOND.

'DEAR SIR,—You wrote to me that you wished to efface all memory of our acquaintanceship, a few days later you ask me to lend you ten pounds.

'To your first letter I answered with courtesy and sincerity, regardless of the tone of your letter. To the second I made no answer. Correspondence between us is impossible. I return your letter and will not receive any in the future. Fully persuaded that I have done nothing unfair in regard to you, I shall remain obstinately silent so long as that is possible, relying on the common sense of every impartial person. A. HERZEN.'

B.

'*Aug.* 23, 1854.

'You are trying to make me fight you as boys are made to fight. It is a matter of complete indifference to me whether you consider me a coward or a brave man, a thief or a counterfeit coiner.

'Do you want to fight me because you are ashamed of having asked for ten pounds from a man with whom you had rudely cut off all relations? If I had given you the money you would have felt no *reconnaissance*,

'I am not going to fight you, because it is stupid, because I have done nothing for which I owe you reparation, and because finally I stand independently on my own feet and am not going to give way to another man's will or insulting language, dictated by some insanity,

'Do not imagine that I am making any secret of this letter. You can read it or not. In fact, do as you please, only don't write to me.

'For my part, I am not going to write or even speak of it, I am so sick of it. A. HERZEN.'

[2] C.—'To send back a letter without reading it is an act of insolence worthy of brave men. To send back a letter on the supposition that it contains a request for money though there is nothing

that some of them are lost; however, the tone is the same in all.

He expected that the letter in which he spoke of cowardice would be followed by my sending him seconds. My conceptions of honour were indeed strange and did not coincide with his. What fun would there be in killing a candidate for Bicêtre or a house of correction, or being killed or maimed by him? And certainly being tried for doing so, giving up one's work—and all this to prove that I am not afraid of him . . . as though mad dogs were the only creatures whose privilege it is to arouse terror without detriment to the honour of the terror-stricken.

Again a pause. Golovin ceased to show himself in our *parages*, caroused at some one else's expense, said insulting things to some one else and borrowed money from some one else. Meanwhile, he was losing the last shreds of his reputation, old acquaintances were cutting him, new ones were avoiding him. Louis Blanc apologised to friends who met him with Golovin in Regent Street; Milner Gibson's house was definitely closed to him, and even remote English simpletons—the stupidest people in the whole world—began to suspect that he was not a prince and not a statesman, in fact not a man at all; none but Germans who know men only from the bookseller's catalogues regarded him as something '*berühmt.*'

In February 1855 a meeting was being prepared at St. Martin's Hall; an impressive but unsuccessful attempt to unite the Socialists of all parties with the Chartists. I have described in detail elsewhere the results of this meeting, and the Marx intrigues against my election. Here I am dealing with Golovin.

of the sort in it, one must be a Jew. To send back a letter without knowing whether it contains something affecting one's honour, one must have a strange conception of honour.'

I did not want to make a speech, and went to the sitting of the Committee to thank them for the honour and to refuse it. It was held in the evening, and as I was going out I met a Chartist on the stairs who asked me if I had read Golovin's letter in the *Morning Advertiser*. I had not. Below the hall was a café, a public-house. The *Morning Advertiser* is in all the taverns —so I went in and he showed me the letter, in which Golovin wrote that it had come to his knowledge that the International Committee had elected me a member 'and asked me as a Russian to make a speech at the meeting, and therefore, *with no motive but love of the truth*, he warned them that I was not a Russian but a German Jew born in Russia,' a race under the special patronage of Nicholas.'

After reading this mischievous sally I went back to the Committee and said to the Secretary, E. Jones, that I took back my refusal. At the same time I showed him and other members of the Committee the *Morning Advertiser*, and added that Golovin very well knew my family history, and 'was lying from love of the truth. Though indeed Jewish extraction could hardly have been an obstacle,' I added, 'since the first exiles after the creation of the world were Jews, *i.e.* Adam and Eve.'

The Committee laughed and accepted my new decision with applause led by the President.

'As for your electing me a member—it is my duty to thank you for it, but to defend the choice is your affair.'

'Yes, yes,' I heard shouted on all sides.

Next day Jones printed a few lines in his paper *The People*, and sent a letter to the *Daily News*:[1]—

'ALEXANDER HERZEN, THE RUSSIAN EXILE

'Some sham democrat has written in the *Morning Advertiser* a libel with reference to M. Herzen, with

---

[1] English in the original.—(*Translator's Note*,)

design to damage, if possible, the approaching demonstration in St. Martin's Hall. The effort is puerile, because that demonstration is one of peoples and principles, and does not in any way depend on the personality of any individuals. But in justice to M. Herzen, we are bound to say that the ridiculous statement about his not being a Russian and an exile is a downright falsehood, and that the statement that he belongs to the same race as Joshua and Josephus is utterly without foundation; not that it is not just as honourable to belong to that once mighty and ever consistent people, as to any other. He was five years a captive in the Ural mountains, and liberated thence only to be banished from Russia, his native clime.

'M. Herzen is at the head of Russian democratic literature, and the most distinguished exile of his country; as such, the representative of its proletarian millions. He will be at the demonstration in St. Martin's Hall, and will, we trust, receive a welcome that will show the world that the English can sympathise with the Russian people, while they desire to strike at the Russian tyrant.'

'*To the Editor of the "Daily News."*

'M. HERZEN.

'SIR,—A letter inserted in one of your contemporaries denies M. Herzen, the well-known Russian exile, the right of representing, in the International Committee, Russian democracy, and even the Russian birthright.

'M. Herzen already has disposed of the second allegation. Allow us, on behalf of the International Committee, to add to M. Herzen's reply a few facts respecting the first one, which very likely his modesty has prevented him from alluding to.

'At twenty years of age, condemned for a conspiracy against the despotism of the Tsar, he was sent to the

[1] English in the original.— (*Translator's Note.*)

frontier of Siberia, where he remained an exile for a period of seven years.

'Pardoned a first time, he knew very soon how to deserve a second condemnation. In the meantime, political pamphlets, philosophical writings and novels secured him one of the most distinguished places in Russian literature.

'However, for the literary and political part played by M. Herzen in this our country, we can do no better than to refer to an article published on the 6th inst. in the *Athenæum*, of which nobody will suspect the impartiality.

'Arrived in Europe in 1847, M. Herzen occupied an important rank amongst the distinguished men who attached their names to the great revolutionary movement of 1848. Since that time he has started in London the first Russian free press, wherein he prosecutes against the Tsar Nicholas and Russian despotism a deadly and most useful war.

'In consequence of these facts, anxious as we were to unite the whole democracy in a common manifestation, we neither hoped nor wished to find in England or in Europe a nobler and truer representative of the revolutionary party in Russia.—Yours, etc.

'(Signed on behalf of the International Committee)

THE PRESIDENT.
Secretaries—ROBERT CHAPMAN,
CONRAD DOMBROWSKI,
ALFRED TALANDIER.'

Golovin remained mute and went away to America.

'At last,' I thought, 'we are rid of him. He is lost in that ocean of swindlers, fortune-hunters and adventurers of all sorts, will there become a pioneer or a digger, a card-sharper or a slave-holder, and whether he grows rich there or is hung by lynch law does not matter so long as he does not come back. 'Not a bit of it—a year later my Golovin popped up in London again and, happening in the street to meet Ogaryov, who did not bow to him, went up to the latter and asked him,' Why, have you been told not to bow to me, eh?' and walked off. Ogaryov overtook him and saying, 'No, it is to please myself that I cut you,' went on his way. I need hardly say that this immediately produced the following note to Ogaryov:—

'As I am about to edit *The Whip*, I do not seek to be on good terms with my enemies, but I do not wish them to imagine all sorts of nonsense about me.

'In a couple of words I will tell you what passed between me and Herzen. I went to his house and begged him not to quarrel. "I cannot agree to that," he said; "I do not sympathise with you, let us start a controversy." I did not do so, but when he sent me back my letter unopened, then I called him a German. It was like Briscorn, who called Dolgoruky a German to make the soldiers laugh. But Herzen was pleased to answer, to give his version, and then to be furious not with himself but with me. But there was nothing offensive in this affair. Admitting that my treatment of him was bad and yours of me good, though you are not twins, still there was nothing to get wild over nor to fight about.

'GOLOVIN.

'*Jan.* 12, 1857.'

We determined to remain absolutely silent: no punishment is so annoying to blusterers and *hâbleurs* as silence, as mute cold contempt. Twice more Golovin tried writing to Ogaryov biting and would-be witty notes, after the style of the following second missive, by now absolutely meaningless and suggestive of real insanity:—

'Berlin, *Aug*. 20.
'I have seen
'The God of the Russian censorship
'And held not my peace.
'Buchberg and I were wrangling for two hours; he sobbed like a calf.
'"*Vous voulez la guerre, vous l'aurez.*"
'Herzen and I have been enemies for two or three years. What has come of it? No good to any one! Does he want to shoot at me? I have an arrow ready, but for the common good it would be better to shake hands!'

'Victoria Hotel.
'You are publishing your complete works: do they smell of a corpse as in Denmark? . . .'

Not a word of answer followed.

And, indeed, he had enough to drive him mad. Little by little all his resources, moral and material, had dried up. The literary enterprises that had maintained his credit were no more, he was undertaking jobs semi-decent, semi-dirty, of all sorts; everything brought him disaster or slipped out of his hands. He was not squeamish as to the means he used. One fine morning—most likely not knowing at whose expense he could have a good dinner—and he was very fond of a good dinner—Golovin wrote to Palmerston and offered his services—it was towards the end of the Crimean War—as a secret agent to the English Government, undertaking to be very useful, owing to his former connections in Petersburg and his excellent knowledge of Russia. Palmerston was disgusted and told his secretary to answer that the Viscount thanks M. Golovin for his offer, but does not require his services at present. For a long while Golovin used to carry this letter with Palmerston's seal on the envelope, and *show it to people*.

After the death of Nicholas he inserted in some paper an abusive article attacking the new Empress, and signed it with a pseudonym; next day he sent a reply to his own attack to the same paper. Our friend Kauffmann, who edited a lithographed sheet, unmasked this proceeding, and there was an outcry about it in dozens of papers. Then he offered the Russian Embassy in London to edit a *Government* Gazette, but Brunov, like Palmerston, had no immediate need of his services.

Then he simply petitioned the Russian Government for pardon, and received it on condition of entering the service. He took alarm, began haggling over the place of his service, begging that Suvorov, then Governor-General of the Baltic provinces, should take him into his. Suvorov consented. Golovin did not go, but wrote a letter to Prince Gortchakov about a dream he had had. He dreamed that the Tsar had invited him to his council, and that he had zealously advised him to undertake good deeds.

Dreams do not always come true, and instead of a place in the Tsar's councils, our now grey-headed rascal almost got into the house of correction. Meeting with a commercial factotum called Stern, Golovin went in for all sorts of speculations without a halfpenny in his pocket, forgetting that as long ago as 1848 his name had been exposed at the Bourse in Paris as a fraudulent speculator. He tried to cheat Stern, but Stern cheated him, and Golovin had recourse to his own method: he sent an article to the papers concerning Stern in which he touched upon his domestic life. Stern was furious and brought an action against him. Golovin went, terrified and distracted, to a solicitor. He was afraid of prison, of a heavy fine, of publicity. The solicitor proposed that he should sign a document to settle it, completely taking back what he had said. The solicitor prevailed, and Stern, after lithographing the document and the signature, sent them to all his and Golovin's acquaintances. I received a copy:—

'4 Egremont Place, London,
May 29, 1857.

'Dear Sir,—You having commenced an action for libel against me in respect of certain statements I have made both verbally and in writing, reflecting upon your character, and you having through the intervention of mutual friends consented to forgo further proceedings therein upon my paying the costs thereof and retracting such statements and also expressing my regret at having made use of them, I thus gladly avail myself of these terms, and beg to assure you, that if anything I may have written or said has tended in the most remote degree to injure you, I can only say that such was not my intention, and that I am very sorry for having adopted the course I did, which shall never be repeated by

'Yours truly,   Golovin.

'E. Stern, Esq.

'*Witness*—H. Empson, Solicitor,61 Moorgate Street, London.'

After that London was absolutely impossible for him. . . . Golovin left it, taking with him a regular portfolio of unpaid bills from tailors, shoemakers, restaurant-keepers, landladies. . . . He went off to Germany and all of a sudden got married. The news of this remarkable event he telegraphed the same day to the Emperor Alexander ii.

Two years later, having drunk up his wife's dowry, he published a sketch in some journal of the misery of a man of genius married to a simple woman who cannot understand him.

After that I heard nothing more of him for over five years.

ATTEMPT AT RECONCILIATION

At the beginning of the Polish rebellion there was a new attempt at reconciliation; 'Our Polish and Russian friends expect it and insist upon it!' I said nothing.

At the beginning of 1865 I met in Paris a bent old man with a sunken face, in a shabby hat and a threadbare overcoat . . . it was windy and very cold. . . . I was going to a recitation at Alexandre Dumas'; which was also windy and vapid. The old man was buried in his coat collar; as he passed, he muttered without looking at me:' Used and done for!' and went on. I stopped . . . Golovin walked on with the same heavy tread without turning—I went on, too. I stopped because on two occasions he had met me in the London streets. Once he had muttered: 'What spite!' On the second, he had mumbled something to himself, probably abusive, but I did not hear; he had not addressed me, and I had no inclination to get up a street row with him. He afterwards told Savitch and Savashkevitch that he had met me and sworn at me, but I had said nothing.

'What is Golovin doing here?' I asked the same Golynsky to whom I have referred.

'He is in a bad way; he has turned *brocanteur* and money-changer, he buys up bad pictures, cheats fools with them, but is more often cheated himself. . . . He is growing old and peevish, he sometimes writes articles which nobody accepts, he cannot forgive you your success and swears at you for all he is worth.'

There was no intercourse between us from that time forth. But every year or so when one least expects it comes a letter . . . sometimes with an offer of reconciliation at the request of some Poles, sometimes simply with abuse. Not a word in reply from us.

I made up my mind, however dull it might be, to record our adventures, and for that purpose looked up letters of his that had been preserved. At the very moment that I had taken up my pen and written the first lines, I was handed a letter in Golovin's writing. Here it is as a worthy epilogue:—

'ALEXANDR IVANOVITCH,—I rarely remind you of my existence, but a rumour has reached me that you "are washing your hands" and retiring from the belfry.

'To my thinking if you put your hand to the plough you should not turn back, your resources would allow you to publish *The Bell* even at a loss. If possible insert the letter herewith enlosed. GOLOVIN.'

'*To Mr. Katkov, Editor of the "Moscow News."*

'DEAR SIR—Pardon me for knowing you neither by your own name nor your father's. I know you only from your blind hatred of the Poles, whom you do not recognise as human beings nor Slavs; I know you also from your ignorance of European questions.

'I am told that in your paper the sentence occurred: The Dorpat pen commiserates Russia and drowns in insignificance, or something of the sort. I do commiserate Russia, I commiserate the *janissaries* and the disorder, I commiserate the nobles who are forced to make forged banknotes and forged lottery tickets, so that at the present moment three winning tickets for the hundred thousand rouble prize have been presented, and no one can distinguish which is the real one. I commiserate the drunken peasants, the thieving officials, and the priests who jabber nonsense; but I know that life in Russia is not a bed of roses.

'His Majesty was pleased not to command me to write in my passport the stupid grade I got in the University, and I have written in His dossier the title of "Well-Intentioned," which will remain in it, since what is written with the pen cannot be chopped away with the axe.

'My fatherland was stolen from me for the sake of political economy; I remembered I was a man before I was a Russian—and I serve humanity, a career far grander than the Imperial service which was laid upon me as a duty.

'In my own eyes I have not sunk lower, but I have risen. I have heard that if I came to Russia I should be shut up in a lunatic asylum; but they would have to let a great deal of blood to weaken my brain—a well-known operation in fifty degrees north latitude, performed on people who have a mind to go out of.

'I have the honour to be your obedient servant,

'IVAN GOLOVIN.

'PARIS, *Feb.* 1, 1866.'